Ontology-based Application Inte

Heiko Paulheim

Ontology-based Application Integration

Foreword by Johannes Fürnkranz

 Springer

Heiko Paulheim
Knowledge Engineering Group
Technische Universität Darmstadt
Germany
paulheim@ke.tu-darmstadt.de

ISBN 978-1-4899-9430-1   ISBN 978-1-4614-1430-8 (eBook)
DOI 10.1007/978-1-4614-1430-8
Springer New York Dordrecht Heidelberg London

Printed on acid-free paper

Springer is part of Springer Science+Business Media (www.springer.com)

*This book is an extended version
of the dissertation
"Ontology-based Application Integration
on the User Interface Level"
at Technische Universität Darmstadt, D17.*

Foreword

There is probably no invention in the history of mankind that had such a profound impact on our lives in such a short time as the World Wide Web. Twenty years ago, Tim Berners-Lee has developed the first versions of HTML which allowed to weave documents into the large hypertext document that we know today. It was soon realized that the potential of this technology is not limited to connecting texts, but may serve as a backbone for a world-wide knowledge base called the *Semantic Web*. Again, Tim Berners-Lee helped to pioneer the vision of data and knowledge being publicly available in a formalized, machine-processable form. Based on standards like RDF or OWL, knowledge and semantics may be freely exchanged between heterogeneous applications. The number of facts stored in public knowledge repositories, so-called *ontologies*, is increasing at a rapid scale. Linked open data are on the verge of permeating our everyday lives.

Now we are facing the next revolution. Not only documents or knowledge will be connected, but computer applications are no longer running on personal computers, but on centralized servers which can be accessed via Web interfaces from a large variety of processors in smartphones, TVs, cars, household appliances, and more. For the end user, this not only relieves them of the burden of the update and maintenance of their software, but allows them to access their applications in a uniform way, everywhere and at every time.

A grand challenge for web-based software design is to integrate different heterogeneous applications into a homogeneous new system that utilizes the familiar existing components but allows a transparent data exchange between these components. Such *Mash-Ups* can be realized at the code level, by reprogramming functions of the individual applications, or at the data or business logic level by formalizing the service description and access of the applications, e.g. in the form of Web Services. Both ways have the disadvantage that aspects of the application have to be reprogrammed in order to allow a standardized data exchange.

This book shows how ontologies and semantic web technologies can be employed to solve the practical problem of integrating applications on the user interface level. It shows how the relevant concepts of user interfaces, such as components and interactions, can be captured in a highly formalized ontology, and puts a strong emphasis on practical aspects of the implementation of an integration framework based on that ontology, such as the scalability of semantic event processing approaches, or the support of seamless cross-technological interactions. Never losing the focus on the end user, it further explores the possibilities ontologies provide to enhance the usability of integrated applications.

The book describes this innovative approach in all aspects. It provides an excellent introduction into ontologies and their applications in user-interface and application design, so that the book can be read without extensive prior knowledge in these areas. All presented concepts and techniques are illustrated with a case study that demonstrates the design of an integrated application for the management of catastrophes, which has been developed in a research project with different partners from the industry and academia, led by SAP Research. The book is thus of interest to both, researchers in ontologies who are looking for an interesting application, and for practitioners who want to find out techniques for combining different applications in a non-intrusive knowledge-based way. I am confident that it will become a key publication in its area.

Johannes Fürnkranz
Darmstadt, July 2011

Acknowledgements

While working on the topic of ontology-based application integration on the user interface level throughout the last three years, I have had valuable support and input from many people, without whom this book would not have become what it is.

Johannes Fürnkranz has encouraged me to pursue the topic of ontology-based application integration, agreed to take over the supervision of my dissertation, and has been continuously supporting me with valuable advice with respect to my research and numerous other topics. Jürgen Ziegler has agreed on acting as my secondary supervisor and has given me very valuable feedback in various discussions.

The topic covered by this book has been evolving out of and largely pursued within the research project *SoKNOS* at SAP Research in Darmstadt. First and foremost, Florian Probst has largely helped me in shaping the topic and taught me how to be formally precise when crafting ontologies in many fruitful (and sometimes exhausting) discussions. Many people both in Darmstadt and in other institutions involved in the SoKNOS project have been creating the atmosphere in which this research work could grow, especially Sebastian Döweling, Karen Tso-Sutter, Anna Lewandowski, and Thomas Ziegert, and everybody else who contributed to the SoKNOS project, in particular Daniel Oberle, Grigori Babitski, and Jörg Hoffmann at SAP Research Karlsruhe, Simon Bergweiler at DFKI, Alexander Walkowski, Christoph Stasch, and Florian Daiber at University of Münster, Stephan Braune and Martin Thoma at B2M, Marcus Hoffmann and Thorsten May at Fraunhofer IGD, and Alexander Behring and Andreas Petter at TU Darmstadt.

After the SoKNOS project was finished, I have continued pursuing my research in the *AdiWa* project and was happy to once more find a stimulating environment with great researchers, especially Benedikt Schmidt, Birgit Zimmermann, Christian Kuhn, Eicke Godehart, and Todor Stoitsev. During my whole time at SAP Research, Knut Manske, Nicole Scholl, and Anna Wypior have been supporting me with all the administrative work, Bettina Laugwitz has taught me interesting details about statistical evaluation that I had long forgotten about, and Andreas Faatz has been giving me valuable advice on very different issues far more than once.

During the work on this book, it was my great pleasure to supervise a lot of very talented students. Rene Abraham helped compiling an initial survey of user interface description languages. Atila Erdogan worked on the implementation of the Flex container for Java user interfaces, and Lars Meyer evaluated different implementation alternatives for improving the performance of the integration framework, as well as he worked on the implementation and evaluation of the Semantic Data Explorer. Roland Plendl contributed to the implementation of the rule-based object exchange mechanism, and Tobias Wieschnowsky built a prototype of a graphical user interface integration tool.

For the prototype implementation of the approach discussed in this book, I have used the system *OntoBroker*, and some people supported me in getting non-standard features implemented and told me about secret configuration options which are not mentioned in the official manuals. At OntoPrise, Saartje Brockmanns and Roman Korf have been patiently answering my questions and revealed various hidden functionalities, and Michael Erdmann has pointed me to using Skolem terms for event processing rules.

It was already two years before I started to dive into the topic of ontology-based application integration that I began working with ontologies. Michael Rebstock and Janina Fengel have sparked my interest in that topic and worked with me for two years. Since then, I have been discussing research ideas with countless colleagues at workshops, conferences, and other occasions, and always gained a lot from those discussions.

Last, but not least, my wife Carolin and my family have been continuously supporting me during the last years. Thank you for everything.

Heiko Paulheim
Darmstadt, July 2011

Contents

1   **Introduction** 1
   1.1   Vision 1
   1.2   Challenges 3
   1.3   Approach 4
   1.4   Contributions 4
   1.5   Outline of the Book 5

Part I System Integration, Ontologies, and User Interfaces

2   **Application Integration on the User Interface Level** 9
   2.1   Fundamentals 9
       2.1.1   Levels of Application Integration 9
       2.1.2   Definition of User Interface Integration 11
       2.1.3   Benefits of Application Integration on the User Interface
              Layer 12
       2.1.4   Requirements and Challenges of Application Integration on
              the User Interface Layer 13
       2.1.5   Design Space of User Interface Integration 14
   2.2   Portals 15
   2.3   Mashup Platforms 17
   2.4   Other Commercial and Established Solutions 19
   2.5   Prototypes from Academia 21
       2.5.1   Snap-Together 21
       2.5.2   OpenInterface Workbench 22
       2.5.3   CRUISe 22
       2.5.4   Mixup and mashArt 23
       2.5.5   The Widget Composition Approach by Kotsalis 23
   2.6   Identified Research Gaps 24
   2.7   Summary 25

3   Ontology-based System Integration 27
  3.1   What is an Ontology? 27
      3.1.1   Definitions... 28
      3.1.2   Languages 28
      3.1.3   Reasoning on Ontologies............................ 33
      3.1.4   Types of Ontologies 35
      3.1.5   Ontologies vs. Software Models 39
      3.1.6   Methodologies for Developing Ontologies 40
  3.2   Top Level Ontologies 42
      3.2.1   DOLCE 43
      3.2.2   SUMO 45
      3.2.3   Cyc... 46
      3.2.4   PROTON 46
  3.3   Infrastructures for Working with Ontologies 49
      3.3.1   Ontology Editors 49
      3.3.2   Ontology Visualization 49
      3.3.3   Programming Frameworks 52
      3.3.4   Storage Solutions 54
      3.3.5   Ontology Matching 55
  3.4   Ontologies in Application Integration 55
      3.4.1   Data Source Level 56
      3.4.2   Business Logic Level 58
      3.4.3   User Interface Level 59
  3.5   Summary 59

4   Ontologies in User Interface Development 61
  4.1   Classification Schema 61
  4.2   Ontologies for Improving Visualization 63
      4.2.1   Information Clustering............................... 64
      4.2.2   Text Generation 64
      4.2.3   Adaptation of User Interface Appearance 65
  4.3   Ontologies for Improving Interaction 67
      4.3.1   Ontology-based Browsing 67
      4.3.2   User Input Assistance 68
      4.3.3   Providing Help 70
      4.3.4   Facilitating Interaction in Integrated User Interfaces 70
  4.4   Ontologies for Improving User Interface Development 71
      4.4.1   Identifying and Tracking Requirements.................. 71
      4.4.2   Generating User Interfaces 72
      4.4.3   Reusing User Interface Components 73
  4.5   Summary 74

Part II Integrating User Interfaces with Ontologies

5   **A Framework for User Interface Integration** 79
5.1   Goals and Assumptions of the Approach 79
5.1.1   Goals 79
5.1.2   Assumptions 82
5.2   Design Decisions.. 83
5.2.1   Web-based vs. Non-web-based Approaches 83
5.2.2   Centralized vs. Decentralized Communication 84
5.2.3   Unified vs. Modularized Ontologies.................... 85
5.2.4   Open World vs. Closed World Semantics 87
5.2.5   Hypothesized vs. Skolemized Instances................. 88
5.3   Ontologies and Rules Used for User Interface Integration 89
5.3.1   Ontologies for Event Annotations 89
5.3.2   Ontologies for Describing Applications................ 91
5.3.3   Ontologies for Capturing Applications' States 92
5.3.4   Integration Rules 92
5.4   Basic Framework... 94
5.4.1   Roles and Tasks in User Interface Integration 94
5.4.2   Technical Architecture.............................. 96
5.5   Case Study: User Interface Integration in SoKNOS 101
5.5.1   The SoKNOS Project................................ 101
5.5.2   Applications Integrated in the SoKNOS Project 103
5.5.3   Example Interaction 105
5.5.4   Special Cases 107
5.5.5   Further Usage of Semantic Technologies in SoKNOS 112
5.6   Summary 117

6   **An Ontology of User Interfaces and Interactions**................... 119
6.1   Existing User Interface Description Languages 119
6.1.1   HTML and XForms 120
6.1.2   XIML... 122
6.1.3   XUL.. 122
6.1.4   TeresaXML and MARIA XML 123
6.1.5   LZX.. 123
6.1.6   WAI ARIA 125
6.1.7   UIML... 125
6.1.8   UsiXML 126
6.2   Design and Implementation of the Ontology 126
6.2.1   Typical Queries.................................. 127
6.2.2   Reused Generic Ontologies.......................... 128
6.2.3   The Top Level 129
6.2.4   The Detail Level 138
6.3   Integration Rules 143
6.3.1   Case Study: Definition of Integration Rules 144

      6.3.2   Global Integration Rules 146
  6.4   Summary 150

7 Data Object Exchange 151
  7.1   Annotation of Class Models 151
  7.2   Problems with Static Annotation 153
      7.2.1   Multi-Purpose and Artificial Classes and Properties 153
      7.2.2   Simplified Chains of Relations 154
      7.2.3   Non-atomic Data Types 156
  7.3   Non-Intrusive, Dynamic Annotation of Class Models 157
      7.3.1   Rules for Mapping Class Models to Ontologies 157
      7.3.2   Rules for Mapping Ontologies to Class Models 161
      7.3.3   Object Exchange with Template-based Filtering 164
      7.3.4   Non-intrusive Implementation 166
  7.4   Case Study: Annotating the SoKNOS Class Model with the
       SoKNOS Domain Ontology 168
      7.4.1   Annotation in SoKNOS 169
      7.4.2   Mismatches in SoKNOS 169
      7.4.3   Example Object Exchange in SoKNOS 171
      7.4.4   Performance Evaluation 173
  7.5   Summary 175

8 Efficient Semantic Event Processing 177
  8.1   Why Efficiency is Important 177
  8.2   State of the Art in Semantic Event Processing 178
  8.3   Implementation Variants and Evaluation 180
      8.3.1   Local vs. Global Event Processing 180
      8.3.2   Pushing vs. Pulling of Instance Data 182
      8.3.3   Local Caching of Instance Data 185
      8.3.4   Design of Connector Rules 186
  8.4   Generalization: Reasoning on Data From Running Applications.... 188
      8.4.1   Generalized Architecture 188
      8.4.2   Performance Evaluations 190
  8.5   Case Study: Performance in SoKNOS 193
  8.6   Summary 193

9 Crossing Technological Borders 195
  9.1   Architecture for Cross-Technological User Interface Integration.... 195
      9.1.1   Extending Containers 195
      9.1.2   Handling Drag and Drop 197
      9.1.3   Extending Information Objects 198
      9.1.4   Combining Heterogeneous Applications with A-Box
             Connectors and Caches 198
  9.2   Case Study: Integrating Java and Flex User Interface components
       in SoKNOS 199
      9.2.1   Scenario 199

9.2.2 Implementing the Flex Container 200
9.2.3 Putting the Pieces Together 205
9.3 Summary 205

Part III The Future of Ontology-based UI Integration

10 Improving Information Exploration 209
10.1 Interaction with the Semantic Data Explorer 209
10.2 Architecture 211
10.3 Evaluation 212
10.3.1 Scenario 212
10.3.2 Evaluation Setup 213
10.3.3 Evaluation Results 215
10.4 Summary 218

11 Towards End-user User Interface Integration 219
11.1 Current Approaches to UI Integration Revisited 219
11.2 Enabling End Users for Ad Hoc Integration 222
11.3 Towards a Visual, Ontology-based Tool for User Interface Integration . . 224
11.4 Summary 226

12 Conclusion and Outlook 227
12.1 Achievements 227
12.2 Summary of Evaluations 228
12.3 Open Research Issues 230
12.3.1 Improving the Development Process of User Interface
        Integration 230
12.3.2 Enhancing the Capabilities of Integrated User Interfaces . . . 231
12.3.3 Possible Influence on Related Fields 232
12.4 Concluding Remarks 233

List of Abbreviations 235

List of Figures 239

List of Tables 243

References 245

Index 267

Chapter 1
Introduction

Abstract While software engineering traditionally has been concerned mostly with the development of individual components, there has been a paradigm shift during the past decades. Assembling applications from existing components and integrating applications to complex systems has become more important with a growing number of existing artifacts. In the future, application integration on the user interface level will drastically reduce development efforts and create customizable, seamlessly integrated systems. However, currently existing approaches and frameworks are still not capable of fully harvesting the benefits of this new style of system development.

1.1 Vision

During the past decades, software engineering has changed. The number of existing applications and software artifacts, such as modules, libraries, components, and services, has grown rapidly. Software systems have become more and more complex. At the same time, the pressure to produce those complex software systems in ever shorter periods of time has grown.

These shifts in the basic parameters has influences on the software engineering process itself. An analysis presented by Blechar (2010, p. 25) identify a

> "trend away from net new *development* of business software systems to *composition* of business software systems."

With the advent of *web mashups* in the course of the *Web 2.0* , the vision of rapid integration of applications, including their user interfaces, has rapidly gained momentum. In 2007, Gartner analysts stated that

> "By 2010, Web mashups will be the dominant model (80 percent) for the creation of composite enterprise applications. Mashup technologies will evolve significantly over the next five years, and application leaders must take this evolution into account when evaluating the impact of mashups and in formulating an enterprise mashup strategy." (Gartner, 2007)

One year later, they once again strengthened the business need for such mashup technologies:

> "Enterprises are now investigating taking mashups from cool Web hobby to enterprise-class systems to augment their models for delivering and managing applications. Through 2010, the enterprise mashup product environment will experience significant flux and consolidation, and application architects and IT leaders should investigate this growing space for the significant and transformational potential it may offer their enterprises." (Gartner, 2008)

In the same year, Forrester analysts predicted

> "that the enterprise mashup market will reach nearly $700 million by 2013; while this means that there is plenty of money to be made selling mashup platforms, it will affect nearly every software vendor. Mashup platforms are in the pole position and ready to grab the lion's share of the market – and an entire ecosystem of mashup technology and data providers is emerging to complement those platforms. Those vendor strategists that move quickly, plan a mashup strategy, and build a partner ecosystem will come out on top." (Young et al, 2008)

In 2010, Gartner analysts stated that

> "composite applications enable increased operational and decision-making efficiency by supporting a single integrated view of a critical business entity – e.g., customer, supplier, product, patient and taxpayer – whose data are scattered across multiple databases and applications" (Blechar et al, 2010, p. 25)

and predicted that

> "most organizations will benefit from using new development methodologies and tools focused on providing sustainable agile AD [Application Development], including support for the creation of composite applications and enterprise mashups." (Blechar et al, 2010, p. 25)

In the same report, the analysts also found that

> "composite applications increase the complexity of the computing environment and result in dependencies that demand cautious management." (Blechar et al, 2010, p. 25)

These quotations point to a need for appropriate, professional tools and mechanisms for integration user interfaces. In the future, a typical software engineer will spend less time on coding and more time on choosing components from an inventory and assembling them to a new product. Existing software applications will be reused and recombined to new products, avoiding the reinvention of the wheel and allowing faster and cheaper software production.

Even nowadays, applications are rarely be built from scratch, starting with an empty sheet of paper and ending up with a one-size-fits-all system. Instead, developers choose from a shelf of ready-to-use components and compose them to complex systems. While this composition is currently a manual task, in the future, there will be intelligent tools that require only little manual efforts, and deliver customized integrated systems to the end users. For the end user, however, these applications will not look like rag rugs, but rather like one-of-a-piece products, allowing interactions that do not show the seams where the original components were stitched together.

1.2 Challenges

The current state of the art still faces some major challenges for harvesting the promised benefits created by the mashup style of developing applications (Ogrinz, 2009, pp. 10 and pp. 311). Today, creating a mashup from different applications involves a lot of manual work and requires deep knowledge about the applications integrated. Badly documented interfaces, heterogeneous data formats and technologies, and the lack of adequate and intelligent tool support make mashup development complicated and difficult, thus, the benefits of mashup development are to large extent eaten up by its costs.

Software components, however, typically do not come with matching screws and bolts that make a seamless assembly an easy task. While numerous solutions have been developed which integrate software components using technologies such as web services, those solutions most often target at system integration at a lower level, i.e., the data or business logic level. Integrating existing user interface components is not possible with such technologies.

So far, existing tools for user interface integration are still very limited. In order to result in a maintainable and customizable software system, it is essential that the components forming an integrated system are only *loosely coupled*. Tight coupling introduces dependencies between the integrated components and thus leads to a system which is hard to maintain and hinders fast adaptations to the resulting software. On the other hand, the end user will want to experience a software product as all of a piece and not find any flaws when interacting with the integrated system, i.e., a *seamlessly integrated* application. As discussed by Schefström (1999, p. 24), these two requirements conflict with each other, leading to the so-called *integration dilemma*: strong cohesion and loose coupling are hard to achieve at the same time. This conflict is particularly strong on the user interface level when implementing seamless interactions.

Especially when it comes to the integration of user interface components, current approaches still lack mechanisms for seamlessly integrating components and allowing cross-component interactions. The problem gets even more complicated when dealing with technologically heterogeneous user interface components, such as Flex, Java, and Silverlight components, developed with different programming languages.

When application integration is performed on the user interface layer, it typically involves the acquisition of knowledge about the applications' internal functionality as well as many hacks and workarounds. When integrating heterogeneous user interface components, code is written in different programming languages, using different paradigms and mechanisms for event processing, data conversion, etc. Translating between those mechanisms requires code that is most often scattered across the integrated system, which leads to code tangling and a monolithic architecture that is hard to maintain.

1.3 Approach

For showing that formal ontologies improve the integration of applications on the user interface level, the book demonstrates the development of a formal ontology of the domain of user interfaces and interactions, following established ontology engineering methodologies and building on the foundations of upper ontologies. A prototype implementation will prove the feasibility of applying ontologies and rules to the given integration problem.

That prototype implementation will be the basis for different experimental evaluations. For showing that an implementation with reasonable performance is possible, different architectural variants are implemented, and their runtime behavior is measured. The possibility of integrating applications based on heterogeneous technologies is shown in a proof-of-concept prototype. Furthermore, the prototype implementation is used in a running case study showing the integration of a larger-scale emergency management system.

In addition to the the the integration framework itself, the benefit of ontologies in integrated user interfaces is shown with a tool for exploring information contained in integrated applications, which is evaluated in a quantitative user study.

1.4 Contributions

In this book, we will introduce an approach for application integration on the user interface level which uses ontologies for formally describing user interface components and the data they process. A middleware based on semantic technologies is employed to fully decouple the individual components and still facilitate seamless integration of heterogeneous user interface components. This approach will show that the idea of ontology-based integration, which has been applied to database integration and business logic integration so far, carries over to the user interface level as well.

This book will provide several contributions to the research community. One central artifact is a detailed formal ontology of the domain of user interfaces and interactions, which allows for describing user interfaces based on strict formal foundations. This ontology may not be used in a middleware for application integration on the user interface level, but also for other purposes requiring a formal model of a user interface, such as providing assistance to the end user, or facilitating user interface adaptation, etc.

Data exchange between applications is a major cornerstone in system integration. This book discusses an approach for dynamically annotating data objects for facilitating exchange at run-time, which is more flexible concerning heterogeneous data models than today's state of the art approaches are.

The works on efficient, high-performance event exchange in user interfaces provide a discussion and thorough evaluation of several architectural alternatives for facilitating reasoning on data from running software systems. As performance today is often a major obstacle for employing ontologies and semantic technologies in real world scenarios, the results presented on that topic will help building scalable and usable ontology-based systems of different kinds.

Finally, a user study on ontology-based information exploration will show how ontologies and semantically annotated information may be used for assisting users with complex knowledge gathering tasks, even if those users do not have any prior knowledge on ontologies and semantic technologies. While ontology-based systems often do not find their path out of the research labs, this evaluation points out a way of carrying the benefits of ontology-based systems from specialized researchers to end users.

1.5 Outline of the Book

This book is divided in three parts. Part I discusses the background and state of the art in application integration on the user interface layer in Chap. 2. Chapter 3 introduces ontologies and discusses their role in application integration. Chapter 4 shows the state of the art of employing ontologies in user interface development.

Part II reports on an in-depth study of employing ontologies for application integration on the user interface layer. Chap. 5 introduces a general framework for application integration on the user interface level. This chapter serves as a basis for discussing various aspects of application integration on the user interface level in more detail in four chapters, which are widely independent from each other:

- Chapter 6 shows the development of an ontology used for formalizing user interface components and for annotating the events passed between the different components.
- Chapter 7 discusses the annotation of class models for facilitating the exchange of data objects between user interface components, i.e., bridging *conceptual* heterogeneities.
- Chapter 8 is devoted to the impact of performance on user interface integration and evaluates different architectural variants with respect to performance.
- Chapter 9 specifically deals with the problem of *technologically* heterogeneous user interface components.

The book is accompanied by a running case study dealing with SoKNOS (Döweling et al, 2009; Paulheim et al, 2009), an integrated emergency management tool that has been developed in a consortium of different companies and research institutions, lead by SAP Research. In that project, the approach discussed in this book has been applied on a larger scale. For each of the Chaps. 5, 6, 7, 8, and 9, the implementation of the approach in SoKNOS is discussed.

Part III gives an outlook on future developments in application integration on the user interface layer. Chapter 10 introduces a tool for information exploration built on top of the framework developed throughout the book. In a user study, it shows how information exploration can be significantly improved in an integrated user interface combined with a suitable visualization. Chapter 11 discusses how end users can be enabled to build custom tailored, ad hoc integrated user interfaces, and introduces the prototype of a tool which hides the complexity of formal ontologies and rules under the mask of an easy-to-use interface.

The book closes with a summary and an outlook on open and related research questions in Chap. 12.

Part I
System Integration, Ontologies, and User Interfaces

Chapter 2
Application Integration on the User Interface Level

Abstract This chapter starts with a definition of user interface integration and discusses how user interface integration differs from other application integration approaches in Sect. 2.1. Current state of the arts approaches are discussed, such as portals in Sect. 2.2, mashups in Sect. 2.3, as well as other popular solutions and academic prototypes in Sects. 2.4 and 2.5. The review of the state of the art discusses the recent advances in the field and points out some currently existing drawbacks in Sect. 2.6, which will be addressed in this book.

2.1 Fundamentals

Application integration on the user interface level is one technique of integrating software applications. Other terms encountered in the literature are, e.g. *front-end composition, integration on the glass* (Blechar, 2010, p. 50), and *integration on the presentation level* or *presentation integration* (Yu et al, 2007, p. 923). However, *user interface integration* is the most frequently used term[1], which we will therefore use throughout this book.

2.1.1 Levels of Application Integration

Application integration can be performed on different levels, following the widely accepted three layer model introduced by Fowler (2003, pp. 19). Figure 2.1 gives an overview on different views on application integration from the literature.

Daniel et al (2007, p. 60) follow the notion of Fowler (2003, pp. 19) that software usually comes in three layers, the data source layer, the business logic layer

---

[1] Google lists about 410,000 hits for "user interface integration" and "UI integration", compared to 47,000 for "presentation integration", 42,000 for "integration on the glass", and 8,600 for "front-end composition".

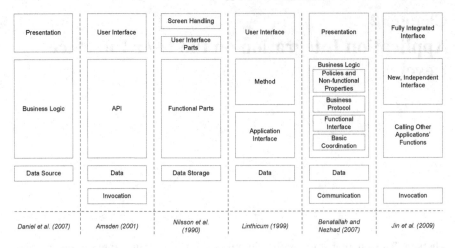

		Screen Handling			
Presentation	User Interface	User Interface Parts	User Interface	Presentation	Fully Integrated Interface
Business Logic	API	Functional Parts	Method	Business Logic / Policies and Non-functional Properties / Business Protocol	New, Independent Interface
			Application Interface	Functional Interface / Basic Coordination	Calling Other Applications' Functions
Data Source	Data	Data Storage	Data	Data	
	Invocation			Communication	Invocation
Daniel et al. (2007)	*Amsden (2001)*	*Nilsson et al. (1990)*	*Linthicum (1999)*	*Benatallah and Nezhad (2007)*	*Jin et al. (2009)*

Fig. 2.1: Different levels of integration: an overview of classifications from the literature.

(originally called *domain layer* by Fowler, but *business logic layer* has become more widespread[2]), and the *presentation layer*. Consequently, the authors derive that there are three layers on which applications can be integrated, which leads to the simplest model of system integration: an *integration layer* can be placed on top of each of the layers, thus facilitating application integration on the data source layer, on the business logic layer, and on the presentation layer.

Amsden (2001) introduces another variation of integration: one application may *invoke* another one, i.e., start it via access to the underlying operating system. It is arguable whether this is really a way of *integration*, since the two applications only run side by side without any interaction after the invocation.

Nilsson et al (1990, p. 442) introduce a separation of integration on the user interface layer: they distinguish the integration of *user interface parts* from the integration on the *screen handling* layer. With architectures such as *X Window* (Scheifler and Gettys, 1986, pp. 79), the implementation of the UI components (called *user interface part* by the authors) is separated from the implementation of the display of and interaction with those components (which is what the authors call *screen handling*). Thus, the authors propose two different strategies of integration: on the UI components and on the screen handling layer.

Linthicum (1999, p. 18) discusses several ways of *enterprise application integration*, i.e., the integration of applications of different enterprises. He distinguishes two types of integration on the business logic level: *application interface integration*, and *method integration*. Application interface integration means that one application calls methods from another one. In contrast, method integration includes that the underlying process models are exchanged, and more complex patterns of interaction

---

[2] About 950,000 Google hits for "business logic layer", compared to 80,000 hits for "domain layer".

between applications, going beyond singular method calls, are supported, such as contract negotiations between companies (Paulheim et al, 2011a).

Benatallah and Nezhad (2007, p. 119) provide an even finer-grained distinction of integration on the business logic layer. Besides Linthicum's distinction of application interface integration (called *functional interface* by the authors) and method integration (called *business protocol* by the authors), they introduce the need for additionally coordinating the message exchange itself (called *basic coordination*) as well as policies such as privacy policies and quality of service agreements between systems. Furthermore, the authors introduce the communication layer as another layer of integration, thereby stressing that when integration distributed applications, the communication protocol heterogeneities must be overcome (Rebstock et al, 2008, pp. 28).

For the rest of this book, we will refer to *user interface integration* as *integration on the user interface* or *integration on the presentation layer*. To provide meaningful, useful integration, the integration layer has to be aware of the data processed by and the operations that can be performed with different user interface components. Thus, regarding the distinction introduced by Nilsson et al (1990), the focus will be on integration on the component layer, however, the screen handling layer will be regarded when performing cross-technological UI integration, as discussed in Chap. 9.

2.1.2 Definition of User Interface Integration

Application integration on the user interface layer, or UI integration for short, is the technique of assembling

> "applications by reusing their own user interfaces. This means that the presentation layer of the composite application is itself composed, at least in part, by the presentation layers of the components" (Daniel et al, 2007, p. 61).

Composing the user interface out of reused user interface components, however, is only the first step. An integrated user interface does not only display different user interface components next to each other, it also has to allow interactions between those components. The integrated user interface has to provide more value than the sum of the integrated applications (Westermann and Jain, 2007, p. 20) – otherwise, any effort of integration would not be justified, as the user could just run the individual applications in parallel instead.

Therefore, UI integration also includes *coordination, synchronization*, and *interaction* between the integrated applications. Actions performed with or state changes occurring in one of the integrated applications can cause reactions in other applications. If this sort of integration is pushed so far that the user can experience the integrated application in as being one of a piece, we use the term *seamless integration* (Paulheim and Erdogan, 2010, p. 303).

Jin et al (2009, p. 5) discuss four levels of UI integration: applications launching other applications, applications calling other applications' functions, several applications sharing one (new) user interface, and fully integrated user interfaces. In the terminology used in this book, only the latter would be regarded as UI integration; the others are merely integration on the invocation level (in Amsden's terminology), and the business logic level.

In the context of enterprise application integration (EAI), the term *user interface-level integration* is used with a different meaning: for systems that have no publicly available API and do not provide direct access to the business logic and data storage, methods such as screen scraping and input emulation on the systems' user interfaces are used to get the data out of those systems (Linthicum, 1999, pp. 79). In contrast, user interface integration, as used in this book, is about facilitating interactions between user interfaces, not about using user interfaces as an entry point for getting data out of IT systems.

Another notion of *user interface integration* has been introduced by Schefström (1999, p. 18): the author does not focus on the composition of different user interfaces, but on the harmonization of the layout and look and feel of integrated applications.

2.1.3 Benefits of Application Integration on the User Interface Layer

There are two main benefits for performing application integration on the user interface level: increasing the usability of software systems, and reducing development efforts for those software systems.

From an end user's point of view, any system that is integrated on a deeper level than the user interface will come with an individually developed user interface (Daniel et al, 2007, pp. 60). Thus, the user will be confronted with a new, unfamiliar user interface and thus have to learn how to work with the system. An integrated system with applications retaining the familiar user interfaces, on the other hand, will result in a steeper learning curve, as the user can continue working with familiar interfaces.

From a software engineer's point of view, reusing existing user interface components, as opposed to developing a new user interface from scratch, means saving time. The user interface is the most expensive part of a software system, the portion devoted to the user interface ranges from 50% (Myers and Rosson, 1992, p. 199) to 70% (Sergevich and Viktorovna, 2003, p. 89) of the total development effort. More sharply phrased: without an approach for integration on the user interface level, the degree of reuse will never exceed 50%. UI integration can therefore reduce development efforts of integrated software systems drastically.

2.1.4 Requirements and Challenges of Application Integration on the User Interface Layer

Performing application integration on the UI layer bears some challenges. Daniel et al (2007, pp. 61) introduce five key requirements for UI integration approaches:

1. defining a common model and language for specifying components,
2. defining a model and language for specifying the integration,
3. supporting interaction and communication among the components,
4. defining a mechanism for visualizing the individual UI components, and
5. developing a mechanism for component discovery and binding.

A framework for user interface integration has to have access to the components to integrate. Therefore, a common model for those components is needed, which defines how to access and control the component. Typically, it is the components' API, which can be a high level API, working on the level of business objects, or a low level API, working on the level of UI entities such as buttons(Daniel et al, 2007, p. 62). As we will show in the subsequent chapters, APIs on both levels are useful for facilitating meaningful user interface integration.

For integrating the user interface components, the developer has to specify the coordination of the different components. This may be done in any general purpose programming language (such as Java), as well as in specialized languages.

To implement interactions between components, some mechanism for communication between components has to be provided. This can be a message exchange facility, event-based communication, etc. Communication between components can be performed either directly or centrally mediated (Daniel et al, 2007, p. 63). As user interface programming itself is most often event-oriented, it seems natural to use event-based communication for UI integration as well (Westermann and Jain, 2007, p. 20).

In an integrated UI, the individual applications' user interface components have to be displayed on the screen. The framework can either delegate the display to the individual components, or perform a unified display, e.g., based on markup, such as HTML.

The last issue is the discovery and binding of components. If the set of applications to integrate is not fixed at development time, components can be registered, e.g., in online repositories, and sought, found, and bound at run-time.

Application integration on the user interface level bears some more specialized challenges. One of those challenges is dealing with technologically heterogeneous components (Hasselbring, 2000, p. 37). In other integration scenarios, such heterogeneities can be "hidden", e.g., behind web service interfaces. UI integration is special, as it requires integration at a deeper level, e.g., for allowing drag and drop between components, which is usually implemented in the UI toolkit used. Implementing such seamless interactions across technologically heterogeneous components is a cumbersome task (Daniel et al, 2009, p. 432). Chap. 9 discusses this aspect in more detail.

Another level of heterogeneity is the use of different data models (Hasselbring, 2000, p. 37). For useful integration, it is necessary that the integrated components exchange data. This raises the need to bridge heterogeneous data models, e.g., by offering data transformation services (Daniel and Matera, 2008, p. 254) or mappings (Pietschmann, 2009, p. 280). A solution for this problem is discussed in Chap. 7.

Furthermore, user interfaces in general introduce very strong performance constraints. Reactivity of an application is a paramount criterion to its acceptance, as widely discussed in the HCI literature, e.g., by Miller (1968, pp. 267) or Shneiderman (1984, pp. 265). Thus, it is very important that the performance overhead of user interface integration is limited as far as possible. Chap. 8 discusses the efficient implementation of an integration framework.

2.1.5 Design Space of User Interface Integration

Paternò et al (2009, pp. 16) define four criteria which can be used to classify approaches for UI integration:

Abstraction Level   As discussed above, models of the integrated UI components are an essential requirement for UI integration. UI integration approaches can be distinguished based on the abstraction level of those models, as proposed by the Cameleon Reference Framework (Calvary et al, 2002, pp. 22), which is discussed in Sect. 6.1. Very abstract models describe only the tasks to be performed with a UI, while more concrete ones describe the user interface itself, be it on an abstract or a concrete level (see Sect. 6.1 for a detailed distinction). On the lowest level, integration can be performed directly on the implementation level, without using any abstraction.

Granularity   UI integration approaches can be distinguished based on the type of elements they integrate, starting from very elemental widgets, such as buttons or lists, up to entire applications.

UI Aspects   According to Paternò et al (2009, pp. 16), integrated UIs may only reuse the data presented by and manipulated through applications, or their behavior. However, following the classification discussed in Sect. 2.1.1, we would classify such an approach as an integration approach on the data and the business logic level, respectively, rather than a user interface integration approach. Furthermore, UI integration may reuse presentation elements. The latter case is the only we refer to as *UI integration* in the sense of the definitions given in Sect. 2.1.1.

Time   Integration can be performed statically at design time, or dynamically at run time, where in the latter case, the set of integrated components may change dynamically.

If regarded as dimensions, those four criteria span a four-dimensional *design space* of UI integration approaches, as depicted in figure 2.2.

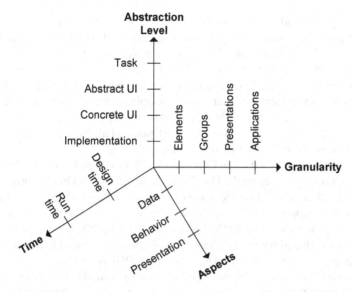

Fig. 2.2: The design space of UI integration, following Paternò et al (2009, p. 16)

2.2 Portals

A *portal* is a web-based integration solution that allows access to different information and applications. Typically, besides providing that access, portals bring additional features such as content aggregation and customization, single sign on (Ogrinz, 2009, pp. 275) for the different applications, etc. (Guruge, 2002, pp. 79; Wege, 2002, pp. 73).

Applications in portals are encapsulated in *portlets*, which run in *portlet containers*. Several portlet containers can be arranged to form one page in a portal, thus integrating different applications in one place (Wege, 2002, pp. 74). Portlets have been standardized in the JSR-286 standard (Heppner, 2008), which defines the portlet API and the life cycle of a portlet within a portal. The standard also foresees communication between events, although events are only identified based on naming conventions, not on a formally defined set of events.

Apache Pluto (Apache Software Foundation, 2010) is a basic, open source reference implementation of the JSR-286 standard. It allows for the integration of Java-only portlets and does not provide any further features than those foreseen by the standard.

Another widely used open source portal implementation is *JBoss Portal*, which has been renamed to *GateIn Portal* as of 2010 (JBoss Community, 2011). It supports the execution of JSR-286 compliant portlets and server-based event mechanisms (Rao, 2009, pp. 228), and also provides means for client-side event exchange between portlets, based on JavaScript. However, reactions to such an event also require a server round trip.

According to a study by Gartner (Gootzit et al, 2009), the four commercial key players in portal technology are WebSphere Portal by IBM, SharePoint server by Microsoft, NetWeaver Portal by SAP, and Oracle WebLogic Portal.

IBM WebSphere (IBM Corporation, 2008), currently availabe in version 6.1.5, allows for the assembling of Java applications, using portlets as defined by the JSR-286 standard. They are arranged and wired in templates, for which a graphical editor is provided. Wirings between portlets are used to passing parameter values between portlets, e.g., for automatically filling forms (Fischer et al, 2006). Portlets can also communicate via shared variables and events.

Oracle WebLogic Portal (Oracle Corporation, 2011), currently availabe in version 11g, also uses portlets based on the JSR-268 standard, as well as Oracle's proprerietary PDK-Java portlets, which provide some extensions to the older JSR-168 standard (Abdelnur and Heppner, 2003) that have become more or less obsolete with the advent of the JSR-286 standard (Desbiens et al, 2010, pp. 83). As foreseen by that standard, events (based on naming conventions) can be exchanged between portlets, which requires a server round trip (Desbiens et al, 2010, pp. 137).

SAP Netweaver Portal (SAP AG, 2011), currently available in version 7.0, supports components both written in Java and SAP's own programming language ABAP. It does not support the portlet standard, the corresponding building blocks are *iViews* (Jay, 2008, pp. 73 and pp. 227). Events between iViews are possible. As in the JSR-286 standard, there is no common event model; events are only based on upon naming conventions.

Microsoft SharePoint (Microsoft Corporation, 2010b), the current version being SharePoint 2010, like SAP NetweaverPortal, does not support the portlet standards. Instead, SharePoint relies on its own mechanisms called *Microsoft Web Parts* (Nazarian, 2009, p. 29). Web Parts can communicate based on events which are processed either with JavaScript or VB Script, and there is a basic set of predefined events, such as `onclick` (an element has been clicked) or `onfocus` (an element has gathered the focus) (Laahs et al, 2001, pp. 250). Basic layout control can be performed visually by assigning a preferred position to each web part.

Table 2.1 sums up the findings for the examined portal frameworks. One key problem which encompasses most of the above mentioned approaches is that the provided event processing mechanism between portlets in a portal always causes a server call and thus requires a re-rendering of the page for displaying effects. Thus, implementing seamless integration, as defined in section 2.1.1, is problematic due to performance issues (see also Chap. 8). For some portal solutions, there are work around for enabling client-side event processing, such as using AJAX (Murugesan, 2007, p. 38) and Dojo (The Dojo Foundation, 2011) in WebSphere (Bowley, 2009, pp. 345).

Regarding event exchange, it is further notable that none of the approaches supports a formal model of events. Events are always defined by using naming conventions, i.e. assigning an arbitrary string to an event. The effect is that for consuming an event, the developer needs to know the naming conventions of the component producing that event – which contradicts the idea of modularity[3]. The same holds for access to the components and state model of other portlets – if possible at all, it is restricted to accessing shared state variables, again identified with naming conventions.

Furthermore, seamless integration such as drag and drop requires exchanging objects between applications, which includes the task of converting objects from one application's data model to the other. Support for an automated conversion of data objects is completely missing in all of the approaches.

	Apache Pluto	JBoss GateIn	IBM WebSphere	Oracle WebLogic Portal	Microsoft Sharepoint	SAP Netweaver Portal
Event Mechanism	Server side only	Client side with server round trip	Server side only	Server side only	Client side possible	Client side possible
Common Event Model	no	no	no	no	Only few basic predefined system events	no
Data Conversion	no	no	no	no	no	no
Component and State Model	no	shared state variables without formal model	shared state variables without formal model	no	no	no
Supported UI Technologies	Java	Java	Java	Java	.NET	Java and ABAP
Layout	JSP Templates	Predefined Layouts	XML Templates	JSF Templates	Predefined and Custom Templates	Predefined and Custom Templates
Visual Editor	no	yes	yes	yes	yes	yes

Table 2.1: Comparison of popular portal frameworks

2.3 Mashup Platforms

While portals are created by professional developers, the idea of mashups is to let end users or people with average technical skills perform the task of integration (Ogrinz, 2009, p. 9). Unlike portals, mashups are rather short-lived, ad hoc developments (Yu et al, 2008, p. 45). Liu et al (2007, p. 335) name *web-based, light weight, reusable,*

---

[3] The problems that naming conventions impose on modular code has been widely discussed, e.g. by Knight and Dai (2002, p. 53).

and *end consumer centric* as the key features of mashups, while portals are considered rather *heavy weight* and *developer centric*. Ogrinz (2009, pp 20) points out the static nature of portals, as opposed to the more flexible and dynamic nature of mashups, which can be directly and deeply influenced by the end user, while portals can be personalized only in the ways foreseen by the vendor, if at all.

There are two views on what a mashup is: it either deals with combining data from different sources (also called "piping"), or with combining different views on that data (also called "wiring" or "clipping") (Hoyer and Fischer, 2008, p. 710; Ogrinz, 2009, pp. 54). In the context of this book, only the latter category of mashup platforms is of interest, because the former are not UI integration approaches following the classification introduced in Sect. 2.1.1. Popular approaches from the first category are *Yahoo! Pipes* (Yahoo! Inc., 2011) or *ARIS MashZone* (Software AG, 2011). There is also an effort of standardizing data-centric mashups with the XML-based EMML (Enterprise Mashup Markup Language) proposed by the Open Mashup Alliance OMA (Open Mashup Alliance, 2009). However, Gartner analysts have questioned a wider adoption of EMML, since many key players are not involved in its development (Knipp et al, 2009, p. 2).

The most well-known mashup platforms for performing UI integration are Google Mashup Editor, Microsoft Popfly (both of which have been discontinued), Intel MashMaker, JackBe Presto, and IBM Mashup Center. Comprehensive overviews are given by Hoyer and Fischer (2008, pp. 708) and Yee (2008, p. 311).

Google Mashup Editor (Google Inc., 2010), a discontinued mashup platform by Google, was one of the first and most well-known mashup platforms, centered around Google's own components, most notably their map component from Google Maps. It uses a set of XML tags to define the mashup, where the XML contains HTML snippets to control the resulting mashup's layout. Events can be exchanged based on JavaScript and naming conventions, and data exchange is done via the XML-based exchange formats Atom (Nottingham and Sayre, 2005) or RSS (RSS Advisory Board, 2009).

Microsoft Popfly is a meanwhile discontinued mashup platform. Popfly mashups are made from so-called blocks, which are provided for encapsulating common web sites and web services. The mashup developer can wire inputs and outputs provided by the different blocks in order to achieve a desired behavior of the mashup (Griffin, 2008, pp. 35). Popfly supports only basic interaction paradigms, such as viewing detail data on items shown by another application, and the developer has to manually code more complex behaviors.

JackBe Presto (JackBe Corporation, 2011) is a mashup platform targeting at visualizing data from different data sources, and concentrates on merging, transforming, and linking such data. Data can be transformed with XPath (W3C, 2010d) expressions. There are various visualization capabilities as well as connectors to different, heterogeneous systems to get the data from. However, the interactions between visualization widgets are limited to data-driven events, i.e. visualizing related data upon selection. Other, more generic interactions are not supported.

Intel Mash Maker (Ennals, 2010) is similar to JackBe Presto as it also aims at providing a universal data visualization. It mashes up different *widgets*, following

	Google Mashup Editor	Microsoft Popfly	Jackbe Presto	Intel MashMaker	IBM Mashup Center
Event Mechanism	Client side wirings defined in XML	Wirings of parameters and methods	Only data-driven	Client side events	Client side events
Common Event Model	Some basic pre-defined events	no	no	Some basic pre-defined events	Some basic pre-defined events
Data Conversion	To/from Atom and RSS	no	XPath based	no	no
Component and State Model	no	no	no	Data from other widgets can be accessed	Shared state variables
Supported UI Technologies	Web-based only	Web-based only	Connectors to different legacy systems exist	Web-based only	Web-based only
Layout	HTML/JSP	HTML	HTML	XML	Pre-defined lay-out templates
Visual Editor	Yes	Yes	Yes	Yes	Yes

Table 2.2: Comparison of popular mashup platforms

Intel's *Widget API*, based on predefined, hard-wired events, such as selection. The data is exchanged in the form of JSON-like trees, and, based on the data given, Mash Maker tries to infer related data and highlight related information, based on heuristic similarity, e.g. trying to visualize data that is structured like a typical address on a map widget (Ennals and Garofalakis, 2007, p. 1117). With Mash Maker, widgets can also access other widgets' data actively, as long as the other widgets' data model is known (Ennals et al, 2007, p. 31).

IBM Mashup Center (IBM Corporation, 2010) is a more versatile platform to mash up different web-based applications. Those applications can use a set of predefined events and also communicate via exposed state variables, both based on naming conventions.

Table 2.2 sums up some of the characteristics of the most popular mashup platforms. As for portal platforms, a similar set of shortcomings can be identified: there is a lack of common component, state, and event models. Data conversion is also an issue for mashup platforms. While there are some ad hoc mechanisms for transformation, they require a deep knowledge about each widget's data model. A detailed survey of mashup platforms is given by Grammel and Storey (2010, pp. 137).

2.4 Other Commercial and Established Solutions

Microsoft has proposed *Composite UI Application Blocks (CAB)* (Microsoft Corporation, 2005) as a solution for UI integration. The solution is restricted to .NET based user interfaces. It allows for exchanging events based on a topic driven publish/subscribe mechanism, and for sharing state variables, both based on naming conventions (Platt, 2008, pp. 121). The layout of the integrated UI has to be programmed in a general purpose programming language, or defined using the graphical layout capabilities of Microsoft's Visual Studio.

A more recent development from Microsoft is *Prism* (Microsoft Corporation, 2010a). It differs from CAB mostly in that it offers more flexible event mechanisms, such as aggregating complex events from elemental ones, or using commands between modules. Like for CAB, both events and commands rely on naming conventions. Prism also offers integration with Silverlight, Microsoft's technology for rich user interfaces on the web (Microsoft Corporation, 2011b).

Another widely used UI integration approach is the open source *Eclipse Rich Client Platform* (Rubel, 2006, pp. 36) (Birsan, 2005, pp. 40), which can be used to provide integration of Java-based applications on the business logic as well as on the user interface level. The basic concept of Eclipse RCP is the *plugin*, which provides a certain functionality. Plugins are connected via extension points, where a plugin defines possible contributions that can be made by other plugins. Those extension points are based on naming conventions. Plugins can also communicate via commands and invoke methods on each other directly (Silva, 2009, pp. 24). Especially the latter requires knowledge about the other plugin's API.

	Microsoft CAB	Microsoft Prism	Eclipse RCP
Event Mechanism	Publish/subscribe	Publish/subscribe, commands, event aggregation	Extension points, commands, direct calls
Common Event Model	No, naming conventions based on URIs	No, naming conventions	No
Data Conversion	No	No	No
Component and State Model	Shared state variables, based on naming conventions	No	No
Supported UI Technologies	.NET based only	Microsoft based only	Java based only
Layout	Programmatic	Programmatic	Programmatic
Visual Editor	Yes	Yes	No

Table 2.3: Comparison of other commercial and established UI integration approaches

Table 2.3 sums up the findings for the investigated approaches. Unlike with portals and mashups, layout is controlled programmatically, i.e. by using explicit means of the underlying programming languages, rather than visual templates. As for portals and mashups, there is no common model for events, components, and states, and performing the integration thus requires detailed knowledge about the integrated components' interna. Explicit conversion support for different data models is neither provided by any of the approaches.

2.5 Prototypes from Academia

Besides the well-known commercial solutions, there are also research prototypes and cutting-edge research projects that have developed mechanisms and techniques for UI integration.

2.5.1 Snap-Together

One of the first approaches to user interface integration has been proposed by (North and Shneiderman, 2000, pp. 128) with *Snap-Together*. The main idea of Snap-Together is to provide coordinated visualizations of data in different applications, which communicate via Microsofts COM (Microsoft Corporation, 2011a). Thus, all applications based on Microsoft technologies can be directly integrated with the SnapTogether approach, and with Java-COM-bridges such as *EZ JCom* (Desiderata Software, 2008) or *JACOB* (Adler, 2004), Java applications can be included as well (North and Shneiderman, 2000, p. 132)

Based on the user actions of selecting and scrolling and the system actions of scrolling and loading, the authors foresee different forms of such coordination:

Brushing-and-Linking   If an object is selected in one application, related information objects are also selected in other applications (Eick and Wills, 1995, pp. 445).

Overview and detail view   If an object is selected in one application (providing the overview view), the object is scrolled into view in another one (providing the detail view).

Synchronized scrolling   Scrolling a set of objects into view in one application causes scrolling related objects into view in another application.

Drill-down   If an object is selected in one application, detailed data about that object is loaded into another one.

Details on demand   If an object is selected in one application, detailed information on that object is loaded into another application. While drill-down is used to provide hierarchical access to large data sets by following part-of relations (e.g. selecting a galaxy and loading all the stars), details on demand deals with arbitrary related data (such as displaying the address of a selected person in an address book).

The Snap-Together approach is limited to coordinating visualization in different user interfaces. Other interactions, such as drag and drop across user interfaces, are not supported. Furthermore, the applications have to use a shared data model. Conversion between data models, such as described in Chap. 7 in this book, has to be developed manually on top of the Snap-Together API.

2.5.2 OpenInterface Workbench

The *OpenInterface Workbench* (Lawson et al, 2009, pp. 245) aims at integrating different heterogeneous user interface components and also includes the possibility to wire different hardware user interface components, not only software components as discussed in this book. The integration framework is developed in C/C++, additional bindings for other user interface technologies can be added. Currently, there are bindings for Java, Matlab, and .NET. A binding uses a proxy developed in C/C++ which translates the messages from and to the respective target technology.

OpenInterface uses CIDL (Component Interface Description Language), a proprietary XML-based description language (Lawson, 2008), as a modeling language for user interface components. Like, e.g., WSDL (W3C, 2007d), CIDL defines the programming interfaces of those components, i.e., their methods and parameters. The workbench also provides to automatically generated the required XML-based component descriptions from the source code in Java and C/C++ (Lawson et al, 2009, pp. 247). The developer can then wire the different programming interfaces together based on those descriptions.

As an API is not self-explanatory, the authors demand that the components' APIs are sufficiently documented. The developer has to take care about the API calls' semantics and ensure that the system functions correctly when performing the wiring. Thus, exchanging a component for another one requires rewiring of the system.

2.5.3 CRUISe

The *CRUISe* approach (Pietschmann et al, 2009b, pp. 473) takes a similar approach. It describes the services provided by a user interface with the a user interface description language called UISDL, which is based on WSDL (W3C, 2007d). This language allows for dynamically retrieving, instantiating and invoking user interface components (Pietschmann et al, 2009a, pp. 217).

The authors discuss an integration framework, which provides a JavaScript-based middleware for linking the different user interfaces based on their service descriptions. *Integration plug-ins* are introduced which encapsulate user interface components developed in different technologies.

The authors' focus is on dynamic retrieval of different user interface components, based on their service descriptions. A developer can provide an abstract representation of the desired application and its control flow. Based on that representation, the CRUISe system finds appropriate UI components, which can then be assembled by wiring the respective service calls. The integration can take the state of the different components into account, however, that state is modeled as a set of arbitrary key-value pairs (Pietschmann, 2009, p. 280). Thus, there is no common model of state, instead, developers have to rely on assumptions about the naming of state parameters in different components.

As the *CRUISe* approach focusses on web-based mashups, with the communication between mashlets coordinated with JavaScript. Thus, all components allowing JavaScript communications can be integrated, such as HTML/JavaScript based components, as well as Flex applications and Java applets (Pietschmann et al, 2009b, pp. 473).

2.5.4 Mixup and mashArt

Mixup is a mashup approach that focuses on integration of web-based widgets, connected by JavaScript. Like CRUISe, Mixup is based on the user interface description language UISDL for defining events and operations. The integration itself is done by mapping events and operations with another proprietary XML-based language called XPIL (for eXtensible Presentation Integration Language) (Daniel and Matera, 2008, pp. 254).

As in CRUISe, events are not formally modeled, but rely on naming conventions. Thus, the developer performing the integration has to know the semantics of the events, either by making assumptions based on the events' names, by consulting the documentation, or by code introspection.

mashArt is a successor of Mixup, which aims at a more universal integration approach, including both UI integration and service integration, i.e., addressing both the business logic and the user interface layer. The languages developed for Mixup are extended to mashArt Description Language (MDL) and Universal Composition Language (UCL), which support user interface and service integration in one language. Transformations between different data models can be implemented with XSLT (Daniel et al, 2009, pp. 436). Both Mixup and mashArt come with visual editors to support the developer of an integrated user interface. Like CRUISe, Mixup and mashArt are web-based approaches, which are therefore capable only integrating only web-based user interfaces.

2.5.5 The Widget Composition Approach by Kotsalis

Kotsalis (2009, pp. 313) describes an approach which targets at integrating smaller-grained widgets (such as trees, selection lists, etc.) developed based on different platforms. The aim of that approach – which currently is at the stage of being a proposal not accompanied by a prototype implementation – is to formally describe these widgets with UsiXML (Vanderdonckt, 2005, pp. 25) (see section 6.1).

Once the components are described bottom-up, a user interface can be specified top-down using MDA methods, and based on the two descriptions, suitable widgets can be selected and assembled to a complete user interface. As UsiXML provides the abstraction in the middle, the composition of heterogeneous widgets is possible in theory. The approach is so far only described as an abstract idea without any details on the implementation.

	Snap Together	Open Interface Workbench	CRUISe	Mixup and mashArt
Event Mechanism	Direct events via COM	Explicit wirings	Publish/subscribe	Explicit wirings
Common Event Model	Only select and scroll events	No	No	No
Data Conversion	No	Only syntactical	No	XSLT transformations
Component and State Model	No	XML-based state model	Key-value pairs based on naming conventions	Shared state variables based on naming conventions
Supported UI Technologies	Arbitrary	Adapters to different technologies available	Web-based only	Web-based only
Layout	None	None	Layout Models	HTML templates
Visual Editor	No	Yes	Yes	Yes

Table 2.4: Comparison of research prototypes for UI integration

Table 2.4 compares the approaches for UI integration from academia. The approach discussed by Kotsalis is not included in the overview because of a lack of detail information provided by the authors.

2.6 Identified Research Gaps

The review of the state of the art in UI integration has helped to identify several strengths and weaknesses of current UI integration approaches. There are sophisticated tools that allow for the authoring (or programming) of integrated applications, and layouting mechanisms, e.g., based on templates and visual editors, are already rather mature.

There are, however, a number of significant shortcomings:

- UI integration in most cases requires a deep knowledge of the different UI components' interna (Jin et al, 2009, p. 5). Such a knowledge has to be acquired by reading documentation or source code. This process of acquiring knowledge slows down the integration process significantly.
- More severely, an integrated UI built based on the knowledge gathered on other UI component's internal implementation is hardly maintainable, since it relies on the invariability of that internal implementation. When the implementation of a UI component changes, or a component is exchanged for another one providing the same functionality, the integrated system itself has to be changed as well.

- Both of those drawbacks are based on the fact that most of the UI integration approaches work on the lowest abstraction level in the design space defined by Paternò et al (2009, p. 16, see also Sect. 2.1.5). There are no abstract models of the integrated UI components, instead, integration is always performed on the implementation level. In particular, there is in most cases no common event model which can be used for coordinating interactions between integrated applications.
- Most frameworks do not offer conversion between heterogeneous data models, and if so, they require conversions for each pair of components, thus ending up with quadratic efforts for defining those conversion (see section 3.4). Building those pairwise conversions is a tedious effort, and it again introduces dependencies between components which lower the maintainability of integrated UIs.
- Most of the approaches are limited to a subset of UI technologies. There are very few UI integration approaches that are able to work with components developed with arbitrary, heterogeneous UI technologies (Daniel et al, 2007, p. 64).

This book discusses an approach that aims at closing these gaps. The areas of layouting and tool support are not subject of this book, as they are already well covered by research as well as commercial developments.

2.7 Summary

In this chapter, we have discussed the spectrum of application integration approaches in general, ranging from data integration approaches to business logic integration and user interface integration approaches. We have discussed the benefits and challenges of application integration on the user interface layer, and taken a look at the state of the art in application integration on the user interface level, or UI integration for short, looking both at commercial and accepted applications as well as research prototypes.

The review of the state of the art in UI integration has helped to identify several strengths and weaknesses of current UI integration approaches. Layouting capabilities and tool support are currently well covered by many approaches. Current shortcomings are that integration in most cases requires a deep knowledge of the different UI components' interna, since there are little abstractions in the form of common abstract models of events, components, and their states. Most frameworks do not offer conversion between different data models, and if so, they require conversions for each pair of components. In addition, the support for generating seamlessly integrated UIs from components developed with heterogeneous technologies is currently very limited.

Chapter 3
Ontology-based System Integration

Abstract Ontologies have been widely used in application integration scenarios, most often on the data and on the business logic level. This chapter gives an overview on ontologies in general and introduces different classification of ontologies in Sect. 3.1, and discusses various general top level ontologies that may be used for application integration in Sect. 3.2. Sect. 3.3 introduces existing infrastructures for working with ontologies, such as editors, storage solutions, or programming frameworks, and Sect. 3.4 provides an overview of the main approaches to employing ontologies in application integration.

3.1 What is an Ontology?

In their frequently cited article "Ontologies: Principles, Methods and Applications", Uschold and Grüninger (1996) point out the usefulness of ontologies for achieving *inter-operability* between IT systems: ontologies are proposed as an *inter-lingua* for information exchange between applications. This section shows different approaches of using ontologies in application system integration.

The term "ontology" comes from the greek words $ov\tau o\varsigma$ ("being") and $\lambda o\gamma o\varsigma$ ("theory", "science"). As a sub area of philosophy, ontology deals with the question of what existence actually is, as well as with categorizations and organizations of existing things. In computer science, an ontology is a formal model of a domain. While in philosophy, *ontology* is used only as a singular word and denotes a field of study, computer science typically deals with many *ontologies*, as there can be more than one formal model of a domain.

3.1.1 Definitions

There is a variety of definitions for ontologies in computer science, the best known of which probably is the following:

"An ontology is an explicit specification of a conceptualization." (Gruber, 1995, p. 200)

This definition is further detailed by Guarino and Giaretta (1995, p. 32), stating that an ontology is

"a logical theory which gives an explicit, partial account of a conceptualization,"

and, even more precisely, by Guarino (1998, pp. 4), defining an ontology as

a set of logical axioms designed to account for the intended meaning of a vocabulary.

While Gruber's definition only states that the specification is *explicit*, i.e., not containing any hidden assumptions, Guarino's definitions demand that it is *formal* ("a set of logical axioms"). Furthermore, Guarino points out that ontologies are *partial*, i.e., they cannot fully capture a domain in every detail. Although Gruber's definition is the more commonly used, it is almost often tacitly assumed that ontologies are captured in the form of logical axioms[1].

Ontologies may contain definitions about categories and their relations (such as CONTINENT and COUNTRY) as well as instances (such as "EUROPE is a CONTINENT"). The first is called *terminological knowledge* and often referred to as *T-Box*, the latter is called *assertional knowledge* and often referred to as *A-Box*[2] (Turhan, 2010, pp. 5).

3.1.2 Languages

The World Wide Web Consortium (W3C) have proposed a set of standardized languages for ontologies, which were originally designed to implement the vision of the *semantic web* (Berners-Lee et al, 2001), a web of information accessible both to humans and to automatic agents. The authors outlined a new web which was not made up of texts that can only be understood by humans, but of information that can be processed by intelligent agents that can, e.g., make an appointment with a doctor. They also sketched the idea of devices that intelligently communicate with each other, e.g., turning down the volume of the stereo when the phone rings. Their vision foresaw the employment of ontologies and formal descriptions for providing the necessary machine readable descriptions of contents and services. Figure 3.1 shows the so-called *semantic web stack*, a reference architecture which illustrates the languages proposed by the W3C for implementing the semantic web.

---

[1] Ironically, this is a hidden, non-explicit assumption.

[2] The spelling *ABox* and *TBox* is also found in the literature.

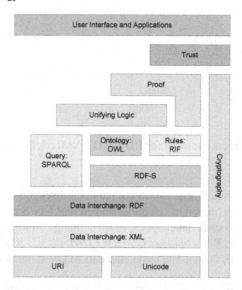

Fig. 3.1: The semantic web stack (Berners-Lee, 2009, p. 14)

The technological foundations on which the semantic web languages are built are the general-purpose eXtensible Markup Language XML (W3C, 2008b), Uniform Resource Identifiers or URIs (Berners-Lee et al, 2005), which are used to reference any kind of defined entity, and unicode (Unicode Inc., 2011) for a standardized, multi-language encoding of documents on the semantic web.

The base language of the semantic web layer stack is the Resource Description Framework (RDF) (W3C, 2004e). RDF allows for formulating sentences of the form *subject predicate object*, e.g., "Tom is a man" or "Tom lives in New York". Because of this strict form that always consists of the three parts subject, predicate, and object, RDF statements are often referred to as *RDF triples*. More complex sentences involving n-ary predicates can be expressed using so-called *blank nodes*, i.e., anonymous resources. Blank nodes allow for expressing sentences such as "There is an (anonymous) person that both Tom and Tina know."

There are different syntactic forms of RDF, the most dominant ones being RDF-XML and the less verbose Notation 3 (N3) (Berners-Lee and Connolly, 2011), in which the sentence-based nature of RDF becomes more obvious (see figure 3.2). For achieving the vision of creating a web of information that can be read both by humans and machines, the W3C further proposed a mechanism for embedding RDF in traditional HTML websites, called *RDFa* (W3C, 2008c).

While RDF is commonly used to express statements about individuals, ontologies are used to define the categories of those individuals, and their relations. Ontologies contain statements about hierarchies, e.g., "each human being is a mammal", relations

```
<?xml version="1.0"?>              @prefix rdf:
<rdf:RDF xmlns:rdf="               <http://www.w3.org/1999/02/
 http://www.w3.org/1999/02          22-rdf-syntax-ns#>.
 /22-rdf-syntax-ns#">              :Tom rdf:type :Man.
 <Man rdf:about="#Tom" />
</rdf:RDF>
```

Fig. 3.2: Different syntaxes for RDF: RDF-XML (left) and N3 (right)

between category members, e.g., "each human being lives in a city"[3], or additional constraints, e.g., "each human has exactly two parents" (see Sect. 3.1.4).

In the semantic web stack, languages used for defining ontologies are RDF Schema (W3C, 2004d), and the *Web Ontology Language OWL* (W3C, 2004b)[4], the successor of DAML+OIL (W3C, 2001). The basic elements of OWL ontologies are:

- Category and sub category definitions (called Class), e.g. defining MAN as a sub category of HUMAN. Set operators may also be applied for defining categories, e.g., defining the category HUMAN as the union of MAN and WOMAN.
- Relation and sub relation definitions (called ObjectProperty), e.g. defining a relation HAS PARENT between humans, and a sub relation HAS FATHER. OWL allows for defining the domain and range of relations by referring to categories. Relations may also be defined as being symmetric, inverse of each other, etc.
- Cardinality restrictions, e.g., defining that each human as exactly one father.

Figure 3.3 shows an example OWL ontology in N3 notation. The ontology defines three categories (humans, men, and women) and four relations between them (has parent, has father, has mother, and has child). It is stated that each human has exactly one father and one mother. As it further stated that men and women are disjoint categories, this implicitly includes that each human has two parents.

OWL comes in the three different flavors OWL Lite, OWL DL, and OWL Full, each having a different expressive power and complexity. The recently proposed OWL 2 language provides further extensions, such as more fine-grained definitions of data types, more precise statements about relations, and *property chains*, which provide a means for defining very basic rules. Like OWL, there are different subsets with different complexity, which are called *profiles* (W3C, 2009a).

Since RDF is used for defining OWL, i.e., each valid OWL document is also a valid RDF document, OWL document can be serialized in all syntaxes that exist for RDF, i.e., RDF-XML or N3. Further possible syntaxes for OWL documents are

---

[3] This is a simplification, since nomads are not covered by the definition. While ontologies in theory aim at providing a formally correct and complete formalization of a domain, such simplifications are often made in practice.

[4] Although the acronym would rather be *WOL* than *OWL*, the latter has been chosen for the sake of simple pronunciation and memorability (Finin, 2001).

```
@base <http ://www. heikopaulheim .com/ex .owl>  .

<http ://www. heikopaulheim .com/ex .owl> rdf : type  owl: Ontology  .

:Human  rdf : type  owl: Class  ;
        owl: equivalentClass  [ rdf : type  owl: Restriction  ;
                                owl: onProperty  : hasFather  ;
                                owl: onClass  :Man  ;
                                owl: qualifiedCardinality

                              ]  ,
                              [ rdf : type  owl: Restriction  ;
                                owl: onProperty  : hasMother  ;
                                owl: onClass  :Woman  ;
                                owl: qualifiedCardinality

                              ]  .

:Man  rdf : type  owl: Class  ;
      rdfs : subClassOf  : Human  ;
      owl: disjointWith  :Woman  .

:Woman  rdf : type  owl: Class  ;
        rdfs : subClassOf  : Human  .

: hasParent  rdf : type  owl: ObjectProperty  ;
            rdfs : range  : Human  ;
            rdfs : domain  : Human  .

: hasChild  rdf : type  owl: ObjectProperty  ;
            owl: inverseOf  : hasParent  ;
            rdfs : subPropertyOf  owl: topObjectProperty  .

: hasFather  rdf : type  owl: ObjectProperty  ;
            rdfs : range  :Man  ;
            rdfs : subPropertyOf  : hasParent  .

: hasMother  rdf : type  owl: ObjectProperty  ;
            rdfs : range  :Woman  ;
            rdfs : subPropertyOf  : hasParent  .
```

Fig. 3.3: Example OWL ontology, written in N3 syntax

the *OWL functional-style syntax* (W3C, 2009c) and the *Manchester syntax* (W3C, 2009b).

RDF and OWL are the basis for *linked data*, an approach for providing distributed data on the web (Bizer et al, 2009, pp. 1). URIs are used for identifying resources in RDF statements, and at the same time, they serve as pointers to RDF documents on the web which contain information on those resources. Thus, URIs in used linked data are supposed to be *dereferencable* (W3C, 2008a), which is not necessary for

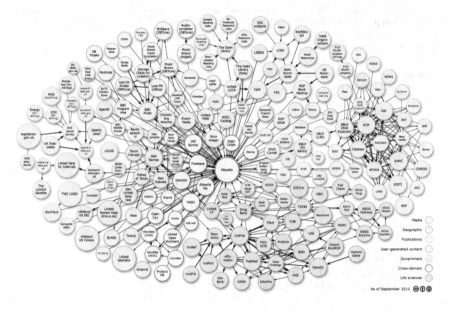

Fig. 3.4: The linked open data cloud (Cyganiak and Jentzsch, 2010)

URIs used in RDF documents in general. There is a large amount of linked data which can be accessed freely on the web, which is known as *linked open data*. Figure 3.4 shows the 200 largest datasets which are currently available as linked data.

Rules can be used to express additional axioms that most ontology languages do not foresee. In the semantic web stack, various rule interchange formats to express rules defined with different individual rule languages, such as the Semantic Web Rule Language SWRL (W3C, 2004f) or the Rule Markup Language RuleML (Boley et al, 2010). Those rule languages allow for more flexible definitions than property chains in OWL 2.

The Rule Interchange Format RIF (W3C, 2010b) provides an abstraction from those rule languages which is based on formal logic. It can be seen as an instantiation of the unified logic layer (Gerber et al, 2008, p. 81).

To query the information contained in the semantic web, or defined in RDF, ontologies, and rules, various languages have been proposed (see the surveys, e.g., by Haase et al (2004, pp. 502) and Bailey et al (2005, pp. 35)). From that variety, the SPARQL query language[5], an SQL-like query language for RDF-based documents (W3C, 2008d), has been establishing as a widely accepted standard.

The layers on top are subject to ongoing research, without any solutions or languages standardized so far (Bénel et al, 2010, p. 159). Based on the formal logic statements expressed in ontologies and rules, a *proof* can be given on every statements deduced from information on the semantic web (Pinheiro da Silva et al,

---

[5] *SPARQL* is a recursive acronym, standing for SPARQL Protocol and Query Language.

2008, pp. 847), and a *trust* level can be assigned, which is especially interesting if a deduction uses information from different potentially unreliable sources (Artz and Gil, 2007, pp. 58). *Cryptography* is planned to be used to securely encrypt and decrypt sensible information on the semantic web.

The top most layer is a placeholder for every application that uses information from the semantic web, as well as any user interface to information from the semantic web, such as semantic web browsers.

Apart from the languages standardized or recommended by the World Wide Web Consortium, there are others that are used both in industry and academia. One of the most often used of those languages (Cardoso, 2007, p. 85) is *F-Logic* (Angele and Lausen, 2009, pp. 45), which integrates ontology definitions and rules in one uniform language (Antoniou et al, 2005a, pp. 61). Other than the semantic web languages proposed by the W3C, which follow the open world assumption, F-Logic uses closed world semantics (Motik et al, 2006, pp. 502) (see section 5.2.4).

The basic building blocks of F-Logic ontologies are:

- Class and subclass definitions.
- Relation definitions. Other than OWL, F-Logic does not support sub relation definitoins.
- Rules. Most of the definitions in F-Logic are based on rules. Like Prolog rules, they consist of a head (i.e., what is stated to be true) and a body (the condition under which the head is true). However, unlike in Prolog, the order of rules does not influence a reasoner's results.

Depending on the implementation, other features are available as well, e.g., the definition of functions and first-order logic predicates. Figure 3.5 shows an example ontology in F-Logic, which corresponds to the OWL example depicted in Fig. 3.3. As sub relation definitions as well as inverse relations are not supported directly, they are defined using the F-Logic rule mechanism[6].

Besides OWL-based languages and F-Logic, there are other widely adopted ontology languages, such as *KIF* (Knowledge Interchange Format), a Lisp-based notation for predicate logic, which is a rich language with built-in support, e.g., for arithmetics or set algebra (Genesereth and Fikes, 1992). Overviews and comparisons of ontology languages are given, e.g., by Calì et al (2005, pp. 14), Gutierrez-Pulido et al (2006, pp. 489), and Su and Ilebrekke (2006, pp. 761).

3.1.3 Reasoning on Ontologies

The knowledge formalized in ontologies can be exploited by *reasoning*, i.e., the deductive deriving of new implicit facts from those explicitly encoded in the ontology (Calì et al, 2005, pp. 6). A well-known example is that from the facts *Aristotle is a*

---

[6] Rephrasing sub property and inverse property relations is only an approximation to the corresponding constructs in OWL, since they only work on the instance level, i.e., schema-level queries (e.g., find all sub relations of `has Parent`) are not possible.

```
:-  prefix  ="http://www.heikopaulheim.com/example#".
:-  module  ="http://www.heikopaulheim.com/"#example.

#Human[].
#Man::#Human.
#Woman::#Human.

#Human[#hasParent=>>#Human].
#Human[#hasFather=>#Man].
#Human[#hasMother=>#Woman].
#Human[#hasChild=>>#Human].

RULE #motherSub:  FORALL P,C C[#hasParent->P] <- C[#hasMother->P].
RULE #fatherSub:  FORALL P,C C[#hasParent->P] <- C[#hasFather->P].
RULE #parentInv:  FORALL P,C C[#hasParent->P] <- P[#hasChild->C].
RULE #childInv:   FORALL P,C P[#hasChild->C] <- C[#hasParent->P].
```

Fig. 3.5: Example F-Logic ontology

man and *All men are mortal*, a reasoner can derive that *Aristotle is mortal* (Russell and Norvig, 2010, p. 4).

Reasoning on ontologies can be used for different purposes. The most dominant use case is *querying knowledge bases*: with a querying language such as SPARQL (see above), queries such as "find all customers that are interested in the semantic web" can be issued. Using formalized axioms such as *if a customer has bought a book about X, s/he is interested in X* and *ontologies are a sub topic of the semantic web*, a reasoner can provide an adequate answer set.

Another important use case for reasoning is the *validation* of ontologies. The consistency of a whole ontology can be evaluated automatically, and conceptual mistakes can be found, such as the definition of two disjoint categories with a non-empty intersection (Calì et al, 2005, p. 8). Another feature offered by some reasoning tools is to provide explanations for the results inferred from an ontology (Turhan, 2010, pp. 15).

There are two dominant implementation flavors of reasoners: tableau-based reasoners (Möller and Haarslev, 2009, pp. 509) and logic programming based reasoners (Motik, 2009, pp. 529). Tableau-based reasoners are the most commonly found type. The underlying algorithm evaluates axioms in the ontology and derives new axioms until no more axioms can be found, or until a contradiction is detected. Logic programming based reasoners translate ontologies into a program in a logic programming language, such as datalog, and use a corresponding interpreter to resolve the queries.

Examples for well-known reasoning tools are Pellet (Sirin et al, 2007, pp. 51), *Fact++* (Tsarkov and Horrocks, 2006, pp. 292) and Racer (Haarslev and Möller, 2003, pp. 27), which are tableau-based implementations, HermiT, which uses an extension of the classic tableau mechanism called *hypertableau* (Motik et al, 2009, pp. 165), and KAON2 (Motik and Sattler, 2006, pp. 227) with its commercial counterpart

OntoBroker (Decker et al, 1999, pp. 351), which are based on logic programming. Overviews and benchmark comparisons of state of the art reasoning systems are given by Weithöner et al (2007, pp. 296), Lee et al (2008, pp. 543), Luther et al (2009, pp. 66), and Dentler et al (2011).

Besides a visual user interface and/or proprietary APIs for different programming languages, most reasoners support the de facto standard DIG (DL Implementation Group), which allows accessing reasoners via HTTP, also remotely on the web in a distributed system (Bechhofer et al, 2003a).

3.1.4 Types of Ontologies

There may be various types of ontologies, developed and employed for different purposes. Various classification approaches have been discussed for comparing and distinguishing those ontologies. One of the oldest classifications is proposed by van Heijst et al (1997, pp. 194), who distinguish ontologies based on two properties: their amount of structure, i.e. their degree of formality, and their subject. Regarding the degree of formality, they distinguish terminological ontologies, which specify a list of terms and their meaning, information ontologies, which specify the structure of data, and knowledge modeling ontologies, which specify a conceptualization of knowledge. Lassila and McGuinness (2001, pp. 4) provide a more fine-grained distinction between the following types of ontologies (see Fig. 3.6):

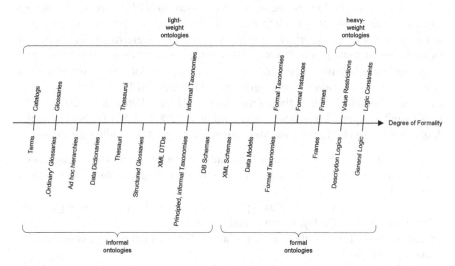

Fig. 3.6: Ontology types based on the degree of formality, following Lassila and McGuinness (2001, p. 4) (upper part) and Uschold and Grüninger (2004, p. 59).

Catalogs   are collections of terms without any further descriptions. They can be used for disambiguating communication by ensuring that the same term is used for the same concepts.

Glossaries   are catalogs that are enriched with descriptions for the terms.

Thesauri   contain additional relations between terms. Typically, those are relations such as *synonym of*, *broader term than*, or *narrower term than*.

Informal taxonomies   arrange the terms in a hierarchy. An example are the concept hierarchies used by web shops.

Formal taxonomies   also use hierarchies, but in a stricter sense. In a formal hierarchy, the constraint $C_1 \subseteq C_2 \Rightarrow (c \in C_1 \rightarrow c \in C_2)$ must always hold. In contrast, this constraint may be violated in an informal taxonomy: a web shop's product hierarchy may define, e.g., that "decoration" is a sub category of "home", while the statement "each decoration is a home" is clearly nonsense.

Formal instances   are taxonomies that also explicitly define instances, such as "Africa is a continent". They are sometimes also referred to as *populated ontologies* (Kalfoglou and Schorlemmer, 2005, p. 4).

Frames   are used to define relations between concepts, e.g., that each food product is made from ingredients.

Value restrictions   impose additional domain and range constraints on such frames, such as that only eatable substances can be used as ingredients for food products.

Logic constraints   are constraints that go beyond domain and range definitions, e.g. stating that categories of objects are disjoint.

The first four are sometimes referred to as *informal ontologies*, that last five as *formal ontologies*. Following the definition of Guarino (1998, pp. 4, see above), which demands an ontology to be formal, only those are considered to be ontologies in a narrower sense. In contrast, the first four are often referred to as *controlled vocabularies* (Rebstock et al, 2008, p. 101), stressing that they are merely defining terms, not the relations between them[7]. Another distinction that is often used is *lightweight* and *heavyweight* ontologies, where the latter include value restrictions and logic constraints, while the former do not (Gómez-Pérez et al, 2004, p. 8). As depicted in figure 3.6, Uschold and Grüninger (2004, p. 59) further refine the classification given by Lassila and McGuinness (2001, p. 4) by adding the following:

Ad hoc hierarchies   are even weaker than informal taxonomies. The hierarchies do not even intend to create correct is-a relations, but only group things that roughly belong together.

Data dictionaries   define complex types of data based on simple ones, e.g., a date being composed of a day, a month, and a year.

Structured glossaries   contain further relations between terms, e.g., synonym and antonym relations.

XML DTDs   are meta descriptions of XML documents. They define which elements in an XML file can exist, and how they can be nested. Those nestings provide informal, unnamed relations between the nested elements.

---

[7] However, the term *controlled vocabulary* is used as a synonym for *catalogs* as well, e.g. by Gómez-Pérez et al (2004, p. 28)

Database schemas   describe tables in a database, their elements, and their relations.

XML schemas   have the same purpose as XML DTDs, but are more expressive.

Data models   refer to models that go beyond database schemas, e.g., UML-based models, possibly with additional constraints.

Regarding the contents of ontologies, van Heijst et al (1997, p. 94) distinguish four types of ontologies:

Domain ontologies   define concepts of one specific domain.

Generic ontologies   define concepts that are general enough to be used across various domains.

Application ontologies   define concepts from a domain that are required for one application, as well as, optionally, some specific extensions that are needed for that application. In contrast to domain and generic ontologies, application ontologies are most often not reusable.

Representation ontologies   define the concepts that are used to define ontologies, i.e., they define concepts such as *term* or *relation*. They can therefore also be regarded as meta-ontologies.

A similar distinction is used by Uschold and Jasper (1999, pp. 18). The authors distinguish three types (or meta-levels) of ontologies:

L_0 or Operational data   defines knowledge about instances, such as "Africa is a continent."

L_1 or Ontologies   defines the concepts and terms of a domain. Ontologies provide the vocabulary to define operational data.

L_2 or Ontology representation languages   provide means for defining L_1 ontologies. The languages listed in section 3.1.2 belong to this category.

The classification proposed by Guarino (1998, pp. 7) distinguishes ontologies by their level of abstraction and their usage, as shown in figure 3.7. Some of the ontology types resemble those in the classification by van Heijst et al (1997) above:

Top-level ontologies   or upper ontologies are equivalent to *generic ontologies*. They contain general concepts that are useful across several domains, most often based on human perception of the world (Kiryakov et al, 2001, p. 48). Section 3.2 gives a closer look at top level ontologies.

Domain ontologies   are equivalent to domain ontologies as defined by van Heijst et al (1997, p. 194, see above).

Task ontologies   define the activities of a task, but without pointing to a specific domain. For example, scientific experiments contain hypotheses, measurements, and evaluations, all of which can be defined agnostic to the actual domain of the experiment, be it molecular biology or sociology.

Application ontologies   are equivalent to domain ontologies as defined by van Heijst et al (1997, p. 194, see above) They the concepts defined in domain and task ontologies to define specific activities. This is done by stating which entities from the domain ontology play which role in an activity defined in the task ontology.

It is notable that the ontologies of the different levels are interconnected with specialization relationships. Thus, ontologies reuse definitions made by ontologies on a higher level, therefore making them modular and comparable.

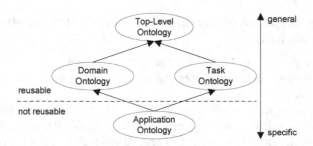

Fig. 3.7: Classification of ontologies based on their level of abstraction, following Guarino (1998, p. 7).

This book puts its focus on the use of ontologies for solving a particular software engineering task. Regarding the role ontologies play in software engineering, Happel and Seedorf (2006, pp. 10) distinguish the domain of discourse (the technical parts of the system, or a real world domain[8]) and the usage time of the ontology (design time, or run time), thus ending with a four-fold categorization, as shown in figure 3.8:

Ontology-driven development   uses ontologies at design time for formalizing the software system's real world domain. A typical example is generating source code from ontologies in a model-driven engineering approach (Gašević et al, 2006, pp. 173).

Ontology-enabled development   uses ontologies at design time for formalizing the software's technical components. A typical example is the use of repositories with annotates software components (Happel et al, 2006, pp. 349).

Ontology-based applications   use ontologies formalizing the real world domain for controlling the software at run-time. A typical example is the use of ontology-based business rules (Antoniou and Bikakis, 2007, pp. 233).

Ontology-enabled architectures   use ontologies for providing an intelligent software infrastructure at run-time. A typical example are semantic web services, as described in section 3.4.2.

Chapter 4 discusses a variety of examples for each of the four areas.

---

[8] The authors use the terms "infrastructure" for the technical parts of the system, and "software" for the real world domain. As we consider especially the latter as confusing, we have not adopted the authors' terminology.

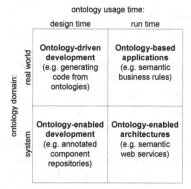

Fig. 3.8: Classification of ontologies in software engineering, following Happel and Seedorf (2006, p. 11).

3.1.5 Ontologies vs. Software Models

From the definitions given above, ontologies seem to be a lot like software models. Models are representations, images, or plans of other things. According to Stachowiak (1973, pp. 131), models have three important characteristics:

- Models are *images* of some originals. Those originals can be of any kind, real or ficticious, existing in nature or made by humans. Even models may serve as originals for other models.
- Models are *reduced* with respect to the original. They do not contain every detail of the original, but only those attributes that have been considered relevant by the person crafting the model.
- Models are used for a *purpose*. They are designed to be used by a certain group of users, in a given time frame, and within certain tasks. Thus, there is not one universally correct model of an original, but only models that are useful in some context.

In fact, ontologies and software models share a lot of common characteristics (Atkinson et al, 2006, p. 57). Models have been widely used in computer science, especially data and class models. Both ontologies and software models are *abstractions* of a domain, i.e., they define the relevant concepts and neglect the irrelevant ones. However, there are some essential differences between models, as they are used in computer science, and ontologies.

The following definition by the Object Management Group (OMG), one of the key consortia driving model driven architecture , points to some essential conceptual differences between ontologies and models, as used in computer science:

"A model of a system is a description or specification of that system and its environment for some certain purpose." (OMG, 2003, p. 12)

Ontologies, at least those on the top and domain level in Guarino's classification, are *generic*, with a focus on precisely capturing the semantics of terms used in a domain. A model, on the other hand, is *specific* for one or more particular purpose, with the focus on an efficient implementation of an application for solving specific tasks in the modeled domain (Spyns et al, 2002, p. 13, Atkinson et al, 2006, p. 49, Ruiz and Hilera, 2006, p. 63). As a consequence, a software engineer would rather trade off precision for a simple, efficient model, while an ontology engineer would trade off simplicity for a precise representation.

Another conceptual difference is that in software engineering, models are most often *prescriptive* models, which are used to specify how a system is *supposed* to behave, while ontologies are rather *descriptive* models, which describe how the world *is* (Aßmann et al, 2006, p. 256). This corresponds to the dual use of the word *model* with the different meanings *image* and *ideal* observed by Stachowiak (1973, p. 129).

The research literature on ontologies and models also states a number of differences which are at least questionable. Atkinson et al (2006, p. 51) state that "ontologies are for run-time knowledge exploitation", "while models are not". Although this may be true for many applications, there are examples where data models are explored at run-time, e.g. in generic database administration tools, while there are also examples where ontologies are only used at design time, as the classification by Happel and Seedorf (2006, p. 11, see above), shows.

One commonly cited difference is that "ontologies are formal, while models are not" Atkinson et al (2006, p. 52). As discussed above, there are also informal ontologies. On the other hand, description means such as UML are rather formal.

Another commonly cited difference is that models follow the closed world assumption, while ontologies follow the open world assumption (Aßmann et al, 2006, pp. 255). While this is true for ontologies modeled with OWL, the statement cannot be generalized to all kinds of ontology languages, such as F-Logic (Atkinson et al, 2006, p. 52). Furthermore, ontologies allow for formal reasoning (see Sect. 3.1.3), while models at least do not provide an out of the box mechanism for reasoning (Atkinson et al, 2006, pp. 51). However, there have been approaches for reasoning on models, e.g., for checking UML class models (Evans, 1998, pp. 102) or ER diagrams (Lutz, 2002, pp. 185) for consistency.

Some of these differences between models and ontologies pose some challenges to employing ontologies in software engineering. One particular aspect is that annotation of models with ontologies has to take into account several potential mismatches between ontologies and models, based on those differences. Chapter 7 examines this problem in detail.

3.1.6 Methodologies for Developing Ontologies

Several approaches have been proposed for developing ontologies, a process also called *ontological engineering* (Fernández et al, 1997, p. 30). The first ontological engineering methodologies were introduced by Grüninger and Fox (1995) and Uschold and Grüninger (1996, pp. 93).

Grüninger and Fox (1995) identify six steps for creating ontologies: first, a *scenario* is identified, e.g., in the form of textually described use cases from the domain that is about to be captured in the ontology. From that scenario, *informal competency questions* are derived, which can be seen as queries which should be solved by using the ontology, but which are not captured formally, but in natural language. Next, the *terminology*, i.e., the concepts used in the competency questions, is formulated in first order theory.

In an iterative process, the informal competency questions are translated into *formal competency questions* in an appropriate query language, and the *axioms* needed to answer the queries are added to the ontology. In a final step, *completeness theorems* are defined, which identify the conditions under which the axioms in the ontology lead to correct conclusions beyond the initial competency questions.

The methodology proposed by Uschold and King (1995) and Uschold and Grüninger (1996, pp. 93) consists of four phases: first, the *purpose and scope* of the ontology are identified, which corresponds to the *scenario* step in the methodology by Grüninger and Fox (1995). The second step of actually *building* the ontology is divided in three sub steps: *ontology capture*, where key concepts and relations are identified, *ontology coding*, where the identified concepts and relations are translated into formal statements, *integrating other ontologies*, whenever some of the concepts and relations identified are known to exist in other ontologies. The final steps comprise the *evaluation* of the ontology, and the *documentation* of both the ontology and the modeling decisions made.

METHONTOLOGY (Fernández et al, 1997, pp. 30) is a more detailed ontology engineering methodology which concentrates on the capturing and coding tasks. It comprises eleven tasks, which follow each other sequentially, but the ontology engineer can step back in the flow if necessary, e.g., when new terms are introduced (Gómez-Pérez et al, 2004, pp. 131). The approach starts with building a flat *glossary* of terms, which is then turned into a *taxonomy*. The third task is to identify *ad hoc binary relations* between the concepts identified. Those ingredients, and optionally instances, are used to build a *concept dictionary*. Based on that dictionary, additional *relations*, *class and instance attributes*, and *constants* are defined. For building a heavy weight ontology, the following tasks comprise the definition of *formal axioms* and *rules*, and, optionally, of instances.

Figure 3.9 shows the three methodologies and their interrelations. It can be observed that they differ both in the individual steps and in their order. For example, the methodology by Uschold and King (1995) foresees an early beginning with actually coding the ontologies' axioms, while this step is taken at later stage when one of the other two methodologies is used. A detailed discussion of different ontology engineering methodologies is given by Gómez-Pérez et al (2004, pp. 148).

Ontology engineering does not have to be all-manual work. There are various techniques of supporting ontology engineers during the various tasks, which are subsumed under the term *ontology learning* (Cimiano et al, 2010, pp. 254) . Those techniques cover extracting relevant terms and synonyms from texts, clustering them

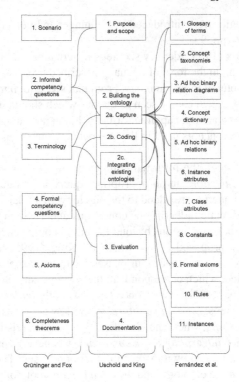

Fig. 3.9: Comparison of different ontology engineering methodologies

and arranging them in hierarchies, as well as extracting relations and their domains and ranges. Ontology learning systems can either work automatically and suggest a complete ontology, or in dialog mode with a user confirming the individual steps.

   Besides the methodologies for building ontologies, there are other tools for improving the quality of ontologies built. For example, *ontology design patterns* (Gangemi and Presutti, 2009, pp. 221) define best practices and provide small, reusable sets of concepts and relations for specific recurring problems. Methods such as *Onto-Clean* (Guarino and Welty, 2009, pp. 201) define a set of modeling guidelines which help the ontology engineer in avoiding typical modeling mistakes which can lead to unwanted behavior when querying the ontologies.

3.2 Top Level Ontologies

Top level ontologies, also referred to as *upper level ontologies* or *foundational ontologies*, (Gómez-Pérez et al, 2004, p. 71), are at the top of the ontology stack suggested by Guarino (1998) (see above). By committing to a standardized or de facto standard upper ontology, different domain ontologies become interoperable and can be more easily compared, aligned, and merged (Noy, 2004, pp. 65). Another motivation for using top level ontologies is enabling the cooperation between different agents or companies without the need to make their whole ontologies public (Mascardi et al, 2007, p. 55).

Mascardi et al (2007, pp. 55) present an encompassing survey of top level ontologies. Besides BFO (Grenon et al, 2004, pp. 20) and GFO (Herre, 2009), which are mainly used in the biomedical domain, and the top-level ontology by Sowa (2000, pp. 67), which has no documented software applications, they name DOLCE, SUMO, Cyc, and PROTON as the most commonly, domain independent used top level ontologies.

3.2.1 DOLCE

DOLCE, the "descriptive ontology for linguistic and cognitive engineering" (Gangemi et al, 2002; Masolo et al, 2003) is a foundational ontology with its roots in cognitive science and linguistics. It provides a top level of categories in which entities can be classified. Notably, the top level category is "particular" – where a particular is something which cannot have direct instances, whereas a "universal" is something which *can* have direct instances. For example, the Eiffel Tower is a universal, since there is a direct instance of it. A building, on the other hand, is a particular, since there is nothing that would be denoted as *the building*. Universals are members of the sets defined by particulars (Masolo et al, 2003, pp. 9).

Figure 3.10 depicts the top level of DOLCE. The four basic categories are EN-DURANT, PERDURANT, QUALITY, and ABSTRACT. An endurant is something whose parts a fully present at a given point in time (like a car), while a perdurant is something whose parts are not fully present at a given point in time (like the process of driving with a car). As a consequence, the parthood relation for endurants is only fully defined when adding a time span (e.g., "Alan Wilder was a member of Depeche Mode from 1982 to 1995"), while the parthood relation for perdurants does not require such a time span (e.g., "the 1980s were part of the 20th century"), as explained by Masolo et al (2003, p. 11).

Typically, endurants *participate* in perdurants (like a car participating in the driving of that car). Important distinctions of endurants encompass physical vs. non-physical and agentive vs. non-agentive endurants. Niles and Pease (2001, p. 5) point out that when adopting the point of view of a four dimensional space where time is yet another dimension, there is no such distinction into endurants and perdurants.

Qualities are entities that can be perceived or measured, like the color and the prize of a car. Every entity may have a set of qualities that exist as long as the entity exists. DOLCE distinguishes physical qualities (such as size or color), temporal qualities (like the duration of a process), and abstract qualities (such as a prize).

Abstracts are entities that neither have any qualities nor are qualities by themselves. A typical abstract is a spatial region or a time interval.

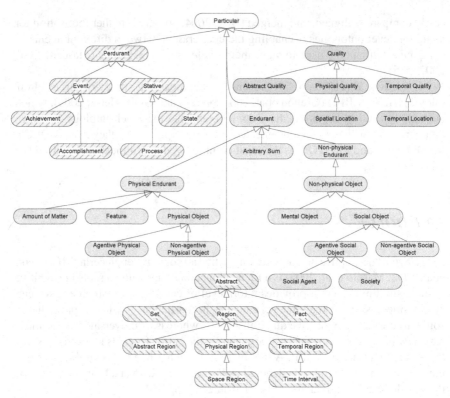

Fig. 3.10: The top level categories of DOLCE, following Masolo et al (2003, p. 14).
The subtrees of the four main categories are marked in different shades.

Several extensions to DOLCE exist. One of the most frequently used is the *DOLCE DnS*[9] (Descriptions and Situations) module, which is used to formalize communication scenarios. As interoperation between computer systems, as discussed above, is a crucial field of application for ontologies, and such an interoperation is a special case of communication, the D&S ontology provides useful concepts for describing such interoperations, such as parameters, functional roles, and communication methods (Gangemi and Mika, 2003, pp. 689). Due to its wide usage, DOLCE and DOLCE DnS are bundled together in one ontology as *DOLCE-Lite*. DOLCE-Lite consists of 37 classes, 70 object properties, and 349 axioms.

Based on the DnS extension, two other extensions to DOLCE have been proposed, which are useful foundations for using ontologies in the field of software engineering. The *DDPO* (Dolce and DnS Plan Ontology) (Gangemi et al, 2005, pp. 23), which defines categories such as tasks and goals, as well as constructs needed to account for the temporal relations, such as preconditions and postconditions. The *information object ontology* (Gangemi et al, 2005, pp. 80) defines information objects (such as

---

[9] Also referred to as *DOLCE D&S*.

printed or digital documents) and their relations to actors and real world entities. Based on those foundations, Oberle et al (2009, pp. 383) have defined ontologies of software and and software components (see section 6.2.2). Table 3.1 sums up the different extension to DOLCE and depicts their sizes.

	Categories	Relations	Axioms
DOLCE-Lite	37	70	349
Temporal Relations	4	25	79
Spatial Relations	0	20	64
Descriptions and Situations	55	114	567
Functional Participation	0	30	107
Plans	22	27	124
Core Software Ontology	45	37	186
Core Ontology of Software Components	6	10	52

Table 3.1: Size of the DOLCE ontologies and extensions

3.2.2 SUMO

The Suggested Upper Merged Ontology *SUMO* (Niles and Pease, 2001) is a top level ontology written in KIF. An OWL version of SUMO is also available. SUMO consists of a top level ontology, a mid level ontology, and several domain ontologies, which, together, encompass the definition of 20,000 terms, using 70,000 axioms (Pease, 2011).

The top level of SUMO is shown in figure 3.11. The top level categories are physical and abstract entities. The first are divided into objects and processes, which are the same as endurants and perdurants in DOLCE. The top level of SUMO encompasses about 1,000 concepts (Niles and Terry, 2004, p. 15).

The abstract entities encompasses four different sub categories. Propositions are any type of informational content, ranging from short utterances to books. Quantities are any observations gained by counting or measuring. Attributes are any sort of qualities that are not used to form individual classes, e.g., instead of forming a class of all red objects, RED is defined as an instance of the attribute COLOR. Finally, sets and classes, are collections of individuals, either as structured tuples or unsorted sets. In SUMO, a relation is a set of tuples, e.g., one tuple for each pair of people married to each other for the relation "married to".

Below the top level, some specific constructs are defined which rather belong to a meta ontology than to a top level ontology, such as BINARY RELATION. Thus, SUMO mixes L_1 and L_2 contents in one ontology (and even on the same level).

The mid-level ontology *MILO* defines more specific concepts than the top level ontology. It has been developed by collecting concepts from several domain-specific ontologies from domains such as geography, finance, and defense, and by considering

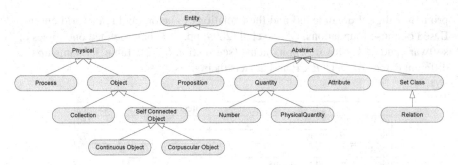

Fig. 3.11: The top level categories of SUMO, following Niles and Pease (2001, p. 5)

frequently used terms from the *WordNet* lexical database (Miller, 1995). The result is a mid level ontology of approximately 15,000 concepts (Niles and Terry, 2004, p. 17).

3.2.3 Cyc

Cyc (Lenat, 1995, pp. 33), the name being derived from en*cyc*lopedia, is the largest top-level ontology. As of 2006, it defined 250,000 terms and 2.2 million assertions. There is also a reduced, freely available subset of Cyc called *OpenCyc*, which is also available in OWL (Cycorp Inc., 2011). OpenCyc contains 47,000 terms and 306,000 assertions (Matuszek et al, 2006, p. 44).

The original intent of Cyc was to codify common sense knowledge in order to build expert systems and prepare the ground for AI applications. Cyc is defined in its own, very expressive language called *CycL*, which is based on first order logic and provides several extensions from higher-order logic (Matuszek et al, 2006, pp. 44).

Cyc is divided into an upper ontology, and several middle and lower ontologies. The upper level is a "classical" top level ontology defining categories such as TANGI-BLETHING, as shown in figure 3.12. Like SUMO, its contents also mix up the upper level L_1 definitions with definitions that are rather on a meta level (i.e., L_2) than on an upper level, such as PREDICATE and BINARY RELATION.

The middle level defines widely used categories such as everyday items or geospatial relationships, while ontologies at the lower level are targeted at specific domains.

3.2.4 PROTON

PROTON (Terziev et al, 2005) is a set of four ontologies (called *modules* by the authors) which can be used as a top level for building domain-specific ontologies. PROTON encompasses about 300 classes and 100 properties. The four modules are

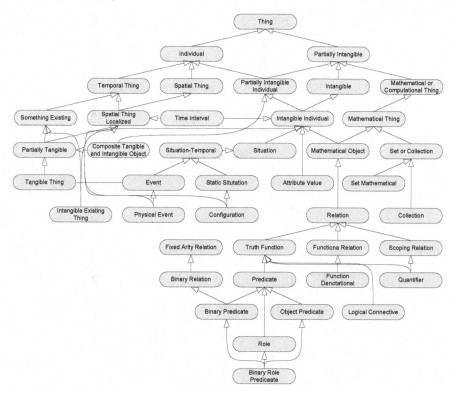

Fig. 3.12: The taxonomy of Cyc's upper level ontology, following Cycorp, Inc. (2002)

system, *upper level*, *top level*, and *knowledge management*. All of them are publicly available as OWL files.

The system module defines very basic categories such as ENTITY or ALIAS. The top level defines basic categories of things that exist in the world, both abstract (such as LANGUAGE or TOPIC) and concrete (such as PERSON or DOCUMENT). Based on that rough categorization, the knowledge management module defines a set of further common upper categories, such as AIRPLANE MODEL or RESEARCH ORGANIZATION. Furthermore, a set of common relations between objects is defined, which can be used, e.g., to express ownership or professions.

Figure 3.13 shows the system and top level categories of PROTON. The top level of PROTON contains some concepts whose adequacy for a top level ontology is at least questionable, such as JOB OFFER, which is a rather specific concept from the domain of employment. Other concepts, such as PRODUCT, are on the border line – PRODUCT can be seen as a concept from the domain of business, which, on the other hand, is generic enough to occur in many domains. However, there are domains in which the concept PRODUCT does not occur, such as astronomy or paleontology.

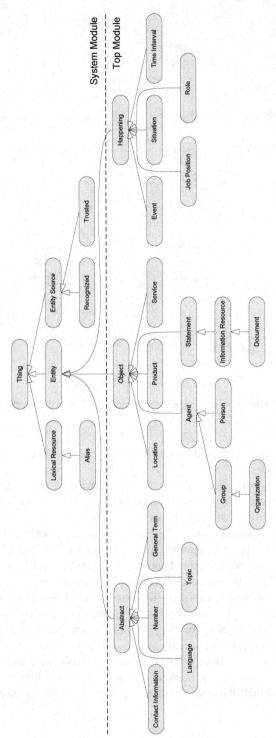

Fig. 3.13: The system and top level categories of PROTON, following (Terziev et al, 2005, pp. 20). Properties are not shown in the figure.

3.3 Infrastructures for Working with Ontologies

Ontologies are not a means in themselves. To build useful systems with ontologies, some more additional ingredients are needed. Editors are used to create and alter ontologies, programming frameworks facilitate implementing ontology-based systems, storage solutions allow for high performance access to ontologies, and ontology matching tools help building systems using a number of different ontologies in parallel.

3.3.1 Ontology Editors

Although it possible to use standard text editors, or, in the case of XML-based formats such as RDF-XML (see Sect. 3.1.2), XML editors for authoring and editing ontologies[10] more sophisticated tools exist. According to Cardoso (2007, pp. 84), the most popular tool is *Protégé* (Gennari et al, 2003, pp. 89), which is used by more than two thirds of the users of ontology editor tools.

Protégé, shown in figure 3.14, is a plugin based tool which allows for authoring OWL ontologies, with additional plugins for rule languages such as SWRL. There are different further plugins for visualization as well as for querying and reasoning with ontologies. Protégé may also serve as a framework for building ontology-based applications with means for editing ontologies (Rebstock et al, 2008, pp. 145).

Other popular ontology editors are *SWOOP* (Kalyanpur et al, 2006, pp. 144), *OntoStudio* (ontoprise GmbH, 2011b), the commercial successor of *OntoEdit* (Sure et al, 2002, pp. 221), and its open source counterpart *NeOn Toolkit* (Haase et al, 2008), *WebODE* (Arpírez et al, 2001, pp. 6), and *Altova Semantic Works* (Altova, 2011). Mizoguchi and Kozaki (2009, pp. 315) provide a detailed comparison of state of the art ontology editors. García-Barriocanal et al (2005, pp. 1) provide an analysis with respect to the usability of ontology editors, finding that there are major usability flaws which prevent the wide adoption of those tools by domain experts and end users.

3.3.2 Ontology Visualization

Many ontology authoring tools and suites come with a number of graphical views of RDF and ontology data. For example, the ontology engineering tool *Protégé* comes with plugins such as *IsaViz*, *OwlViz*, or *Jambalaya*, all providing different visual representations of ontologies and RDF data. Among the variety of other generic RDF

---

[10] In fact, the survey by Cardoso (2007, pp. 84), conducted with more than 600 researchers and practitioners in the semantic web area, observed that text editors are used by more than 10% of the survey participants, making them score as the fourth popular tool in a list of 14 different tools.

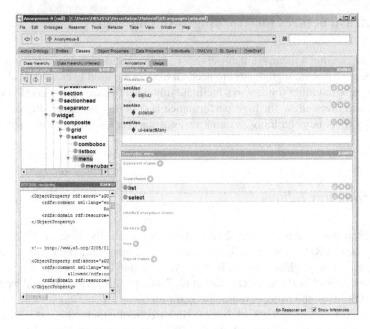

Fig. 3.14: Screenshot of the ontology editor Protégé

visualization tools, two of the best-known are *RDFGravity* (Goyal and Westenthaler, 2004), and the visualization provided by the W3C's RDF validation service (W3C, 2007a). RDF graphs can also be interactive, as demonstrated in (Schmitt et al, 2010). Although mc schraefel and Karger (2006) have argued that mere graph-based visualizations are not helpful for end users, those are by far the most prominent. In Chap. 10, we will show that simple graph-based visualizations are very well suited for generating benefit for end users.

For browsing the web of linked data, several browsers providing different means of visualizations have been developed. *Tabulator* (Berners-Lee et al, 2006) was one of the first tools for browsing linked data. Its basic view presents a tree-like structure of the starting concept, with each relation unfolding a new level containing the related concepts, as shown in figure 3.15. Furthermore, it contains specialized map and timeline views for visualizing spatial and temporal relations. *Fenfire* (Hastrup et al, 2008) provides a straight-forward graph view of linked data, allowing the user to start from a resource and see all the linked resources. The user can follow links to browse the graph of linked data.

Humboldt (Kobilarov and Dickinson, 2008) and *Explorator* (de Araújo and Schwabe, 2009) are linked data browser based on facets, i.e., domain-specific filters for browsing RDF data. The recently discussed extension *RExplorator* (Cohen and Schwabe, 2010) allows for reusing and recombining those facets. *VisiNav* (Harth, 2010, pp. 348) combines tabular, graph-based and faceted browsing, and also pro-

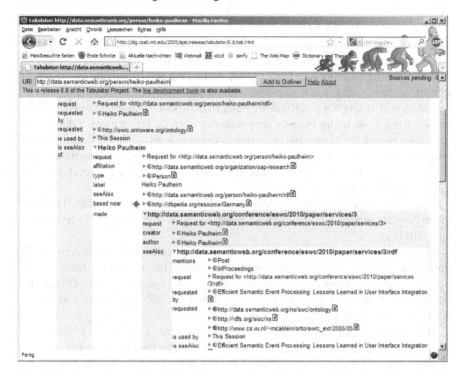

Fig. 3.15: Screenshot of the Linked Data explorer *Tabulator*, showing data from the Semantic Dog Food server (Möller et al, 2007, pp. 802).

vides a timeline-based view for showing temporal data, such as birth and death dates of persons.

visR (Weiss et al, 2008) is a tool for browsing and editing linked data. It features a hybrid view, showing the RDF triples as well as a graph view of the underyling data in parallel in two synchronized views. The authors also present a user study with a group of semantic web engineers where they both evaluate qualitative feedback, as well as quantitative data such as the completion time for different tasks.

RelFinder (Lohmann et al, 2010, pp. 421) is a specialized tool which, unlike the ones discussed so far, does not use *one*, but *two* concepts within an RDF graph to start with, and finds and visualizes links between those two concepts.

ThinkPedia and *ThinkBase* (Hirsch et al, 2009) provide a *hybrid view* on Wikipedia and Freebase, respectively, combining an RDF graph view with the original user interfaces. The authors present a qualitative, but not a quantitative user study. A similar approach is presented with *SemanticWonderCloud* (Mirizzi et al, 2010, pp. 138), which provides a visual interface to DBPedia, combining explicit relations with statistical information, such as the usage of concepts for tagging.

Surveys and comparisons of ontology visualization methods and tools are given, e.g., by Katifori et al (2007) and Lanzenberger et al (2009, pp. 705).

3.3.3 Programming Frameworks

For implementing software systems using ontologies, programming frameworks or application programming interfaces (APIs) are needed, which provide functionality to load, process, query, and manipulate ontologies.

Puleston et al (2008, pp. 130) distinguish frameworks using *direct programming models* from those using *indirect programming models*. When using a direct programming model, the classes the programmer operates with are on the domain model level, e.g., `Customer` or `Banking Account`. Indirect programming models are domain independent, they provide classes on the ontological meta level, such as `Class` or `Relation`.

There are various examples for APIs using direct programming models. They can be further categorized into generative, intrusive, and non-intrusive APIs (Paulheim et al, 2011b).

Generative approaches use the ontology to automatically generate the corresponding domain-specific classes in the target programming language (e.g., Java). Examples for generative approaches are *RDFReactor* (Völkel and Sure, 2005), *OWL2Java* (Kalyanpur et al, 2004, pp. 98), *OntoJava* (Eberhart, 2002, pp. 102), and *agogo* (Parreiras et al, 2009, pp. 342).

RDFReactor uses an RDF Schema as input and creates a set of Java objects such that each `rdfs:class` in the RDF Schema is represented by a Java class. The resulting code allows accessing RDF data both by using an abstract RDF API as well as the generated concrete Java API.

OWL2Java uses a similar approach, but takes the more expressive OWL Full as input to the code generator, incidentally trading the loss of computational completeness for expressiveness, as computational completeness is not an essential property for working with the generated Java classes. Integrity checkers are generated from constraints on relations e.g. restricting the cardinalities. Thus, integrity checks on the Java objects can be performed automatically in the generated code.

OntoJava uses RDF Schema and RuleML as input to the code generator, thus allowing more expressive models. In addition to the restrictions that can be formulated in RDF-S, rules may be used as constraint rules for defining further consistency checks, as production rules for automatically completing data, and as reaction rules which trigger the call of a Java method on certain conditions.

Unlike these approaches, agogo does not use existing ontologies as input to the code generator, but relies on its own input language, which uses SPARQL statements for defining operations on the classes to generate. The input language also provides means for defining reusable design patterns, which leads to more maintainable models.

When using dynamically typed scripting languages, the class model may also be generated on-the-fly at run-time. Implemented examples include *ActiveRDF* (Oren et al, 2007, pp. 817) for Ruby and *Tramp* (Swartz, 2002) for Python. For the developer, such approaches are more comfortable, since they do not require additional tools such as a code generator, but work directly out of the box by invoking an API.

Intrusive approaches do not generate new Java classes from an ontology, but modify (i.e. intrude into) an existing class model by adding additional code fragments. While these approaches can be applied if a class model already exists, e.g. in projects where the use of ontologies has not been foreseen from the beginning of the development, they demand more discipline from the developers, as they have to take care about the synchronicity of the class model and the ontology themselves.

Quasthoff and Meinel (2009, pp. 443) have derived a number of design patterns have been proposed for mapping class models to ontologies from the design patterns for mapping class models to database models introduced by Fowler (2003, pp. 33). The authors discuss *otm-j*, an implementation of their approach based on Java annotations[11]. Similar frameworks are introduced with *Sommer* (Story, 2009), *Texai KB* (Reed, 2007), *RDFBeans* (Alishevskikh, 2011), *Jenabean* (Cowan, 2008), and *P-API* (Wagner et al, 2009, pp. 99), which are also based on Java annotatations. Sect. 7.1 gives a closer look at those intrusive frameworks using direct programming models.

Non-intrusive approaches are still very rare. One example is ELMO (openRDF, 2009), a framework which provides both intrusive and non-intrusive mechanisms. While the intrusive mechanisms, like the approaches above, rely on Java annotations, the non-intrusive ones use run-time registration.

Another example for a non-intrusive approach is described in (Hillairet et al, 2008, pp. 5). The authors propose a mapping between between EMF (Eclipse Modeling Framework) class models (Steinberg et al, 2008) and OWL ontologies, using a proprietary mapping language. With these mappings, data can be transformed between RDF and OWL at run-time. The framework discussed in that paper is also capable of generating an OWL ontology from EMF.

With an API based on an indirect programming model, the developer does not work on domain specific classes, but on classes specific for the respective ontology meta model. One of the most well-known ontology programming frameworks with an indirect programming model is the *WonderWeb OWL API*, often referred to as *OWL API* only (Bechhofer et al, 2003b, pp. 659). Its focus is on providing Java interfaces and classes for OWL language constructs of all three OWL language dialects (see 3.1.2). As interfaces and implementations are strictly separated, developers can add their own specific implementations to support particular features. Although the OWL API does not contain a reasoner, it foresees extension points for adding external reasoners. The basic version of OWL API supports in-memory computation only, which poses certain limitations on scalability when working with larger ontologies.

Another well-known ontology programming framework is *Jena* (Carroll et al, 2004, pp. 74). Instead of directly working with OWL constructs, it adds a level of abstraction and works on general *graphs* (Bechhofer and Carroll, 2004, pp. 266), which allow for the processing of ontologies in RDF(S) , all OWL dialects, and their predecessor DAML. Jena supports in-memory processing as well as processing of persistent ontologies with a lazy loading mechanism (Fowler, 2003, pp. 200) and is thus suitable for implementing highly scalable applications working with large-scale

---

[11] Note that *Java annotations* are a language construct in Java which can be used to add arbitrary metadata to Java classes, methods, and attributes. Those Java annotations are not necessarily *semantic* annotations, but can be used for various purposes (Sun Microsystems, 2010).

ontologies (Rebstock et al, 2008, p. 142). It contains a simple set of built-in reasoner and supports the DIG interface (see 3.1.3) for using external reasoners.

A third example for indirect programming models is the *KAON2* programming framework (Motik and Sattler, 2006, pp. 227) and its commercial counter part *Ontobroker* (Decker et al, 1999, pp. 351). It supports OWL DL, F-Logic, and rules formulated in SWRL (see 3.1.2). For each of those variations, it provides a built-in reasoner. Detailed comparisons of programming frameworks are given by Bizer and Westphal (2007) and Rebstock et al (2008, pp. 139).

3.3.4 Storage Solutions

Almost all software systems using ontologies require some mechanism of storing those ontologies. In the simplest case, ontologies are stored as files. However, whenever there are strict requirements regarding performance or scalability, a file-based solution, e.g., storing individual OWL files, will not carry, since starting off parsing a file when answering a query leads to longer response times, and loading files into main memory as a whole limits scalability to larger ontologies. Therefore, more sophisticated storage solutions, often referred to as *triple stores* (Shadbolt et al, 2006, p. 98), are developed. Such solutions typically support querying the ontologies with query languages such as SPARQL, transaction management, and bulk loading of large amounts of data (Wilkinson et al, 2003, p. 145).

Some of semantic web programming frameworks, such as Jena, allow for storing ontologies directly in data bases by using three-column tables for storing the ontologies' triple representations. Possible optimizations include the use of index or the usage of particular tables for predicates that are often used (Heymans et al, 2008, pp. 90).

A well known data base oriented storage system is *Sesame* (Broekstra et al, 2002, pp. 54). It offers different interfaces such as HTTP, RMI, and SOAP. Sesame is able to use different underlying data base management systems. Each ontology query is translated to one or more database queries, where an optimization algorithm tries to produce only few data base queries that can be processed efficiently.

Another ontology storage system is *3Store* (Harris and Gibbins, 2003), developed in C and using a MySQL database. Like Sesame, 3Store uses optimized database queries to minimize the query answering times. Furthermore, additional hash tables are employed to speed up queries, and particular inferred facts are redundantly stored in the data base (Harris and Shadbolt, 2005, pp. 236).

Virtuoso is a commercial database system developed by OpenLink Software, which can uniformly storage relational data and RDF triples. It provides several bridges between the relational and the triple storage, e.g., SPARQL statements nested into SQL queries, and the conversion of legacy relational data into RDF data (Erling and Mikhailov, 2009, pp. 7).

OWLIM is a storage and reasoning solution developed by Ontotext AD, which aims at fast and scalable storage and querying of large RDF datasets, supporting

OWL reasoning for query answering. There are different editions encompassing the free *SwiftOWLIM* and the commercial *BigOWLIM*, where the latter provides several optimizations, allows for full-text search, and can be run on clusters for load balancing (Kiryakov et al, 2005, pp. 182).

Like OWLIM, *AllegroGraph*, a commercial solution developed by Franz Inc., is an RDF storage solution which provides several reasoning capabilities. Besides standard OWL reasoning, it can deal with spatial and temporal reasoning as well as with Prolog rules (Franz Inc., 2010).

The development of efficient storage solutions for ontologies is a vital area of research, and there are various comparisons of different storage solutions, such as Lee (2004), Liu and Hu (2005), and Bizer and Schultz (2009).

3.3.5 Ontology Matching

There are scenarios in which multiple ontologies are to be used in parallel, e.g., if different organizations have developed individual ontologies of the same or related domains. In these cases, it is necessary to have a mapping between those ontologies. Such a mapping can be a set of correspondences as well as complex mapping rules.

Since creating such a mapping manually is a tedious and time consuming task, *ontology matching* tools can either produce a mapping automatically, or assist the user in a semi-automatic process. Typically, ontology matching tools use a combination of element based (e.g., name similarity) and structural (e.g., common sub and super categories) techniques, as well as external knowledge, such as thesauri (Euzenat and Shvaiko, 2007, pp. 65).

Recent comparisons of ontology matching tools are discussed by by Alasoud et al (2009, pp. 379), Euzenat et al (2009), and (Euzenat et al, 2010). According to the latter, the most powerful tools currently available are *ASMOV* (Jean-Mary et al, 2009, pp. 235), *RiMOM* (Li et al, 2009, pp. 1218), *AgreementMaker* (Cruz et al, 2009, pp. 1586), and *SOBOM* (Xu et al, 2010). Besides improving recall and precision of the tools, current research challenges in the field of ontology matching address issues such as performance and scalability, automatic configuration of matching tools, the use of reasoning for refining mappings, and the involvement of end users (Shvaiko and Euzenat, 2008, pp. 1164).

3.4 Ontologies in Application Integration

Ontologies have been widely used in application integration tasks. Uschold and Grüninger (1996) have pointed out that ontologies are useful for integrating applications, serving as an inter-lingua between systems which may reduce the complexity of translating between those systems from $O(n^2)$ to $O(n)$.

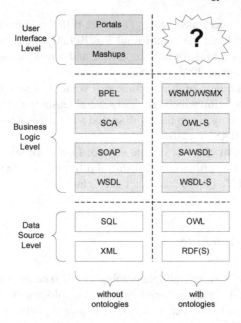

Fig. 3.16: Examples for integration on the different layers, with or without ontologies. Adapted from Benatallah and Nezhad (2007, p. 124). There are currently no approaches employing ontologies on the user interface level.

Figure 3.16 shows examples of ontology-based and non-ontology-based integration techniques on all layers, adapted from Benatallah and Nezhad (2007, p. 124). So far, there have been no attempts to employ ontologies for integration on the user interface level.

3.4.1 Data Source Level

Integration on the data source level is the oldest integration approach using ontologies, dating back to the 1980s – even if at that time, the term *ontology* was not yet common, semantic integration of databases using so called *conceptual schemas* was already discussed then (Batini et al, 1986, pp. 323).

Ontologies are typically used in database integration to provide a common schema for heterogeneous databases, as shown in Fig. 3.17. To this end, the database schemas of the integrated databases are mapped to that common ontology. A query interface then uses the ontology to query the underlying databases; based on the mappings, the ontology-based queries are translated to SQL queries, and the query results from the databases are translated back. Thus, *SPARQL* (see Sect. 3.1.2) can be used as an abstract, ontology-based language for querying databases.

Using an ontology, additional domain knowledge defined in that ontology can be implicitly used for better query answering, and reasoning can draw conclusions from facts that are contained in different databases (Dou and LePendu, 2006, pp. 463).

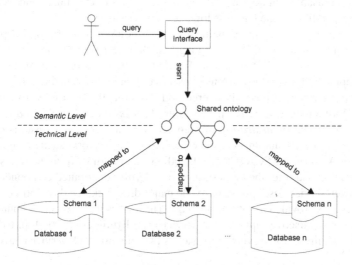

Fig. 3.17: Ontology-based database integration, following (Doan and Halevy, 2005, p. 83).

The basic approach of ontology-based database integration maps tables to classes in the ontology, and column to object or data relations (Berners-Lee, 1998). An example for such a light-weight approach is *SquirrelRDF* (Seaborne et al, 2007).

However, mapping database models and ontologies with a 1:1 mapping is not always desirable (see Chap. 7 for a detailed discussion). Thus, more sophisticated approaches such as *Triplify* (Auer et al, 2009), *D2RQ* (Bizer and Seaborne, 2004), and *R2O* (Barrasa et al, 2004), also allow the definition of non-trivial mappings, based on rules and/or complex SQL statements. A recent state-of-the-art survey is given by Sahoo et al (2009). Current research directions in this area encompass the automatic generation of mappings, scalability to large databases, and visual tools for defining mappings between the database schemas and the ontology.

Another highly acclaimed approach to integration on the data source level is the *Semantic Desktop* (Sauermann et al, 2005; Cheyer et al, 2005). Here, data encapsulated in different applications on one machine – such as e-mail contacts, calendar entries, and documents – is made accessible via a central query interface. Users can browse their personal data using a unified view based on RDF data which is acquired from integrating the underlying applications' data sources, as well as annotate and link them.

3.4.2 Business Logic Level

As discussed in Sect. 2.1.1, data source integration makes the data of different applications reusable, but does not reuse business logics of existing applications. To that end, integration on the business logic level is necessary.

Web services have become a mainstream technique for performing integration on the business logic level. With languages such as the *Web Service Description Language WSDL* (W3C, 2007d) and the *Simple Object Access Protocol SOAP* (W3C, 2007c), application logic, encapsulated by services that can be called remotely across the internet. Services can be discovered and dynamically assembled to complex systems. With languages such as the *Business Process Execution Language BPEL* (OASIS, 2007), the *orchestration* of web services into complex systems can be formally described and automatically executed. Some frameworks such as the Service Component Architecture SCA (Chappell, 2007) further abstract from the web service implementation and offer the orchestration of *arbitrary* distributed components.

Those web service descriptions have one major drawback: the description of what a service does is provided in natural language. This makes it impossible for automatic tools to reliably discover appropriate services (de Bruijn et al, 2009, p. 617). To overcome this limitation, several approaches for semantic web services have been proposed.

WSDL-S (W3C, 2005d) and *SAWSDL* (W3C, 2007b) are similar approaches[12] that propose the extension of WSDL in order to support semantic annotations. With SAWSDL, operations, parameters and data types can be annotated using ontologies. Thus, a formal definition of the respective elements can be provided, which allows for better discovery and orchestration of web services.

While WSDL-S and SAWSDL aim at extending existing standards for web services, OWL-S (W3C, 2004a) and WSMO (W3C, 2005c; Fensel et al, 2007b, pp. 57) propose new standards for semantic web services. While OWL-S is an OWL ontology, several languages for WSMO exist, which are subsumed under the *Web Service Modeling Language WSML* (W3C, 2005b; Fensel et al, 2007c, pp. 83). Those different languages encompass variants based on OWL DL as well as on F-Logic and on logic, rule-based programming.

Both OWL-S and WSMO provide ontologies that can be used to define web services; those ontologies define categories such as WEB SERVICE, as opposed to the ontologies used in WSDL-S and SAWSDL, which describe the domain the web service is used for (see section 5.2.3 for a detailed discussion of this distinction).

OWL-S and WSMO allow for describing preconditions, postconditions, and effects of operations, which can be used for more sophisticated composition of web services, e.g. by ontology-based orchestration engines such as the *Web Service Execution Environment WSMX* (W3C, 2005a). Furthermore, WSMO allows for defining *mediators*, which can be employed for transformations between heterogeneous data models, such as described above for data base integration. Both languages provide

---

[12] After SAWSDL became a W3C recommendation, WSDL-S has been discontinued (de Bruijn et al, 2009, pp. 632).

means for adding constructs in other languages, such as SWRL or F-Logic, in cases where a higher expressivity is needed. There are also other proposed ontology-based add-ons to semantic web services, e.g., describing non-functional properties such as Quality of Service (Maximilien and Singh, 2004, pp. 84).

Several tools have evolved in the landscape of semantic web services, which enable the developer of web services to provide annotations and descriptions in the respective languages. Such tools range from generators which automatically create at least parts of the annotations, and editors which allow for a simplified creation and maintenance of web service annotations without having to code ontologies manually (Ankolekar et al, 2007b, pp. 311).

3.4.3 User Interface Level

As discussed by Benatallah and Nezhad (2007, p. 124), and supported by a careful review of the literature, there have not been any attempts to employ ontologies for user interface integration (see figure 3.16). Despite the added value that ontologies have brought to integration on the data source and business logic level, as sketched above, and a general notion that ontologies could help in integration on the UI level (Ankolekar et al, 2007a, p. 830), and that current ontology-based approaches on the business logic level cannot be trivially transferred to the UI level (Dettborn et al, 2008, p. 110), no ontology-based approach to UI integration has been proposed so far. A possible reason is that UI integration itself is still a young field, compared to, e.g., database integration.

3.5 Summary

In this chapter, we have introduced ontologies and their role in application integration. In existing research works, ontologies have brought significant contributions to application integration. However, no approaches exist so far that employ ontologies for providing a versatile mechanism for UI integration allowing for arbitrary interactions, which stresses the scientific contribution of this book.

Chapter 4
Ontologies in User Interface Development

Abstract There are various approaches that use ontologies in UI development. To summarize those approaches, we use the term "ontology-enhanced user interfaces", defined as user interfaces "whose visualization capabilities, interaction possibilities, or development process are enabled or (at least) improved by the employment of one or more ontologies." (Paulheim and Probst, 2010c, p. 37). As discussed in a position paper by Rauschmayer (2005), ontologies and semantic web technologies can potentially be used for various purposes in the field of user interfaces, such as reduction of information overload, context-sensitive adaptation, providing help, integrating different user interface components, and support for particular work-flows. This chapter introduces a classification of ontology usage in user interfaces in Sect. 4.1, and provides an overview of state-of-the-art approaches, illustrated using representative examples of using ontologies for improving visualization (Sect. 4.2), interaction (Sect. 4.3), and the development of user interfaces (Sect. 4.4).

4.1 Classification Schema

As discussed in Sect. 3.1.4, there are various classifications of ontologies and their employment, each following a certain purpose and thus having a particular bias. We adopt some of the criteria proposed in those works and enhance them with criteria which are useful for categorizing user interfaces.

Since the development of user interfaces is a sub-area of software engineering, we follow the schema introduced by Happel and Seedorf (2006, pp. 10) and take the ontologies' domain and the time of its employment into account. Furthermore, we adopt the ontology complexity criterion from van Heijst et al (1997, pp. 194) and Gómez-Pérez et al (2004, p. 8), as this is a useful criterion for tackling the requirements when it comes to decide for an ontology language and a matching programming framework.

Regarding the domain, Happel and Seedorf (2006, p. 11) distinguish two types: the real world domain for which the software is build, and the domain of software systems. We introduce a third domain, namely users and the roles they have (Kagal et al, 2003, pp. 63). Roles are most often roles a person takes in the real world. However, roles may also affect the way that person can interact with a system (e.g., whether that person has certain rights within a system) or is supposed to perform certain tasks. Thus, they cannot be clearly assigned to any of the two domains introduced by Happel and Seedorf. Therefore, we propose users and roles as a domain of its own.

Regarding the complexity, it is beneficial to further classify highly formal ontologies into decidable and non-decidable ontologies, as reasoning plays an important role in many ontology-based systems (Antoniou et al, 2005b, p. 13).

We augment these three criteria by two additional ones that target specifically at user interfaces, based on the fact that user interfaces usually serve two main purposes: a) presenting information to the user, and b) allowing interaction with a system. For ontologies in user interfaces, we therefore propose the following two additional criteria: a) how the ontology is presented to the user, and b) how the user can interact with the ontology.

In ontology-enhanced user interfaces, the ontologies used and the information contained therein may be, at least partially, presented to the user. Therefore, the question *how* the ontology is presented is particularly interesting. There are different options:

No presentation.   The ontology is completely hidden.

Lists.   Lists of categories from the ontology are shown without making relations between those categories visible. Those lists may be actual selection lists as well as the names of single concepts from the ontology appearing as text blocks in some places of the user interface.

Graphical.   Relations between concepts are visualized, e.g., in form of trees (most often showing the taxonomy) or graphs (including non-taxonomic relations). A detailed survey of ontology visualization techniques is given by Katifori et al (2007), encompassing various graphical representations in 2D and 3D.

Verbalized.   A textual representation of the axioms contained in the ontology is provided.

Source code.   The ontology's source code, e.g., in OWL or F-Logic, is shown to the user.

At first glance, it may be questionable whether we are still talking about ontology-enhanced user interfaces if those ontologies are completely hidden, or whether the ontologies are rather used in the business logic or data layer when they are not visible in the user interface. However, we will show some examples in the next sections where hidden ontologies can directly influence the user interface and thus conform to our definition.

Besides the visualization, there may be different types of interaction with the ontologies used in an ontology-enhanced user interface. In some cases, the ontologies may only be viewed, in others, the user can also extend and alter them. We distinguish three types of interaction with ontologies:

No interaction.   The user cannot interact with the ontology.

View only. The user can view the ontology or selected parts thereof. The view can be static (e.g., in form of texts or graphs) or dynamic and interactive (i.e., allowing to browse between concepts, zoom in and out, etc.)

View and edit. The user can modify the contents of the ontology. Such modifications can either be limited to refining the ontology (i.e., adding new subcategories or relations), or allow full modification, such as changing and deleting existing concepts.

In most cases where ontologies may be altered, this functionality is only accessible by a selected group of users, such as administrators.

Thus, we end up at a characterization schema comprising five criteria, as depicted in Fig. 4.1. In the rest of this section, different uses of ontologies in the field of user interfaces are discussed and classified in this schema.

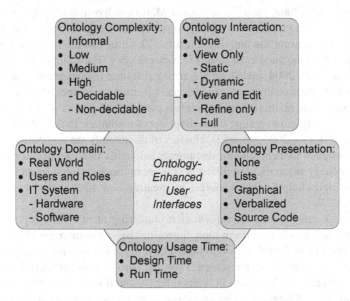

Fig. 4.1: Characterization schema for ontology-enhanced user interfaces (Paulheim and Probst, 2010c, p. 39)

4.2 Ontologies for Improving Visualization

Ontologies may be used for improving the appearance of a user interface, i.e., the way information is presented to the user. This means that given a set of information items, the transformation into visual items on the screen is influenced by ontologies. The determination of the initial set of information items, however, is not a task performed in the user interface, but in the underlying business logic. Therefore, approaches such as ontology-based information filtering are out of scope here, unless combined with an ontology-enhanced user interface.

4.2.1 Information Clustering

When retrieving information, it is possible that a large number of information items is returned. Therefore, the user may want some assistance in handling the query results. One possible approach is *information clustering*: Here, information items are subsumed to groups which stand for a set of single items. Each of these groups is represented by one visual item on the screen (Herman et al, 2000).

One example for ontologies-based information clustering is the *Cluster Map* project (Fluit et al, 2003, pp. 415). In Cluster Map, search results (e.g., from a web or database search) are visualized as connected sets (painted as balloons), which contain small dots representing the individual results. The user can navigate the ontology and get an idea of the number of results in each category. The *Courseware Watchdog* project (Tane et al, 2004, pp. 1), an e-learning resource management system, uses ontologies to provide an intuitive way to access e-learning resources. Here, taxonomic and non-taxonomic relations between classes can be displayed as well, allowing the user a flexible way of navigating through the set of resources. In the *SWAPit* project (Seeling and Becks, 2003, pp. 652), clusters of documents are computed from the metadata assigned to them, and the documents belonging to different categories in a domain ontology are marked in different colours in those clusters. In each of those cases, ontologies help finding resources by creating new visualizations apart from simple lists.

Ontologies can be used for information clustering at run-time to provide the groups and their labels for information clustering. By subsuming each information item to a class in the ontology's class hierarchy, those items can be clustered, and the classes are visualized on the screen. Thus, the ontology is characterizing the real world domain that the information items refer to, and it has to consist of at least a class hierarchy (although additional relations may be visualized as extra guidance). Both lists and graphical visualizations are possible, where in the latter case, the user may also navigate through the visualization interactively.

4.2.2 Text Generation

Information contained in ontologies is usually encoded in machine-readable languages that only experts can understand. When trying to make that information available to the user, it can be beneficial to transform it into a language that can be understood by the end user. To that end, different ontology verbalizing algorithms have been developed (Kaljurand and Fuchs, 2007).

An example for using verbalized ontologies is the *MIAKT* project (Bontcheva and Wilks, 2004, pp. 324): in that project, information about medical cases gathered from an information base in the form of RDF triples is turned into human-readable reports. The RDF triples and the definitions from the corresponding ontology are verbalized and turned into a small text describing a medical case.

There are other examples where not full text, but only text fragments are generated from information contained in ontologies. One promising strategy is to use texts that already exist and augment them with additional information taken from ontologies. In the *COHSE* project (Carr et al, 2001, pp. 334), text documents are augmented with links to related documents and categories as lists of links added to the texts. Here, ontologies defining the documents' domain of discourse can help identifying the correct anchor terms in the document, and ontology-based information retrieval may be one step in finding relevant documents to link to the anchor terms. Depending on whether the documents are directly linked to the anchor terms or link lists based on categories from the ontologies are generated, the ontologies are either invisible or visualized as lists. One appealing vision of applying this approach is to have a large information base, such as Wikipedia, interlinked and enhanced by using ontologies (Völkel et al, 2006, pp. 585). In this scenario, the user could even enhance and alter the ontology in a collaborative setting.

For verbalizing knowledge with ontologies, those ontologies have to be at least fairly complex, otherwise, no reasonably interesting text can be produced (only short sentences such as "a cat is an animal" can be generated from less complex ontologies). Reasoning over more complex ontologies can also be useful to provide better natural language representation, since statements which are not explicitly contained in the ontology can also be added to the text (Carr et al, 2001, pp. 34). Text generation may be performed both at design-time (in cases where a set of documents is compiled prior to using the system) as well as run-time (in cases where reports etc. are produced on demand). Although editing verbalized ontologies in collaborative settings is possible, most approaches only foresee viewing ontologies.

4.2.3 Adaptation of User Interface Appearance

Apart from the information displayed in a user interface, the appearance of the parts of a user interface itself may also be directed by ontologies. Most commonly, the user interface is adapted to the user's needs. If both the user interface elements and the user's profile are defined by using highly formal ontologies, a reasoner can determine the appearance which fits the user's needs best and thus personalize the user interface.

One particularly interesting application is the adaptation of user interfaces for users with special needs, such as in the *Semantic Life* project (Karim and Tjoa, 2006, pp. 77) or the W3C's *WAI ARIA* initiative (W3C, 2011a). Such adaptation includes adjusting font size, colours (for partly colour-blind people), and the organization of contents on the screen. In the Semantic Life project, the ontology models users' impairment and appropriate visualizations, i.e., it covers parts of the user as well as the system domain, so a reasoner can determine appropriate visualizations. In WAI ARIA, only the system parts are modeled in an ontolgy, and the selection of appropriate visualizations is left up to an agent (which is not specified any further). In both approaches, the underlying ontologies are evaluated at run-time for adapting the user interface, but they are not visible to the user.

Ontologies may not only be used for software adaptation, but also for *hardware adaptation*. One example is the *Context Studio* application developed by Nokia (Korpipää et al, 2004, pp. 133). Here, the user may create rules defining how mobile devices are supposed to provide information to the user in given situations (e.g., "if the display is turned down, do not ring aloud"). To this end, an ontology of the mobile phone and context situations is defined, which can be utilized by the user to create rules on how they want their mobile devices to behave (and thus extend the underyling ontology). The ontology is presented to the user when defining rules in the form of selection lists (although graphical assistance in defining those rules would also be possible), but is invisible outside the rule definition mode. In the case of mobile phones, the user's context may additionally be acquired, e.g., from GPS sensors of the mobile device, thus allowing adaptation of mobile applications based on the user's spatial context (Lee, 2010).

Another approach for hardware adaptation is shown in the *MaDoE* project (Larsson et al, 2007, pp. 704): here, user interfaces are distributed across different hardware devices. An ontology of devices and their capabilities is combined with a set of rules to make sure that each user interface component is displayed by a hardware component that has the required capabilities.

In the examples above, the rules for adapting user interfaces have been actively defined by the developer or the user, either at design or at run-time. Another approach is observing the user and learning those rules from the user's behavior during runtime, or off-line from log files. Such an approach is described by Schmidt et al (2008b, pp. 736). Here, learned rules, based on ontologies characterizing both the IT system and the real world domain, are used to optimize the information presentation in a portal. Information items that are more likely to be relevant for the user are given more prominent positions on the screen than others.

Another adaptation mechanism is the selection of visualization modules (software widgets, algorithms, or even hardware devices) that are suitable for a given information. This requires an ontology of those modules (i.e., the system domain software and/or hardware) in a degree of formality which allows reasoning to answer the queries for appropriate visualization modules. Such an approach is shown by (Potter and Wright, 2006, pp. 151), where input and output devices are selected automatically at run time given the current information and visualization needs.

Ontologies for adapting user interfaces can be used both at design and at run time, depending on whether the user interfaces is supposed to adapt dynamically, or if pre-adapted user interfaces are to be shipped. It may take place in the background, with the ontologies completely hidden from the user, or visibly. The user may also be granted the possibility to express their own rules for adaptation. Since the reasoning employed for adaptation is fairly complex, the ontologies also have to be highly expressive. Information about the real world, the IT system to adapt, and the user may be included for adaptation.

4.3 Ontologies for Improving Interaction

Besides visualizing data, the second important purpose of a user interface is to provide an access point to a system's functionalities. To this end, the user has to interact with the system by entering data, selecting items, issuing commands, etc. There are several approaches for employing ontologies to improve the interaction with IT systems.

4.3.1 Ontology-based Browsing

While we concentrated on information visualization as a run-once task so far (i.e., a given set of information items is visualized in an optimal form), the user usually interacts with these visualizations by browsing from one information item to another. Ontologies can be used to improve this browsing process. Hyvönen et al (2002, pp. 15) use the term "semantic browsing"; however, we prefer the term "ontology-based browsing" since any kind of browsing information always requires a semantic understanding of that information (which, on the other hand, does not need to be formalized in an ontology).

One example of a semantic browser is *Ozone* (Burel et al, 2009). Ozone uses RDF embedded in web pages as RDFa (see Sec. 3.1.2) to provide so-called "semantic overlays", i.e., textual and/or graphical information provided on demand when selecting an information item. For example, city names in texts annotated with concepts from an ontology defining their geographical position can be displayed on a map when selected.

Embedded RDF, however, is currently rather rare on the web. The browser *Magpie* (Dzbor, 2008, pp. 34) uses overlays like Ozone, but does not rely on embedded RDF. Instead, HTML pages are pre-processed, and the annotations are generated automatically. This is an approach also followed by *PiggyBank* (Huynh et al, 2005, pp. 413): here, so-called "screen scrapers" automatically transform web page contents into RDF. This RDF can then be used to provide additional information on the web page's contents. Piggy Bank also allows the user to store and share the RDF information gathered from scraping the web.

Another popular approach for ontology-based browsing is *faceted browsing*. Here, data (such as product information, or websites) is annotated with ontologies. The user can then select from different lists of ontological categories and orthogonal property values to view filtered lists of relevant information (Heim et al, 2008, pp. 49). While the basic faceted browsing approaches only use list-based views, there are some interesting extensions. The *SearchPoint* web search interface presents a graph of topics (which can be filled from an ontology) and their relations, and the user can click on any point in the graph to view the search results which belong to the topics which are displayed closest to the selected point (Pajntar and Grobelnik, 2008). The faceted browsing approach introduced by Hussein and Münter (2010) allows for defining arbitrary as well as domain-specific interaction elements (called "facet decorators") for different facet types, e.g., sliders for numeric values, maps for geographic values, etc.

Ontology-based browsing cannot be performed on the web alone. The *Semantic Desktop* (Sauermann et al, 2005; Cheyer et al, 2005) allows for browsing data contained in different applications on a single desktop computer. For example, there may be papers from authors (stored as text files), some of the authors may also be email contacts (stored in an email client program), and their web pages are bookmarked in a standard web browser. Semantic Desktop software links this data and explicitly presents these links to the user, so that the user can navigate from one resource to another, even if they are stored in different programs.

When resources are annotated with ontologies, an ontology-based browser can point to relevant other resources. Unlike finding related documents by measuring text similarities or access correlations, the user can also be informed about *how* the documents are related. Ontologies of low complexity (in the simplest case topic lists) about the documents' real world domain are sufficient for providing ontology-based browsing, but more sophisticated browsing functionality requires at least medium complexity. Visualization can range from invisible ontologies (in case related documents are proposed with help of the ontology, but without showing the ontology itself) to lists of concepts and more sophisticated graphical visualization.

4.3.2 User Input Assistance

In most kinds of interfaces, the user has to enter data into the system at a certain point, either in the form of textual input or by selecting values from predefined lists. In a form-based user interface, not every combination of input options is feasible. An ontology formalizing knowledge about the domain of the objects whose data is entered in a user interface may be employed to provide plausibility checking on the user's input.

It may be argued that plausibility checking is a functionality of the business logic, not of the user interface. Nevertheless, when being applied *during* the input process and not *afterwards*, plausibility checking can help *reducing the complexity of input forms*, e.g., by dynamically removing invalid options or providing direct feedback. Thus, plausibility checking can improve the usability of a user interface.

An example is introduced by Liu et al (2005, pp. 254). In a flower shop application, the customer has to step through an input wizard consisting of different forms. If a male person is selected as the recipient of a bouquet, then options such as "mother's day greeting card" are not included in subsequent selection lists. Here, an ontology reasoner can decide that a male person cannot be a mother and will therefore not receive a mother's day greeting card. Another example for a real world setting is e-government, where ontologies can be used to ease input in a large amount of forms, as shown in the *SeGoF* project (Stadlhofer and Salhofer, 2008, pp. 427). Another setting where filtering selection lists is useful are user interfaces for configuring complex products, as demonstrated in the *CAWICOMS* project (Ardissono et al, 2002, pp. 618).

Feasible input options can also be extracted from context information at run-time. In the semantic e-mail client *Semanta* (Scerri et al, 2009, pp. 36), for example, the content of an e-mail is extracted at run-time (e.g., it contains a meeting request), and possible answers (e.g., accept or decline the request) are determined by a reasoner and shown to the user in a selection list for automatically generating an answer mail. Here, the complex input task of writing an e-mail is simplified and reduced to selecting a template and filling the gaps.

In addition to supporting the user in selecting from pre-defined values, ontologies may also be employed *improving textual input*. In the case of searching for information, as shown, for example, in *OntoSeek*, the number of search results can be increased by not only searching for documents containing one term, but also for those containing a term related to the one the user entered, where those related terms are defined in an ontology (Guarino et al, 1999, pp. 70).

Another way of improving textual input is the provision of *autocomplete functionality*, where the user types the beginning of a word, and the system proposes completion based on terms defined in an ontology (Hildebrand and van Ossenbruggen, 2009). This ensures that the user only enters terms that the system understands and follows the idea of using ontologies as a shared vocabulary (Gruber, 1995, p. 908). In this scenario, the ontology again contains domain knowledge, but it requires only little formalization, since no reasoning is applied, and it is invisible for the user.

In many ontology-based systems, large knowledge bases are created, e.g., in the field of life sciences (Mendes et al, 2008, pp. 432). While querying those knowledge bases is very useful, it is a difficult task for the end user who is not familiar with querying languages such as SPARQL. Therefore, assistance in *query construction* is a desirable feature in those applications. This approach requires an ontology which models the real world domain the knowledge base is about, and its complexity can range from informal (when only single query terms are selected) to high (when complex queries are issued). In most cases, lists of concepts are shown to the user, although more sophisticated visual interfaces are possible (Spahn et al, 2008, pp. 1).

In the simplest case, query construction can be done by selecting terms from a list. More sophisticated query construction interfaces let the user specify additional properties and relations of the selected concept. For example, the user selects the concept "employee" and then restricts the query by adding the relation "works for" and providing a value for the relation, thus querying for all users working for a given company, as shown in the projects *QuizRDF* (Davies et al, 2004) and *TAMBIS* (Paton et al, 1999, pp. 138). A similar mechanism is used in the online news portal *PlanetOnto* (Domingue and Motta, 1999, pp. 103): here, the user may also store their queries and get notifications when there are new results. Other systems such as

SEWASIE try to construct the first cut of the query from natural language input and allow further graphical refinement of that query (Catarci et al, 2004, pp. 103).

The ontologies are usually not visually presented to the user. As it is typically information from the real world domain (e.g., customer data) which is entered into a form, the ontology used for plausibility checking at run-time has to model that domain in a highly formal way to enable reasoners to decide whether an input combination is plausible. While plausibility checking may also take place in the background without any visualization, ontologies are often presented in the form of lists (e.g. selection lists in forms) or graphs, as in the case of query construction support.

4.3.3 Providing Help

More general approaches of user assistance provide help for the user, especially in form of help texts, which can range from tool tips of a few words to large, inter-linked help documents. Examples are projects such as *SACHS* and *CPoint* (Kohlhase and Kohlhase, 2009), where ontologies are used to generate user assistance. That process is called "Semantic Transparency" by the authors. User assistance *making the system more transparent* can be created in the form automatically generated help documents, small tooltips displayed on demand (Paulheim, 2010a, pp. 66), and graphical visualizations of how the system works.

Gribova (2007, pp. 417) presents an approach which accounts for the user's context. Besides the system and its real world domain, the ontologies have to model the user's possible tasks as well. By observing the user's activities and the system's state, the system determines the user's current task. Based on this information, context-sensitive help can be provided on demand, thus freeing the user from searching the relevant help text sections themselves.

Approaches for providing help for the user employ ontologies characterizing both the system itself as well as parts of its real world domain and present them to the user in verbalized form. As discussed above for text generation, the provision of useful help texts requires at least a medium level of formality and can be done at design-time or at run-time.

4.3.4 Facilitating Interaction in Integrated User Interfaces

When performing a complex task, the user often does not only use one application, but several ones in parallel. This generates additional workload for the user for coordinating work with the different applications, such as finding related information stored in different applications, or copying and pasting data from one application to another.

To provide *unified views on data* stored in different applications, portals or mash-ups displaying different applications as *portlets* or *mashlets* at the same time can be used, as discussed in Chap. 2. A few projects exist in which ontologies are used enhancing web portals. The approach described by Dettborn et al (2008, pp. 109) uses semantic web services to retrieve related data in different applications unified in one portal. Thus, applications can display data which is relevant according to the data displayed in other portlets. A similar approach for mashup development is shown by Ankolekar et al (2007a, pp. 825).

Díaz et al (2005, pp. 372) discuss an approach which allows pre-filling form fields in different applications based on data from other applications. The input and output data are annotated by using ontologies defining the real world domain, and based on those annotations, data pipes between the different forms are defined.

The approach discussed in this book also falls into this category. While the approaches discussed above are restricted to a particular type of interaction, e.g., establishing data pipes between forms or selecting relevant data to display, our approach facilitates arbitrary interactions between user interface components, based on formal models.

In all of those approaches, the ontologies are evaluated at run-time for coordinating the behavior of integrated user interfaces. The ontology is not visible to the user, in fact, the user may not even know that the integration is based on ontologies. Both the technical components as well as the real world information they process have to be formally characterized in an ontology to automate the coordination of user interface components.

4.4 Ontologies for Improving User Interface Development

Ontologies can be used at different stages in the software development process; starting from requirements engineering and ending up with maintenance (Hesse, 2005; Calero et al, 2006). This also holds for user interface development. Whereas in most of the approaches shown above, the ontologies are used at the system's run time for supporting the user, the following approaches most often employ ontologies at a system's design time, and the end user of the system does not see the ontologies, nor interact with them.

4.4.1 Identifying and Tracking Requirements

The task of *identifying the requirements* of a software system includes modeling the real world domain to a certain level. In the case of a form-based user interface, for example, it is necessary to define the real-world concepts for which data is entered, the ranges of their relations, etc. The approach described by Furtado et al (2002, pp. 25) how such ontological models can be used in user interface development. Such an approach helps decoupling domain knowledge and user interface code and allows reuse of the domain ontology when developing different user interfaces for related applications in the same domain.

After a user interface has been developed from the requirements originally identified, those requirements may change, e.g., due to adaptation of business processes. In that case, parts of the system, including the user interface, have to be rewritten, and it is not always trivial to *track the requirements* and identify those parts. The approach presented by Sousa (2009, pp. 325) uses ontologies for modeling both business processes and the user interfaces. Based on these ontologies, rules describing the dependencies between elements in the user interfaces and in the business processes can be defined. In case of business process changes, those rules are used to find the spots where the user interfaces need to be adapted.

Adaptations of a user interface may not only be triggered by changes in business processes, but also by changes in technical requirements, e.g., support of additional platforms. Such *system migrations* require decisions on which components and widgets of a platform to use for a given component. Modeling the system as well as the target platforms in formal ontologies can help assisting developers with those decisions (Moore et al, 1994, pp. 72) and thus improve the migration process.

In all the cases discussed, reasoning is employed to assist the developer, therefore, formal ontologies are required. To model requirements, both the real world and the IT system have to be taken into account.

4.4.2 Generating User Interfaces

An area which has been increasingly gaining attention is the automatic generation of user interfaces from ontologies. This can be seen as a special case of model driven architectures (MDA), where software is generated from models (not necessarily ontological models).

Similar to the problem of system migration described above, platform independent models in MDAs can also be used in conjunction with rules defining the mappings of UI components to specific widgets and components on different target platforms (Calvary et al, 2003, p. 289). Similarly, combining the system ontology with ontologies of users and user preferences, personalized versions of user interfaces can be created, like shown in the *OntoWeaver* project (Lei et al, 2003, pp. 54).

Luo et al (2009) discuss an approach for generating user interfaces from ontologies which also takes the generated user interface's layout into account. They measure the similarity of the concepts involved in a user interface and group elements related to more similar concepts together. Furthermore, the authors analyze the user's current task and order user interface elements by their relevance with respect to that task. For calculating both the similarity and the relevance, distance measures on the ontology are used.

For being able to automatically derive a software system from an ontology, this ontology has to model the system as well as parts of its the real-world domain.

Although reasoning is not necessary, the ontology has to be complex enough to model the system on a reasonable level of detail (Liu et al, 2005, pp. 254; Sergevich and Viktorovna, 2003, pp. 89; Shahzad and Granitzer, 2010, pp. 198).

4.4.3 Reusing User Interface Components

The development of a system's user interfaces consumes about 50% of the overall development efforts (Myers and Rosson, 1992). Thus, reusing existing user interface components is especially desirable.

Reusing software components requires *finding suitable components* as a first step. Similar to defining and retrieving web services in the field of semantic web services, those components are annotated with ontologies describing their functional and non-functional properties. Base on these annotations, developers can find components suitable for their specific problems based on more precise queries then text-based search. One example for a component repository (dealing with software components in general, not specifically UI components) implementing these ideas is *KOntoR* (Happel et al, 2006, pp. 349).

User interface components are not restricted to software components. Besides standard input and output components (keyboard, mouse, screen), more specialized and advanced devices have recently been developed. From a more general point of view, selecting suitable components for developing a user interface therefore also includes choosing the right hardware devices. There are ontologies which can be used to define hardware devices, such as the *GLOSS ontology* (Coutaz et al, 2003, pp. 447) and the *FIPA device ontology* (Foundation for Intelligent Phyiscal Agents, 2002). With the help of those ontologies, the process of *selecting suitable hardware devices* can be supported efficiently as a larger number of highly specialized devices becomes available.

Similarly to components, design practices and patterns can also be stored in annotated databases and retrieved by developers. Ontology-based pattern languages have been proposed to formalize those patterns (Gaffar et al, 2003, pp. 108). With the help of such ontologies, developers can query a knowledge base of patterns in order to find patterns suitable for their problems and find additional information such as related patterns, patterns that can be combined, etc. (Henninger et al, 2003).

Reusing UI components does not only encompass the *retrieval* of those components, but also assembling them to a complete system. Thus, the approach discussed in this book also belongs to this category.

To provide a formal model of a user interface component, both the component itself as well as the real world information it processes has to be modeled in the ontology. For finding components in a repository, a hierarchy of concepts is sufficient, although more complex ontologies can be employed to specify more concise queries and retrieve more accurate results.

Peng et al (2010) discuss an approach for creating mashups on mobile devices. By annotating both the sensor information provided the mobile device (such as a

GPS sensor) and the data provided and consumed by applications, the system may propose certain combinations and assist the user in constructing useful mashups. As the mashup platform runs on a mobile phone with limited resources, no formal reasoning is employed in their approach.

Table 4.2 summarizes the approaches discussed and their characterization in our classification scheme. In the following section, we will discuss some of the findings from this survey in more detail.

4.5 Summary

This chapter has provided a survey on the use of ontologies in user interface development. We have introduced a characterization schema for organizing the survey, which allows for a clear analysis of the state of the art in ontology-enhanced user interfaces. The survey shows that there is a large amount of applications of ontologies in user interfaces, and it also points to some research gap, e.g., the development and use of advanced visualizations, or the exploitation of highly formal ontologies in user interfaces.

Purpose	Approach	Domain	Complexity	Visualization	Interaction	Usage Time
Improving Visualization Capabilities	Information Clustering	W	L+	L,G	V	R
	Text Generation	W	M+	V	V,E	D,R
	Adaptation of UI Appearance	W,S,U	H	N,L,G	V,E	D,R
Improving Interaction Possibilities	Ontology-based Browsing	W	I+	N,L,G	V	R
	Input Assistance	W	I+	N,L,G	N,V	R
	Providing Help	W,S,U	M+	V,G	V	R
	Facilitating Interaction in Integrated User Interfaces	W,S	L+	N	N	D,R
Improving Development	Identifying and Tracking Requirements	W,S	H	N	N	D
	Generating UIs	W,S	M+	N	N	D
	Reusing UI Components	W,S	L+	N	N	D

Table 4.2: Summary of approaches for ontology-enhanced UIs (Paulheim and Probst, 2010c, p. 53). Legend: Ontology Domain (W=Real World, S=IT System, U=Users & Roles), Ontology Complexity (I=Informal, L=Low, M=Medium, H=High, + indicates a minimum level of formality required), Ontology Visualization (N=None, L=Lists, G=Graphical, V=Verbalized), Interaction with the ontology (N=None, V=View only, E=Edit), Usage Time (D=Design Time, R=Run Time)

Part II
Integrating User Interfaces with Ontologies

Chapter 5
A Framework for User Interface Integration

Abstract This chapter gives a high-level view on a framework for application integration on the user interface level. This chapter will be the basis for various refinements and detailed explanations in the subsequent chapters. Section 5.1 discusses the goals of the approach and defines some axiomatic assumptions. From those goals and assumptions, a set of design decisions are derived, which are sketched in Sect. 5.2. Section 5.3 shows the different types of ontologies used and how they are employed in the framework, and Sect. 5.4 discusses the technical architecture of the framework. In Sect. 5.5, we will introduce the SoKNOS system, an application from the emergency management domain, which has been implemented using the framework discussed in this chapter, and which serves as a running case study throughout this book.

5.1 Goals and Assumptions of the Approach

This section lists the goals of which the approach discussed in this book is supposed to fulfill. Furthermore, a set of axiomatic assumptions is presented, which are considered as invariants for the approach.

5.1.1 Goals

The overall goal of the work presented in this book is to develop an approach for integrating different applications on the user interface level, which is to be implemented as a software framework. Several subgoals have been identified.

5.1.1.1 Modularity

The idea of building software in a modular fashion is almost as old as software engineering itself (Naur and Randell, 1968, p. 39). Well modularized software decomposes into a set of components with as few interdependencies as possible (Szyperski, 2002, p. 40). A central criterion for assessing the quality of modularization is *information hiding*, i.e., the use of minimal and stable interfaces between modules, where developers do not need to know the implementation of the components providing those interfaces (Parnas, 1972, p. 1056).

An integrated system is made from different applications that are integrated with each other. However, the integrated applications should still be agnostic of each other, i.e., no application should directly depend on any other application. An integrated system of n applications is considered to be modular if, after removing m applications, the remaining $n - m$ applications still work (although the functionality may be limited), without the need of modifying and/or recompiling any of the applications or the integrated system.

The idea behind this strict sense of modularity is that an integrated system should still be flexible. It should be possible to recombine applications in different integration scenarios without having to revert adaptations that have been made for one particular integration scenario. Thus, the applications themselves should be agnostic towards the fact that they are integrated with others.

Modularity in that sense has some implications. It forbids direct method calls and invocations from one application in another. Thus, some indirection is needed for allowing applications to exchange messages and information.

Another requirement imposed by the goal of modularity is that the interfaces of the integrated applications must not change. As those interfaces, as discussed, are only used via an indirection, e.g., a message exchange, it means that the format of messages emitted and consumed by applications must not change.

5.1.1.2 Extensibility

It should be possible to extend an integrated system without affecting the applications that are already integrated. In a weak sense, extensibility means that adding m applications to an integrated system of n applications, the n original applications still work, and all interactions implemented between those applications are still possible.

The extensibility goal can also be formulated stricter: if an application a_1 can interaction with an application a_2, it should also be able to interact in the same way with a similar application a_3 which serves the same purpose, without having to alter a_1 when exchanging a_2 for a_3. This goal leads to the requirement of using a commonly agreed upon message format that all applications use. Together with the communication indirection imposed by the goal of modularity, such a commonly agreed upon message format fulfills the strict extensibility goal.

5.1.1.3 Domain Independence

The approach should not rely on any specific real world domain, such as banking, travel, or emergency management. The implemented framework is supposed to be agnostic of any specific domain and allow for application integration in general, regardless to the contents of those applications. It may even be beneficial to combine applications from different domains, e.g., production, logistics, and billing, for certain use cases.

5.1.1.4 Support for Heterogeneous Systems

Integrated applications are possibly heterogeneous. Thus, the framework should be able to deal with heterogeneous applications. There may be different types of heterogeneity, and dealing with those is considered to be a central and challenging task within application integration (Hasselbring, 2000, p. 37).

Applications can be *technologically heterogeneous*, i.e. developed with different programming languages, or different technological platforms. While such heterogeneities are already solved for lower levels of integration, e.g., by using web service interfaces to existing heterogeneous systems, dealing with such heterogeneities on the user interface level is a difficult issue so far, especially when it comes to more sophisticated types of interaction, such as dragging and dropping objects from one application to another (Daniel et al, 2007, p. 64). Such interactions need special solutions that cannot be provided by state of the art techniques, such as web services.

There may also be *conceptual heterogeneities* between applications. When applications are built independently from each other, it is likely that they use different internal data models, even if the same things (such as travels or bank accounts) are represented in the applications. As integrated applications will have to exchange data, an integration approach has to be able to deal with that sort of heterogeneity.

5.1.1.5 Usability

An integrated system should not have worse usability than a system with a user interface which was built from scratch. In the first place, this means that the interaction capabilities of the integrated user interface should be the same as those provided by a one-of-a-piece user interface. *Seamless integration*, i.e., facilitating drag and drop between components, should be achieved.

Furthermore, the reactivity of the user interface is a crucial usability factor. The HCI literature states that the reaction time of an information system should not exceed two seconds, as discussed, e.g., by Miller (1968, pp. 267) and Shneiderman (1984, pp. 271). Those limits should not be exceeded by integrated applications as well.

5.1.2 Assumptions

When defining the goals that our approach is supposed to fulfill, we also defined a number of assumptions that we regard as invariants.

5.1.2.1 Preselected Applications

Our approach is not designed to automatically select applications that can *potentially* be integrated with each other in a meaningful way. Instead, we leave this a manual preparatory task. Once the selection is done, our framework supports the integration of those preselected applications. Daniel et al (2007, p. 63) call this approach "hybrid binding": the selection of applications happens at design time, while the actual integration is performed at run-time.

5.1.2.2 Availability of Suitable Wrappers

The implemented software framework will be based on some particular programming language p_0. For integrated applications, two cases are possible: they are also developed in p_0, or they are developed in a different programming language.

Some kind of communication between the framework and the integrated application is required, e.g., by calling methods of the integrated applications, or catching events thrown by the integrated application. For applications also written in p_0, this is possible without any additional efforts.

Applications written in a different programming language p_1 have to use a *wrapper* encapsulating the application and making it accessible in p_0, e.g., as an object if p_0 is an object oriented programming language, or via a set of functions. Therefore, applications written in programming languages different from p_0 can be integrated given the existence of a suitable wrapper, e.g., using techniques such as JNI (Gabrilovich and Finkelstein, 2001, pp. 10) for accessing non-Java components in Java programs.

As it is possible in theory for containers to bridge operating system boundaries, e.g., with tools such as *Cygwin* (Red Hat, Inc., 2011), *Wine* (CodeWeavers Inc., 2011), or *Parallels Desktop* (Parallels Holdings Ltd., 2011), the availability of a suitable container may also facilitate integrating applications developed for different operating system.

5.1.2.3 API and Data Access

Integrating applications requires that the integration framework accesses some of the applications' interna, e.g., via API calls for invoking functionality, and by accessing the data processed by the applications.

Thus, it is required that the integrated applications provide means to be accessed in that way. The applications have to provide the respective APIs, those APIs must not be obfuscated (Collberg et al, 1997) and should be reasonably documented. For applications in different programming languages, the respective wrappers have to have access to the APIs, as discussed above.

The minimum requires for the APIs are:

- For each operation that should be triggered by a cross-application interaction, a method has to be accessible which invokes the operation.
- For each event that can trigger in a cross-application interaction, the application has to provide means for publishing that event, e.g., by allowing an event listener to register.
- For each type of component involved in a cross-application interaction, the application has to provide access to the instances of those components.
- For each data object that is involved in a cross-application interaction, the application has to provide access to that object.

Each of the requirements and its impact on the implementation of the prototype framework will be discussed throughout this chapter in more detail.

5.2 Design Decisions

In this section, we discuss some of the basic design decisions which lead to the framework's architecture and the underlying ontologies.

Figure 5.1 shows the characterization of the approach discussed in this book, using the schema developed by Paternò et al (2009, pp. 16), which was introduced in section 2.1.5. Our approach uses abstract user interfaces as an abstraction level, as we do not restrict ourselves to a particular implementation platform. Granularity-wise, we integrate applications as a whole, although more fine-grained operations may be triggered, such as highlighting particular components. We reuse data, behavior, and presentation of the integrated application, and aim at integration that can be performed dynamically at run-time.

5.2.1 Web-based vs. Non-web-based Approaches

Many of the approaches to UI integration discussed in Sect. 2 are web-based, such as portals and mashups. Although web-based approaches are quite frequent, non-web-based approaches are also possible.

Web-based approaches can leverage a large number of existing applications which have a web-based interface, and integrated systems can therefore draw from a lot of existing applications. Furthermore, due to the large body of work in web-

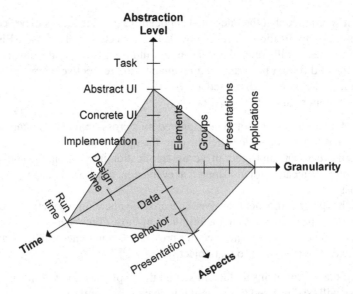

Fig. 5.1: Characterization of the approach in the schema introduced by Paternò et al (2009, pp. 16).

based portals and mashups, the ground is well paved when developing web-based integration approaches.

On the other hand, when developing interactive web-based approaches running a browser, programming is reduced to the use of client-side scripting languages. More complex operations, such as the processing of ontologies and rules, requires either server-side processing or the installing of a specialized browser plugin. Server-side processing of events creates unacceptable latencies (Schmidt et al, 2008b, p. 737), while the requirement to install a browser plugin for viewing a web application hinders a wide adoption of that application and contradicts the idea of making applications accessible via the web using a standard browser.

Because of those drawbacks, we have decided to develop our prototype using a non-web-based approach. As our framework shows a proof-of-concept implementation, the findings may be even carried over to web-based approaches once more sophisticated means for client-side programming become available, or increased network bandwidth compensates for the latencies created by server round trips.

5.2.2 Centralized vs. Decentralized Communication

To coordinate interaction with different integrated applications, those applications have to communicate with each other. As discussed by Daniel et al (2007, p. 63), there are different alternatives for implementing such a message exchange:

- Applications may communicate directly with each other, or indirectly via a central mediator.
- Messages may follow a synchronous communication protocol of invoking a method and waiting for a return value, or an asynchronous protocol of publish and subscribe, where each application sends out a message, and every application "interested" in that particular message listens to it.

The strict sense of modularity introduced in 5.1.1 imposes some restrictions on the choice regarding those alternatives. As we demand that no application must rely on the presence or non-presence of another, some sort of indirection needs to be introduced in the communication. We use a central mediator for decoupling the applications.

As integration does not only imply the exchange of messages, but also of data (e.g., objects in an object-oriented setting), different data formats need to be translated in such an exchange. As discussed in Sect. 2.2, Uschold and Grüninger (1996) have pointed out that ontologies as an inter-lingua help reducing the complexity of such an exchange significantly.

Since user interface integration is strongly based on events exchanged between the integrated applications (Daniel et al, 2007, p. 62; Yu et al, 2008, p. 52), we have taken over that paradigm, which leads to an approach that does not use invocation of methods, but an event mechanism. We have decided to use a centralized event processing engine which listens to all events produced by all applications and notifies those applications that require notification.

5.2.3 Unified vs. Modularized Ontologies

The ontologies used for formalizing user interface components, behaviors, and for unambiguously annotating events have to describe various types of information: descriptions of components and activities that they can perform are required as well as characterizations of the type of information they process and represent. In other words: both information about the *system* and the *real world* has to be formalized in ontologies.

These information may be contained in one ontology, or distributed across different ontologies. Both approaches have their advantages and disadvantages. As discussed by Wang et al (2007), modular ontologies are of advantage with respect to scalable and distributed processing, reusability, as well as improving the performance of reasoning processes. On the other hand, the effect of modifications to the ontology can be handled more easily with one unified ontology than with modularized ontologies (Stuckenschmidt and Klein, 2003, pp. 900).

As stated above, domain independence was one goal for the design of the framework. As, on the other hand, means for formalizing user interface components and behaviors have to be an integral part of the framework, we have decided to separate the real world domain ontology from the system ontology, as depicted in figure 5.2. Thus, such an ontology is not included in the framework; when assembling a system

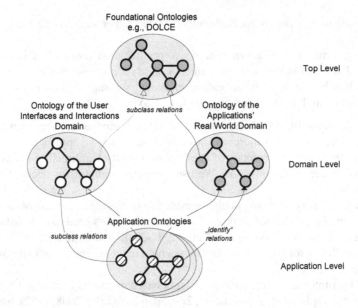

Fig. 5.2: Ontologies used in the integration framework, following Paulheim and Probst (2010a, pp. 1106). The real world domain ontology can be grounded in a foundational ontology, but it does not necessarily have to be.

for a particular domain, a suitable real world domain ontology has to be developed and/or reused.

While the domain ontology of user interfaces and interactions is not targeted at any specific user interface component (such as a Microsoft Outlook mail window), the actually integrated user interfaces are described in *application ontologies*, which specialize the categories defined in the domain level ontology by adding links to the real world domain ontology. For example, while SELECTABLE LIST may be an abstract concept from the ontology of user interfaces and interactions, the sub concepts SELECTABLE LIST OF OBJECTS IDENTIFYING CUSTOMERS[1] would belong to an application ontology, referring to the CUSTOMER concept from the real world domain ontology.

---

[1] Although one would be tempted to speak of a "list of customers", it is more exact to speak of a list of objects identifying customers, as the customers themselves are not elements of the list. The distinction is particularly relevant when the same set of ontologies is used for describing, e.g., manufacturing and e-commerce systems. While in the first, there may be a component which actually creates a product, the latter may only create objects identifying a product.

5.2.4 Open World vs. Closed World Semantics

An important decision when dealing with ontologies is whether to employ open world or closed world reasoning. A reasoner following the *closed world assumption* assumes that everything not explicitly stated in axioms is implicitly false, while a reasoner following the *open world assumption* assumes that everything not explicitly stated in axioms is not known (Russell and Norvig, 2010, p. 417). From a reasoning point of view, the open world assumption allows for *monotonic reasoning*, which means that conclusions once computed do not have to be discarded when new facts are added to the ontology, while the closed world assumption requires *non-monotonic reasoning*, which has to foresee the invalidation of computed conclusions (Drabent, 2010, pp. 32).

In Sect. 3.1.2, different ontology languages have been introduced, some of which inherently assume open world semantics, while others assume closed world semantics. Thus, deciding for a particular language in most cases means deciding for exactly one of the two paradigms.

Dealing with software applications typically involves a mixture of both paradigms. As discussed above, the ontologies used may formalize both the software system and the real world objects that it holds information about. While there is only incomplete information about the real world items (e.g., we may store a customer's name and home address, but not her shoe size), the information about the computational objects in the software system is complete (figuratively speaking, we may look through the RAM starting from $0x00000000$ to the upper limit and find each and every computational object). In other words: the computational objects form a closed world, while the real world objects form an open world.

Therefore, when performing reasoning on user interface components, e.g., processing events in user interfaces, closed world semantics is a natural choice. This is illustrated by the following example from the domain.

Consider a category SELECTACTION with two sub categories SINGLEOBJECTS-ELECTACTION and MULTIPLEOBJECTSELECTACTION, where the first describes the action of selecting exactly one object, while the latter describes the action of selecting multiple objects. Given the axiom

$$SelectAction(a_0) \wedge use\_of(a_0, o_1), \tag{5.1}$$

which states that object o_1 is used in the action a_0, we want to decide whether SINGLEOBJECTSELECTACTION(a_0) or MULTIPLEOBJECTSELECTACTION(a_0) holds. Using open world semantics, this decision cannot be made, since it respects the assumptions that objects other than o_1 exist that are also involved in the action. Using closed world semantics, on the other hand, adheres to the assumption that if no objects other than o_1 are explicitly given, they do not exist. A reasoner following the closed world assumption would therefore decide that SINGLEOBJECTSELECTACTION(a_0) holds.

As depicted in figure 5.2, the ontologies used in our framework foresee the definition of components and actions in application ontologies, which are *sub categories* of the objects defined in the domain ontology of user interfaces and interactions, and which *refer to* categories from a real world domain ontology. Thus, as long as reasoning is performed on objects from the application ontologies, closed world semantics are appropriate. Therefore, we have chosen to use a language and reasoner based on closed world semantics, i.e., F-Logic (Angele and Lausen, 2009) and OntoBroker (Decker et al, 1999) in our framework.

5.2.5 Hypothesized vs. Skolemized Instances

Processing events by means of reasoning may involve reasoning on objects that do not (yet) exist. For example, when asking a reasoner "which actions are triggered by an event e_0", the answer will comprise a set of actions that have not yet been performed, i.e., they do not exist as instances. Typically, a rule evaluated such a query has the form

$$EventA(e_0) \Rightarrow \exists e_1 EventB(e_1) \wedge triggered\_by(e_1, e_0) \qquad (5.2)$$

This rule states that for every event of type *EventA*, there exists an event of type *EventB* that is triggered by *EventA*, i.e., every event of type *EventA* triggers an event of type *EventB*. Unfortunately, such rules are not supported by most rule languages due to the existential quantifier in the rule head (Boley et al, 2007, p. 286).

In principal, there are two different possibilities of solving this challenge. Terenziani and Anselma (2003, pp. 37) propose using *hypothesized instances*, i.e., instances representing those possibly existing instances. They are marked in order not to be confused with actually existing instances, or stored in an separate A-Box, as proposed by Junghans et al (2010, p. 24). When querying via a reasoner, the result set may also contain such hypothesized instances. A possible reformulation of 5.2 using hypothesized instances would be

$$EventA(e_0) \wedge EventB(e_1) \wedge HypothesizedInstance(e_1) \Rightarrow triggered\_by(e_1, e_0) \qquad (5.3)$$

This rule states that for an event of type *EventA* and a hypothesized instance of *EventB*, that hypothesized event is triggered by each event of type *EventA*. Given that a hypothesized instance e_1 is generated before the rule is evaluated, the reasoner can compute the effect of event e_0 appropriately. However, the approach has some limitations. For example, consider two events e_0 and e_0' occurring at the same time. The reasoner would compute only one resulting event e_1 with both e_0 and e_0' as triggers, instead of two distinct events, as the desired result would be.

The other possibility is the use of skolem functions for constructing instances in rules. Skolem functions are functional expressions that create instances, such as:

$$EventA(e_0) \Rightarrow EventB(f(e_0)) \wedge triggered\_by(f(e_0), e_0) \qquad (5.4)$$

This equation defines an event $f(e_0)$ for each event e_0 and states that the event $f(e_0)$ is triggered by e_0. The mechanism for removing existential quantifiers in rule heads (i.e., transforming rule 5.2 to rule 5.4) is called *skolemization* (Russell and Norvig, 2010, p. 346). As e_0 is used to generate an identifier for the new instance of *EventB*, the problem described above for hypothesized instances does not occur. In the case discussed above, two distinct instances $f(e_0)$ and $f(e_0')$ would be created.

Rules with skolem functions need to be crafted carefully. Rule 5.4, for example, would not be a feasible rule. Given an event e_0, it would state the existence of an event $f(e_0)$. Applying the rule to $f(e_0)$ would state the existence of another event $f(f(e_0))$, and so on. Thus, the rule possibly produces an infinite sequence of events – in an unlucky setting, this may not only lead to wrong results, but completely hinder termination of the reasoning process. Thus, when implementing rules with skolem functions, additional conditions ensuring the termination of a query are therefore needed.

While hypothesized instances are a straight-forward approach, skolem functions are more versatile, as shown in the example above. Furthermore, in the case of larger ontologies and many rules, the number of hypothesized instances to insert in the ontology's A-Box may be fairly large, especially when those instances may have different attribute sets. This combinatorial explosion may lead to a large A-Box which significantly slows down the reasoning process, while skolem functions create only those instances that are actually needed, and the developer does not need to take care about creation and deletion of those instances. For those reasons, we use skolem functions instead of hypothesized instances in our framework.

5.3 Ontologies and Rules Used for User Interface Integration

Ontologies and rules are used for different purposes within the framework. As discussed above, we use four types of ontologies: on the top level, foundational ontologies pave the common ground for defining domain-specific concepts. On the domain level, ontologies describe user interfaces and interactions in general, as well as the objects from the real world the application deals with (such as customers). On the application level, the actual components of the integrated applications are described.

5.3.1 Ontologies for Event Annotations

The most important use case for ontologies in our framework is the annotation of events. Events emitted by an application have to be universally understood by all other applications. Thus, it is necessary that the applications commit to the same set of ontologies, and that they annotate the events they send using those ontologies.

Processing events based on such annotations is called *semantic event processing* (Teymourian and Paschke, 2009).

Westermann and Jain (2007, pp. 23) introduce six aspects of event annotation:

The temporal aspect   describes *when* an event takes place. Such a description may be absolute or relative to other events.

The spatial aspect   describes *where* an event takes place. The spatial aspect may refer to different reference systems, such as geographical coordinates, or arbitrary systems (such as zip codes or room numbers). As for the temporal aspect, spatial descriptions may be absolute or relative to other events.

The informational aspect   describes the nature of the event. This may include the type of an event (e.g., a button was pressed), as well as involved actors (e.g., who pressed the button) and objects (e.g., which button was it that was pressed).

The experiential aspect   describes meta data of the event, such as the sensors that were used to capture the event.

The structural aspect   allows for the description of complex events as aggregations of less complex ones. For example, a drag and drop event consists of (at least) a mouse button pressed event, a mouse moved event, and a mouse button released event.

The causal aspect   describes causal relations to other events, i.e. the original event that has caused an event (such as a mouse click which caused a window open event).

In the context of application integration on the user interface level, not all of these aspects are equally relevant.

Temporal aspects are not treated in our approach. To facilitate coordination between integrated applications, it is necessary to react on single events (such as a button click). The history of past events is not directly needed to compute a suitable reaction on that event. As past events may have changed the system's change, and information about that state can be used to control event processing, past events may have an *indirect* influence on the event processing mechanism. Such an indirect influence, however, does not require temporal information about the stream of events. Furthermore, we respect the causal aspect, which does include a minimal notion of a temporal aspect, since the cause of an event has to happen before the event itself.

Spatial aspects are also only treated indirectly. By capturing the UI components that are involved in an event (which belong to the informational aspect), spatial aspects may be indirectly covered, since those components may have a position. That position can be given in an abstract reference system, such as screen coordinates, or in a physical one, e.g., when dealing with tangible objects.

The experiential aspect is not treated by our framework. As it is our aim to abstract from the actual technical implementation, we do not use any information about how an event was detected technically.

The annotation of an event in our framework thus comprises the nature of the event (i.e., which action does it inform about, such as a button click), and the involved objects, which may be both UI components, such as buttons, as well as information objects identifying real world objects, such as a table row which contains customer data. For describing the information objects, the real world domain ontology is used. As the focus of our approach is on single user systems so far, we have not included information about the actor who has caused an event.

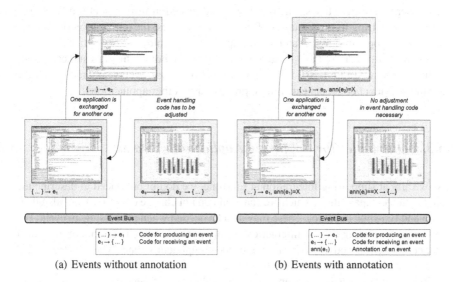

(a) Events without annotation   (b) Events with annotation

Fig. 5.3: Improving modularity with event annotations (Paulheim and Probst, 2010b)

Figure 5.3 illustrates how the use of annotated events can improve the modularity of integrated applications. When reacting to events issued in other applications, the reacting application has to analyze the event that has been raised. Without annotation, this means that the reacting application has to be aware of the raising application's event format. Using a common annotation, on the other hand, decouples the applications, since the reacting application does not have to work with the event itself, but with the annotation, which remains constant even if the underlying implementation changes.

5.3.2 Ontologies for Describing Applications

For supporting a meaningful integration of applications, those applications have to be unambiguously described. This includes the description of the components that make up the applications, as well as their capabilities, i.e., the tasks that can be performed with them, and, specifically for user interfaces, the interactions they support.

As discussed above, we modularize the ontologies used in our framework in a way that each application is defined in its own ontology. Based on the concepts defined in the domain ontology of user interfaces and interactions, the capabilities of each application are described, using concepts from the application's real world ontology for a precise capturing of the semantics of the objects involved.

The basic concepts that are provided by the domain ontology on user interfaces and interactions comprise a basic categorization of user interface components, as well as of user and system tasks. The ontology is described in further detail in Chap. 6.

By committing to the same set of domain ontologies, the application ontologies become interoperable. For example, two application ontologies may define their own, specialized SELECT ACTIONS, but as long as they are both defined as sub categories of the category SELECT ACTION in the domain ontology, events annotated with the application-level concepts can still be processed by other applications.

5.3.3 Ontologies for Capturing Applications' States

As we aim at supporting integration at run-time, we do not only need to describe the applications' capabilities (which are static and do not change over time), but also their state and run-time behavior. These may also be needed when processing an event. For example, for stating that an interaction is only possible with a certain component if that component is activated, the notion of the component's state (whether it activated or not) needs to be formalized in the ontology.

The set of instances of components already creates a very basic notion of state. For example, if a certain set of sub components of an application is present at a given time, their presence already defines part of the applications' state. Another important part of state information is the connection of components and information objects: the reasoner may need to know which component currently processes (and, specifically for user interfaces, displays) which information objects.

Apart from those basic notions of state, the application ontologies may also support more sophisticated properties describing the applications' states, such as visibility, order, relative position (for movable objects), etc.

Figure 5.4 depicts an example application and the ontology-based representation of its state. All sub components and their parthood relations, as well as the information objects processed, are reflected in the user interface and interactions ontology's A-Box. In the real world domain ontology's A-box, the domain objects (in the example: problems and measures in an emergency scenario) are captured, as well as their interrelations. A reasoner has accessed to both A-Boxes for making decisions.

5.3.4 Integration Rules

Integration rules are the glue that put the pieces, i.e., the individual applications, together. They define how applications react to events issued by other applications. Basically, they are ECA (event, condition, action) rules. An ECA rule consists, as the name suggests, of the definition of an event, a condition, and an action. It states that

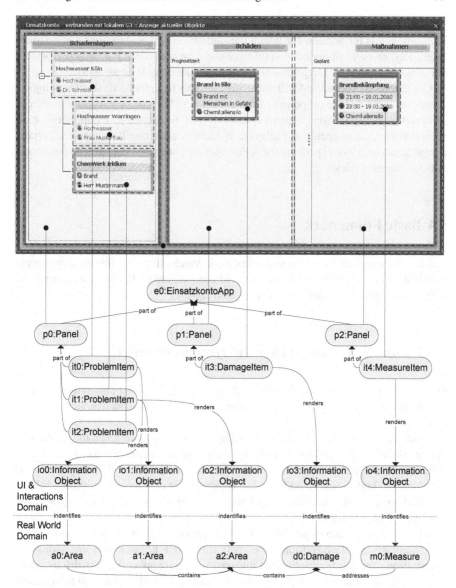

Fig. 5.4: Schematic view of an application and the logical representation of its state at run-time

when an event E occurs, and the condition C holds, an action A is performed. ECA rules can be expressed with different formal languages, such as RuleML (Paschke et al, 2007) or Datalog (Anicic and Stojanovic, 2008, pp. 394). In our framework, we have decided to use F-Logic (see Sect. 3.1.2) as a language for formulating the rules.

As explained above, ontologies are used for annotating and describing events. The same holds for actions, for which the same means of descriptions can be used: essentially, an event in our context informs about an action that has been performed, thus, its description to a large extent comprises a description of an action.

Conditions are formulated with the using concepts from the same set of ontologies. Conditions may refer to properties of the events, e.g., the type of information objects involved in event. Another type of condition may be related to components, e.g., an action may be triggered by an event if there is an active instance of a certain component which would perform the action. Simple conditions may also be combined to form complex ones.

5.4 Basic Framework

The design decisions have lead to a framework which allows for fulfilling the necessary tasks in UI integration. A prototype of the framework has been implemented using Java and OntoBroker (ontoprise GmbH, 2011a).

5.4.1 Roles and Tasks in User Interface Integration

Our framework foresees several roles that are involved in the UI integration process, and different tasks that have to be performed. Figure 5.5 gives an overview of those roles and tasks.

As discussed in 5.3, there are two ontologies on the domain level: the real world domain ontology, and the ontology of the user interfaces and interactions domain. The former is developed by a *domain expert*, while the latter is provided by the *framework developer*. In both cases, an additional *ontology expert* may have a consulting role in cases where the respective people lack the necessary skills in ontology engineering (Babitski et al, 2011, p. 192).

The *application developer* is responsible for developing the application to be integrated. Besides the provision of the application itself, he has to do some additional preparation steps for facilitating the integration of the application. As discussed in section 5.3, an application ontology has to be crafted for each application to integrate. As these application ontologies extend concepts from the two domain ontologies – the ontology of the user interfaces and interactions domain and the real world domain ontology – changes to those ontologies may be considered necessary when developing the application ontologies[2]. As for domain ontologies, an ontology expert may help with this task.

---

[2] Although it is possible to define the extensions in the application ontologies without altering the domain level ontologies, it may be reasonable to pull those extensions into the domain level ontologies if the extensions are general enough to be used in other application ontologies as well. Otherwise, duplicate definitions of the same concepts in different application ontologies would

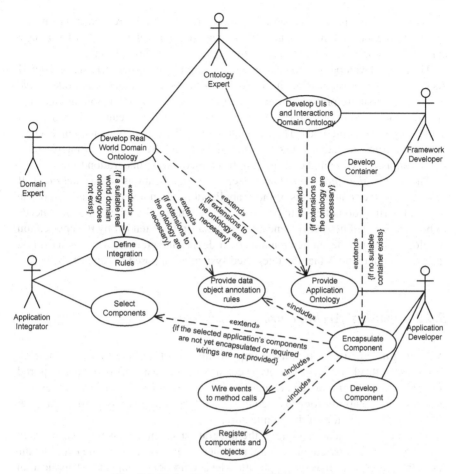

Fig. 5.5: Roles in and tasks in UI integration

Furthermore, the UI components of the application have to be encapsulated in a container. In case no suitable container for the respective UI technology exists, such a container has to be developed, a task which is typically carried out by the framework developer. There are three main activities included in encapsulating a UI component. First, mapping rules between the application's class model and the real world domain ontology have to be defined for all objects that the application needs to exchange with other applications. In the simplest case, those mapping rules are simple 1:1 mappings relating classes in the class model to categories in the real world domain ontology. Chapter 7 will deal with that step in detail. As when defining the application ontology, the developer may identify the need for extensions to the real world domain ontology during this step.

---

lead to non-interoperability of the objects annotated with those concepts and thus foil the use of ontologies.

Second, events have to be wired to method calls. As the reasoner will notify applications about actions computed from integration rules, the developer has to take care that the appropriate method calls are triggered upon those events.

Third, the developer has to take care that components and objects are registered. As the reasoner needs instance information about about the objects and interactive components that are present in the application, the developer has to announce the creation and destruction of those objects to the reasoner. Typically, this is done by calling registration methods. Those registration methods that, e.g., announce a new interactive component to the reasoner, have to be called dynamically during run time, but the appropriate method calls need to be defined during integration time.

The *application integrator* first selects those applications to be integrated. If the user interface components of those applications are not yet encapsulated or the required wirings do not exist to provide a desired interaction, the component needs to be encapsulated first, or the encapsulation has to be extended by the application developer. Second, the application integrator defines integration rules which express the desired interactions that the integrated system is supposed to support.

5.4.2 Technical Architecture

We have implemented a prototype implementation of the integration framework discussed in this book. This prototype consists of the basic infrastructure required for application integration, and containers for two technologies – Java and Flex – to demonstrate the ability for cross-technology integration (see Chap. 9). Figure 5.6 shows a high-level view of the architecture.

The core component facilitating the integration at run-time is the *central event processor*, which is based on a central reasoner. That reasoner uses the two domain-level ontologies as well as one application-level ontology per integrated application as T-box information, provided by the *T-Box connector*, as well as instance data provided dynamically by the *A-Box connector*.

Every integrated application runs in a *container*, which offers certain services to the developer performing the integration. Those services encompass drag and drop handling, event handling, object transformation, and a linked data provision service which provides data to the reasoner.

In addition to integrated applications, *extensions* the framework foresees the addition of *extensions*, which are simpler and more generic. An extension only provides a link to the event bus and allows for arbitrary software components to interact with each other and with the integrated applications via events.

5.4.2.1 Containers

Each container encapsulates one integrated application. Containers are instantiated by the user of the integrated application, although the use of the container is transparent:

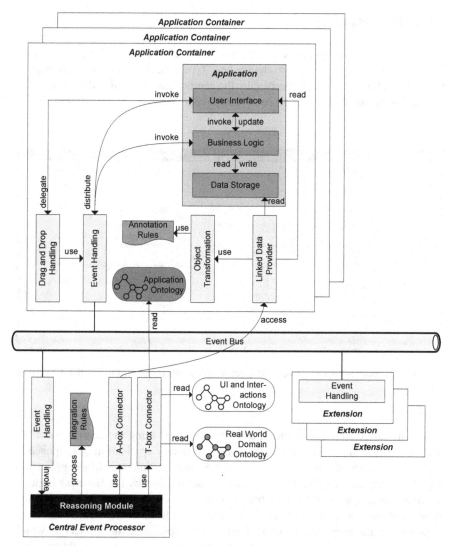

Fig. 5.6: High level view on the implementation of the integration framework. Each application is encapsulated in a container, which a

the user asks the system to open a new instance of an application, which causes the corresponding container to start. The container in turn is responsible for instantiating the application. Containers are represented visually on the screen as windows in which the applications are displayed. Thus, in the terminology of Nilsson et al (1990, p. 442, see Sect. 2.1.1), the container performs the integration on the *screen handling* level, and it offers services which allow the framework for performing the integration on the *user interface parts* level.

5.4.2.2 Event Handling

Events are the central communication means for the integration. To this end, each container is connected to an event exchange bus. Typically, applications will broadcast their events, those events are received by the central reasoner, which determines suitable reactions and notifies the respective applications, again via the event exchange bus.

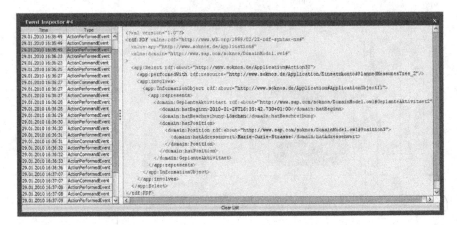

Fig. 5.7: Screenshot of the event inspector, showing the annotation of an event in RDF

Events raised in the application can be distributed using the central event bus if they are essential for the integration, i.e., if another application is supposed to react on that event. Events may be risen both by the user interface of an application, e.g., by some user action such as clicking a button, and by the business logic of an application, e.g., a new object has been created, or an object has been deleted. Whenever such an event is detected and supposed to be distributed, it has to be forwarded to the event handler of the container encapsulating the application which has raised the event. The developer has to make sure the event is caught and map the technical implementation of the event (which may be, e.g., a Java object, or an interrupt with a numerical code) to a suitable annotation. The annotated event is then distributed via the event exchange bus.

Figure 5.7 shows a screen shot of the event inspector, a debugging tool which is part of the framework prototype and which can be used for displaying the annotation of an event. On the left hand side, a list of recently raised events is shown. On the right hand side, the events' annotation is displayed in detail, using RDF for serialization.

5.4.2.3 Drag and Drop Handling

Drag and drop is a particular kind of interaction that requires special support in our framework. While the other interactions discussed so far followed the schema that an action performed with one application causes a reaction of another application, drag and drop is an action which is started in one application and completed in another, i.e., a user action which itself spans two applications.

For supporting drag and drop, application developers can define both drag sources and drop targets. The basic container implementation provides mechanisms for registering a component as a drag source and as a drop target. For components registered as a drag source, there is an additional callback method which asks for the object that has been dragged from the component, and the developer has to make sure this method is properly implemented.

When a component is registered as a drop target, it will accept dropped objects, request the dragged object from the originating application, and emit an event stating that the respective object has been dropped to the component. If a rule is defined stating how the application is supposed to react on that event (e.g., display the dropped object), additional user support can be provided based on that rule: upon a drag event, the reasoner can evaluate which components would be suitable drop locations for that particular type of object and highlight them. Based on the action defined in the integration rule, the reasoner may also generate a tooltip informing the user about that action. Details on the implementation are explained in Sect. 6.3.2.

Implementing drag and drop across different technologies is particularly difficult, since each technology usually uses its own mechanism for supporting drag and drop, and thus, more tweaks have to be applied. Details on implementing drag and drop with heterogeneous technological platforms are discussed in Sect. 9.1.2.

5.4.2.4 Object Transformation

When sending and receiving events, those events typically contain information about the objects that are involved in the event, as discussed in Sect. 5.3.1. To be included in the annotation, the events thus need to be transformed into a common format which corresponds to the common real world domain ontology, e.g., into RDF. This is done by the object transformation service. That service takes as input the mapping rules created by the application developer which define the correspondences between the application's class model and the domain ontology, and execute those mapping rules on objects in order to transform them into RDF.

Likewise, when an event is received, the object transformation service ensures that the objects contained therein are automatically transformed to objects in the receiving application's class model. Thus, the developer has to make sure to map the event to a suitable method call in the integrated application, but she does not need to take care about converting the object.

The coupling of two object transformation services facilitates an end-to-end object exchange between two applications, as shown in figure 5.8. When an event is

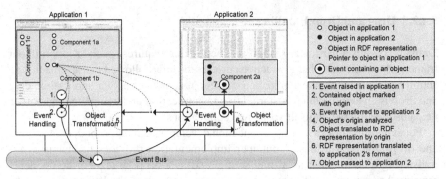

Fig. 5.8: Object exchange between applications, following Paulheim (2010b, p. 125). The reasoning part of processing the event has been omitted for reasons of simplicity.

raised, a pointer to the object involved in that event is included in the event which is broadcast. Following the linked data paradigm (see below), we use a URI to identify an object in the original application. As the URI can be non-ambiguously related to the originating application, it serves as a stamp for identifying the object's sender. When the object is received, the respective application's object conversion service may be called in order to provide a RDF representation of the object. The receiving application's object transformation service turns that representation into an object in the application's own format.

5.4.2.5 Linked Data Providers

The central event processor's reasoner may need to have access to information about the application's individual components, their states, and the information objects they process. To this end, the applications need to provide that data to the reasoner. As that data is provided as instance data annotated according to a shared ontology and linked to other data objects, it can be regarded as *linked data*[3] (see Sect. 3.1.2).

In order to generate linked data representations of their data, the object transformation service of the respective container is used. When starting a container, it is assigned a *base URI* by the framework, so all objects can get a unique identifier.

There are different possibilities of connecting the linked data providers to the reasoner. In a *pushing approach*, the reasoner maintains its own unified A-Box of instance data, and all linked data providers actively send updates to the reasoner. In a *pulling approach*, the reasoner dynamically queries the individual linked data providers when answering a query. Both approaches have their advantages and drawbacks, especially with regard to performance. Details on the variants and their implementation can be found in section 8.3.

---

[3] As discussed in Sect. 3.1.2, one key ingredient of linked data are *dereferencable URIs*, accessible via HTTP. Although it would be possible to have each application container run an HTTP server, we have decided for an implementation with a smaller protocol overhead.

5.5 Case Study: User Interface Integration in SoKNOS

The framework introduced in this book has been used in the SoKNOS project for developing a prototype for an integrated emergency management system. This integrated system will be used as a means for demonstrating different integration issues throughout this book.

5.5.1 The SoKNOS Project

SoKNOS (*Service-orientierte ArchiteKturen zur Unterstützung von Netzwerken im Rahmen Oeffentlicher Sicherheit*, German for *service oriented architectures for supporting networks in the field of public security*) was a research project funded by the BMBF, the German federal ministry of education and research, which has been conducted from 2007 to 2010. Lead by SAP AG, the project consortium consisted of ten partners and six sub contractors from academia and industry, as well as from the application domain (SoKNOS Consortium, 2009).

The central idea of SoKNOS was to develop a system for supporting decision makers in large-scale emergencies, such as large floodings or fires, which require the cooperation of different organizations, such as fire brigades, the police, the military, or the Federal Agency for Technical Relief (THW). To coordinate measures directed against such disasters, decision makers need support in finding, combining, and rating the required information, in gathering an overview of the situation at hand, and in planning and conducting the actual measures.

Working with domain experts, such as fire brigade and police officers, on a fictitious, yet realistic emergency scenario, a number of requirements for a suitable emergency management system have been identified (Döweling et al, 2009, pp. 254). Those can be categorized as requirements concerning visualization and user interaction, information service integration, information aggregation and generalization, and information creation.

In the context of this book, the requirements in the area of visualization and user interaction are particularly relevant. Among those, *ease of use* is a paramount criterion. Fortunately, emergency management systems are not used very often. This means, even given a decent amount of training, that users are not accustomed to every detail of those systems. Furthermore, mistakes made with such a system can have severe results, including danger to life or physical condition, and emergency management systems are most often operated in stressful situations. Thus, it is important that the system is as easy to use and as self explanatory as possible.

For supporting the optimal provision of the end user with relevant information, different views – such as maps, time line based diagrams, tables etc. – are employed. In order to keep an overview across the variety of different views, it is important that *objects can be tracked across different views*. Furthermore, an *adjustable level of detail* is needed to avoid information overload, while at the same time being able to provide required detail information on demand.

Further requirements related to visualization and user interaction include the possibility for collaborative work – both locally as well as remotely – and the personalization of the system.

The employment of user interface integration meets some of those requirements. Since the integration of IT systems in general was a central aspect in SoKNOS, a strategy for integration was needed, which, as discussed in section 2.1.1, could reside on different levels. As discussed in section 2.1.3, integrated user interfaces reusing the interfaces of applications that are already known to the end user can lower the learning barrier of the integrated system and thus increase the ease of use. Seamless integration, as defined in section 2.1.2, can be used to provide tracking of objects by implementing brushing-and-linking (see page 21).

Figure 5.9 shows the different components in the SoKNOS prototype that address the different requirements. In the context of this book, the *Portal*[4] is particularly interesting, as it coordinates the different views, i.e., user interface components (called *plugins* in SoKNOS, as this supports the notion of being able to compose the user interface *dynamically*). For developing the SoKNOS prototype, the framework discussed in this book has been used as means to that end.

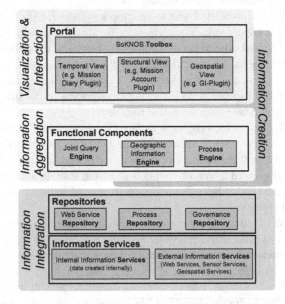

Fig. 5.9: Overview of the SoKNOS prototype (Döweling et al, 2009, p. 258)

---

[4] Although not a web-based portal as introduced in Chap. 2.2, the integration framework is referred to as *portal* in the SoKNOS project.

5.5.2 *Applications Integrated in the SoKNOS Project*

As shown in Fig. 5.9, the SoKNOS prototype consists of several different modules and applications, some of which have been developed particularly in the project, some of which are reused applications. From an information processing point of view, those applications can be roughly categorized (with a few overlaps) into applications for *information integration, information aggregation, information creation,* and *information visualization and interaction.*

Although not all of the modules and applications have user interfaces, many of them do. In SoKNOS, the most important ones are:

- A mission account application, which is used for displaying an overview of the measures which are currently planned or carried out or have been completed, as well as the resources assigned to those measures.
- A resource management application, which displays the set of available resources (such as cars, helicopters, etc.). The application can be used to view different sets of resources from different organizations.
- A geographical information application, which displays a map containing the individual problems and measures of an emergency, as well as various other information, such as weather and traffic conditions, or objects like schools or hospitals, which may also be crawled from the world wide web (Fritz et al, 2010). In SoKNOS, the commercial product *ArcGIS* (ESRI Inc., 2010) is used a geographical information application.
- A mission diary application, which shows problems and measures in a time line based view.
- A messaging application, which is used to send and receive messages to and from other organizations, as well as units in the field.
- A planning application, which manages templates for various measures, such as evacuations. From the planning application, measures may be instantiated.
- A web service repository shows available web services of various types, such as geographical information, sensor data, or web service based access to other organizations' SoKNOS systems.

Figure 5.10 shows a screenshot of the SoKNOS prototype with a set of applications and some example interactions that are possible between those applications, depicted by red arrows:

- When an object is selected in one application, related objects in other applications are highlighted, following the *linked views* paradigm (Eick and Wills, 1995, pp. 445). Examples are objects on the map and their corresponding representations in planning modules, e.g., resources such as trucks, or problems and measures such as fires and ongoing evacuations. Whenever an object of that kind is selected, the other corresponding objects are highlighted.
- Objects can be linked by using *drag and drop* interactions, e.g., linking an incoming message to a running measure. Thereby, the links which can be exploited in linked views are created. Furthermore, it is possible to control system behaviors by

using drag and drop, e.g., by dragging a web service onto the map for displaying sensor data provided by that web service.

While most of the interactions in the SoKNOS prototype belong to either one of those two categories, there are other interactions as well. For example, actions performed with one application can change the state of other applications, e.g., creating a new measure in the mission account application switches the geographical information application to edit mode so that the user can draw the corresponding shape on the map.

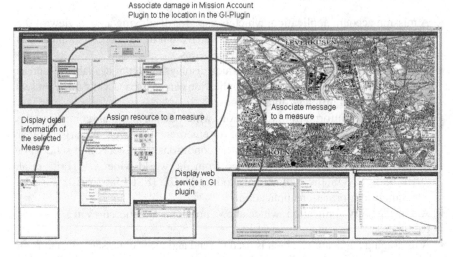

Fig. 5.10: Screenshot of the SoKNOS prototype with a set of UI modules and possible interactions (Paulheim et al, 2009, p. 1440)

Workflows in SoKNOS most often encompass different applications. Typical examples for working with SoKNOS are:

Getting an overview on the situation   The central application for getting an overview on the situation typically is the geographic information application. It is linked to other applications via the brushing-and-linking paradigm, i.e., when selecting an item, such as a measure or a problem, it is highlighted in other applications. Furthermore, geographical information services may be used with the geographical information application, such as water levels, traffic and weather data. Those can be accessed via the web service repository application and dragged and dropped to the geographical information application.

Capturing new problems and creating new measures   Problems and measures are entered into the system using the mission account application. Since problems and measures also have a spatial extension, the user is prompted to draw a polygon in the geographic information application after entering the data in the mission account application.

Assigning resources to measures   Resources are shown in the resource management application. The user can search for resources in that application and assign
them to measures by dragging and dropping them to a measure in the mission
account application. When performing the assignment, the user can directly issue
a command to the commander of the resource, which may delivered, e.g., using a
smart phone application.

Finding and executing plans   Emergency management staffs usually have plans for
typical scenarios, such as floodings or earthquakes. The planning application is
connected to a repository of such plans. When loading a plan, the user may execute
the workflow expressed by the plan. At each step, a corresponding measure may
be created in the mission account application (which again causes a prompt for
providing the spatial location in the geographical information application, as
described above).

Handling messages   Messages play an important role in emergency management.
They are used to coordinate the work within the staff, with unit commanders in the
field, and with other organizations. Messages are mainly handled in the messaging
application, but they may be also linked to problems and measures by dragging
and dropping them on items in the mission account application. Such links may be
used for improving the gathering of information and the reconstruction of events.

Since those central use workflows encompass the use of different applications
in parallel and require information exchange between those applications as well as
a means for cross-application interaction, the framework for UI-level application
integration was used for implementing the SoKNOS prototype.

5.5.3 Example Interaction

As discussed above, dragging and dropping objects between applications is a common
interaction in SoKNOS. One typical example is dragging a resource object (such as
a fire brigade car) from the resource management application and dropping it to a
planned or running measure (such as extinguishing a fire) in the mission account
application for linking the resource to the measure.

Figure 5.11 depicts how that interaction is processed in the integration framework.
First, the framework itself is initialized (1). This includes that the reasoning module
included in the central event processor loads the domain ontologies, as well as the
integration rules.

Application containers are instantiated whenever an application is started in the
framework (2). In the example, two containers are initialized: one for the resource
management application, and one for the mission account application. Upon initializing, two important steps are taken. First, the container's linked data provider
is wired to the reasoner's A-Box connector, so that instance information from the
application can be used by the reasoner. This includes the assignment of a base URI
to the container for facilitating the creation of unique identifiers for objects in the
A-Box. Second, the respective application ontology is loaded into the reasoner, so

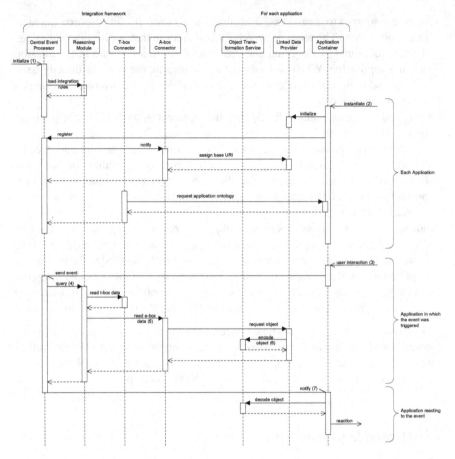

Fig. 5.11: Coordinating interaction in the integration framework (Paulheim, 2011, p. 4). The figure only depicts the components of one application container for reasons of simplicity.

that the specialized concepts used by the application are known to the reasoner. After these initializing steps, interactions between the loaded applications are possible.

In the example, the user drops a resource object to a measure object in the mission account application (3). This causes a drop event with references to the respective dropped object (which originates from the resource management application) as well as to the measure object that served as a drop location. The event is handed over to the reasoning module for computing reactions, i.e., a query for events that are triggered by the given event is issued (4).

To answer that query, the reasoning module processes the integration rules loaded. Given a rule stating that dropping a resource object on a measure object triggers some event, that rule may fire due to the given event. To decide whether the rule is applicable or not, the reasoner may need T-Box and A-Box information (5): T-

Box information is used to properly classify the event and the involved objects and is provided by the T-box connector statically. A-Box information is required to get detail information about the instances involved in both the triggering as well as the potentially triggered event (e.g., has the reacting application been properly initialized?). This information is provided by the A-Box connector (see Sect. 8.3.2 for details on how the connector is used in rules). To provide that instance data, objects are transformed and encoded in a format that can be processed by the reasoner (6). That process is described in further detail in Chap. 7.

Once the reasoner has decided which rules are supposed to fire, a result list is generated, which contains the events that are to be created (identified by skolem identifiers, as discussed in Sect. 5.2.5), the applications that are to be notified, and the information objects involved in the triggered events. From that result list, the central event processor creates event objects and sends them to the respective applications (7). As the result may involved objects originating from other applications, such as the resource object that has been dropped, the container may have to transform the object into the format used internally by the reacting application.

In our example, the mission account application has been notified with a event asking it to link the dropped resource to the respective measure. After the resource object has been transformed to a format that can be processed by the mission account application, the reaction is triggered in the application by calling a method in the application.

5.5.4 Special Cases

The SoKNOS prototype is a complex system with different integrated applications and a large number of supported interactions. Besides the general functionalities of applications integrated on the user interface layer, it provides a number of particular features which are not covered by the framework out of the box. This section sketches those features and their solutions in the framework.

5.5.4.1 The SoKNOS Toolbox

As discussed above, the requirements of SoKNOS included the possibility for personalization, support for collaboration, adjustable level of detail, and ease of use. Guided by those requirements, we developed the SoKNOS toolbox (see figure 5.12), which acts as a common point of interaction to all applications. The toolbox may be personalized for each user.

The applications developed for SoKNOS have been designed, as far as possible, in a way that they omit own menus and buttons in favor of externalizing those as tools in the toolbox. The toolbox can be moved around in the SoKNOS portal and docked to plugins (see figure 5.12(b)). When docked, the tools belonging to the application encapsulated in this plugin are activated.

There were different rationales behind this decision (Paulheim et al, 2009, pp. 1443):

- There are some general functions that can be performed with many applications, such as creating, editing, or deleting objects. To make the application more consistent and easier to use, those functions should always be invoked with the same tools. The toolbox contains a set of such standard tools as well as a space for specialized tools which can be individually defined per application.
- The complexity of system functionality that is potentially available should be reduced according to the user's role, rights, and IT skills (see Fig. 5.12(a)).
- To drive personalization even further, users should be able to equip their toolboxes with the tools they often use, arrange them in a way that is logical and comfortable for them, and use those tools on different SoKNOS workstations they log on to.
- Collaboration of different users on large displays should be supported. Here, using a toolbox reduces conflicts, as only one toolbox can be docked to the same plugin and hence, only one user can operate with one plugin at a time (while different users can collaboratively work on the overall system). Furthermore, as long as every user works only with her own toolbox, it is ensured that no user can invoke functions beyond his rights, and it can be reconstructed which user performed which action.

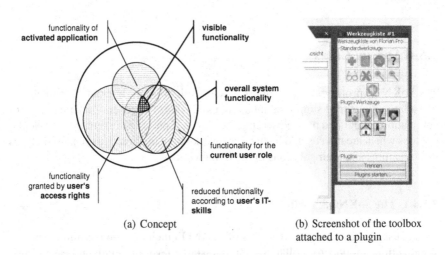

(a) Concept   (b) Screenshot of the toolbox
                                                    attached to a plugin

Fig. 5.12: The SoKNOS toolbox (Paulheim et al, 2009, p. 1443)

Technically, the toolbox is implemented as an application container. Each application ontology defines which tools are supported by the corresponding plugin. When docked to a plugin, that information is used to determine the set of tools to activate. The wiring of tools to actions in an application is done via integration rules: using the tool produces an event, which can cause an integration rule to fire and invoke, e.g., a functionality in the application the toolbox is plugged to. Likewise, activation and deactivation of tools can also be done dynamically based on the state of applications using an integration rule which fires upon an event from the application and triggers the activation or deactivation of a particular tool.

As it is an essential condition for integration rules that the toolbox is docked to a particular plugin, i.e., the rule states that *if tool T is used and the toolbox is docked to plugin P, then action A is invoked on the application wrapped by P*, this information is needed by the reasoner. Therefore, in SoKNOS, the information which plugin the toolbox is currently docked to is made available to the reasoner as part of the plugin's state.

5.5.4.2 The External Link Storage

As indicated in the interaction examples, links between information objects contained in different applications play an important role in SoKNOS: they can be created by dragging and dropping objects onto each other, and they are used for supporting tracking of objects.

Those links need to be stored. If different applications are integrated that do not foresee those links, an external storage is required. For example, in SoKNOS, messages can be linked to measures in order to keep track of those measures' state, but the neither data model of the messaging application nor the data model of the mission account application foresees such a link. Therefore, it is necessary to store those links in a link repository which is external to the integrated applications (Paulheim, 2011, p. 5).

The external storage has been developed as an extension (see Sect. 5.4.2) in the framework, as depicted in Fig. 5.13. It provides data to the reasoner, so that links can be used as conditions in rules such as *if the user selects a measure M, the messaging application A highlights all messages linked to M*. Likewise, the creation of a link can be triggered by an integration rule such as *if the user drops an incoming message I on a measure M, link I to M'*. Such an integration rule requires a means for the reasoner to notify the link storage extension. As with applications, this done via an event. Thus, the link storage extension also requires a connection to the event bus.

5.5.4.3 The Update Service

In SoKNOS, different front ends could share the same back end components. For example, staff members at different workstation may plan single measures individually. Those measures are stored in the same back end system accessed by all mission account applications on the different workstations. Thus, they need to be synchronized. Although such a synchronization could also be do hard-wired for each application, the SoKNOS system also foresees a generic mechanism: the *update service*, an event mechanism from the back end components to the front end portals, has been developed.

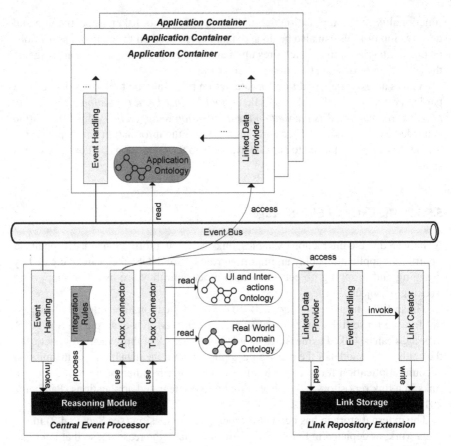

Fig. 5.13: The link storage extension in the integration framework (Paulheim, 2011, p. 7). The containers are depicted in a simplified manner; see figure 5.6 for a detailed view.

In SoKNOS, the update service was used for two purposes: first, external system could enter data into the SoKNOS system. An example are mobile applications run by the units in the field: as they enter update information about certain objects, e.g., modifying the completion status of a measure, that information can be stored directly in a back end system, and the update is distributed to all systems using that back end, so that they can, e.g., adapt their visualization.

The second use case was the coordination of interactions with several SoKNOS systems running in the same organization. Data from central back end systems, such as the local situation service storing all problems and measures, was usually used in different SoKNOS systems. Using the update service ensured that the applications all remained up to date. Message exchange between staff members was also coordinated using the update service.

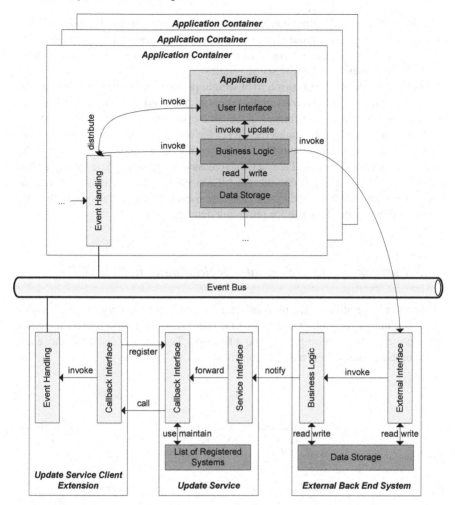

Fig. 5.14: The update service extension in the integration framework. The containers are depicted in a simplified manner; see figure 5.6 for a detailed view.

The different portals and back end systems can register to the update service. The client to that service is implemented as an extension in the framework, which forwards events from the back ends to the framework's event bus. Integrated applications can then react to those events with integration rules just like they would react to events from other applications, e.g. with a rule such as "if a new measure is created, display the measure in the mission account application".

Figure 5.14 shows how the update service is used in the framework. The client is an extension which has a callback interface used by the update service. Upon startup of the extension, the extension registers with the *callback service*. External backend systems, which may be used by applications in the same integrated system, in other integrated systems, or by other non-integrated applications, can use the update service to distribute events. The update service is used as an additional indirection in order to decouple the back end systems from the actual integrated applications using the service, which may be a volatile set of systems.

The update service itself uses a light weight protocol, in order to keep it easy to use and general enough to cover many potential back end systems: it only notifies about the action that was performed in the back end (e.g., creation, modification, or deletion of an object), and contains the URI of the object affected as well as a category from the real world domain ontology depicting that object, plus an identifier of the originating back end system. Thus, a typical message from the update service is "the object http://foo.bar/ex0 of type MEASURE has been created". Applications using data from that back end system are supposed to address that system directly through the interfaces they use for retrieving detailed data.

5.5.5 Further Usage of Semantic Technologies in SoKNOS

Application integration on the user interface layer was not the only usage of ontologies and semantic technologies in SoKNOS. There have been various other use cases in the project where ontologies played a key role. This section discusses those use cases, based on Babitski et al (2011, pp. 183).

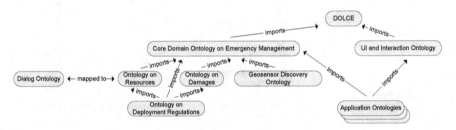

Fig. 5.15: Ontologies used in the SoKNOS project (Babitski et al, 2011, p. 183)

Different ontologies have been developed and used in SoKNOS, based on the formal DOLCE ontologies (see Sect. 3.2). Figure 5.15 shows the stack of those ontologies. The right hand part of the figure contains the ontologies used in the integration framework introduced in this book, as shown in Fig. 5.2. On the domain level, a core domain ontology on emergency management has been developed, which has several specializations: an ontology on resources contains a fine-grained taxonomy of units, such as fire brigade cars and helicopters, and an ontology on damages contains a fine-grained taxonomy of damages, such as fires and floodings. Both are used by an ontology of deployment regulations, which defines which unit is suitable for which damage (Babitski et al, 2009b). Furthermore, a geosensor discovery ontology is used for describing services provided by sensors, and a dialog ontology is used in a dialog system which supports searching for units with a speech-based dialog system.

Six core use cases for ontologies and semantic technologies in disaster management have been pursued during the SoKNOS project. We classified the use cases according to two criteria. First, the use cases provide functionality applicable during design time (before or after an incident) or during run time (during the incident). Second, the functionality is either targeted to the end users (firefighter, emergency management staff, etc.) or to software engineers. Figure 5.16 shows an overview on these ontology-based contributions developed in SoKNOS according to the described dimensions.

5.5.5.1 System Extensibility

In disaster management, users typically encounter a heterogeneous landscape of IT systems, where each application, used by one or more organizations, exposes different user interfaces and interaction paradigms, hindering end users in efficient problem resolution and decision making. Thus, it is required to be able to extend and combine existing systems, and to add new application functionality at little cost. In SoKNOS, we have used a framework for application integration on the user interface for dynamically combining applications. This framework is discussed throughout this book in detail.

5.5.5.2 Simplified Database Integration

Besides interacting with different heterogeneous systems at the same time, users of disaster management software require access to data contained in numerous distributed databases. One typical example in SoKNOS are databases of operational resources (e.g. fire brigade cars, helicopters, etc.), maintained by different organizations, such as local fire brigades. Since larger incidents require ad hoc cooperation of such organizations, it is necessary that such databases can be integrated even at run-time. Only by being able to access those resources in a uniform way, a sound capability planning is possible.

In the SoKNOS prototype, we have used OntoBroker as an infrastructure for integrating databases. As discussed in (Angele et al, 2008, pp. 258), OntoBroker can make instance data stored in relational databases or accessed via web service interfaces available as facts in the ontology. The SoKNOS "Joint Query Engine" (JQE) uses that infrastructure to connect different heterogeneous resource databases in the disaster management domain owned by different organizations.

For the end users, the resource management application (see section 5.5.2) provides a simple graphical user interface to the various databases. The JQE processes the query by unifying different names of input-concepts like, e.g. "helicopter", defined in the SoKNOS resources ontology, which is mapped to the different underlying databases' data models. The query is then translated to a number of queries to the connected databases, and the results are unified and returned to the querying application. As discussed in detail in Chap. 8, directly passing the queries to underlying data sources is faster than materializing the facts from the databases in the reasoner's A-Box. For more sophisticated use cases, such as plausibility checking (see below), the JQE also supports reasoning on the connected data sources.

For establishing the mappings between the ontology on resources and the different databases' data models, SoKNOS provides a user interface for interactively connecting elements from the data model to the resources ontology, which is used at design time. We have enhanced the interface described in (Angele et al, 2008, pp. 260) by adding the SAP AutoMappingCore (Voigt et al, 2010, pp. 2281), which makes suggestions for possible mappings based on different ontology and schema matching metrics. Internally, the mappings created by the user are converted to F-Logic rules which call database connectors (see Sect. 8.3.4 for examples for connector rules). By using those techniques, a unified and powerful interface to heterogeneous databases is provided to the user.

5.5.5.3 Improved Search

One of the key challenges in disaster management is to quickly and reliably find suitable and available operational resources to handle the operation at hand, even under stressful conditions. To make the interaction as intuitive and natural as possible, the JQE (see above) has been combined with a spoken dialog system in SoKNOS. This approach enables domain experts to pose a single query by speech that retrieves semantically correct results from all previously integrated databases.

With that combination, domain experts may formulate queries using flexible everyday vocabulary and a large set of possible formulations referring to the disaster domain. Natural spoken interaction allows a skillful linguistic concatenation of keywords and phrases to express filtering conditions which leads on one hand to more detailed queries with more accurate results, while, on the other hand, shortening the conventional query interaction process itself. For example, the spoken query "Show me all available helicopters of the fire fighters Berlin" results in the display of the two relevant available helicopters in Berlin along with an acoustical feedback "Two available helicopters of the fire fighters Berlin were found".

The core components of the spoken dialog system are a speech recognizer and a speech interpretation module. The recognized speech utterances are forwarded to the speech interpretation module, which decomposes the speech recognizer result into several sub-queries. The speech interpretation module relies on an internal ontology-based data representation, the so called dialog ontology, which defines domain knowledge and provides the basic vocabulary that is required for the retrieval of information from natural language. Based on this dialog ontology this module can resolve ambiguousness and interpret incomplete queries by expanding the input to complete queries using the situational context. For processing the spoken queries with the JQE, the dialog ontology is mapped to the SoKNOS resources ontology, as shown in figure 5.15. Implementation details on the dialog system are described by Sonntag et al (2009, pp. 974).

The spoken dialog system translates the natural-language query into the formal queries which the JQE processes to deliver search results (see above). As the most of the interactions in emergency management are time-critical, the development of the dialog system was focusing on rapid and specific response to spoken domain-specific user input, rather than on flexible input by broad common vocabulary.

Simple measurements, carried out on a standard desktop PC, have shown that the complete processing times of all integrated parsing and discourse processing modules are in the range of milliseconds. This examination shows that the processing of speech input will take place within the dialog platform in real time. However, with increasing complexity of the knowledge domain, the vocabulary and thus the complexity of the generated grammar also increase, which in turn affects the runtime of the developed module.

5.5.5.4 Improved Discovery of External Sensor Observation Services

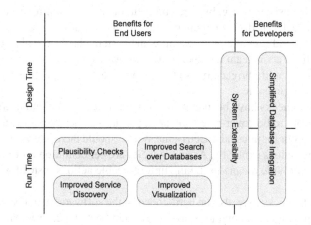

Fig. 5.16: Six use cases for semantic technologies covered in the SoKNOS project (Babitski et al, 2011, p. 186)

Another important task in SoKNOS is gathering an overview of an emergency situation. This requires the integration of dynamic information sources, such as weather, water level, or traffic data, in a semantically correct way. As this is sensor information in a broader sense, such data can be delivered by web services using the Sensor Observation Service (SOS) specification, enriched with semantic annotations.

To ease the search for such services, a geo sensor discovery ontology has been developed in SoKNOS, which formalizes both observable properties (for example wind speed, substance concentration etc.) and the feature of interest (e.g., a particular

river, a lake or a city district). The annotation is performed by extending the standard
service description with URLs pointing to the respective categories in the ontology.

To facilitate discovery, we have established a way to determine the observable
property of interest, based on the ontology. The crisis team member specifies a
substance or geographic object (e.g., river) to which the observable properties may
pertain (e.g., water level, or stream velocity). The latter are then determined through
the relation between an observable property and its bearer, as formalized in the
ontology. To get sensor data, the end users finally specify the area of interest by
marking this area on a map, provided by the geographic information application (see
Sect. 5.5.2), and by specifying the desired time interval. Details of the implementation
can be found in (Babitski et al, 2009a, pp. 103).

5.5.5.5 Plausibility Checks

Mistakes in operating an emergency response system can cause severe problems, e.g.,
when issuing inappropriate, unintended orders. On the other hand, the stress level
in the command control room is high, which increases the risk of making mistakes
increases over time. Therefore, it is important to double check the users' actions for
adequacy and consistency, e.g. by performing automatic plausibility checks. Missing
plausibility checks in disaster management solutions further increase stress and
hence errors on end user side. For example, the system checks the plausibility of an
assignment that a crisis team member issues and warns the user if the assignment of
tactical unit (e.g., a fire brigade truck) to a planned task (e.g., evacuating a building)
does not appear plausible.

Plausibility checks have been considered very useful by the end users, however,
they do not want to be "over-ruled" by an application. Therefore, it is important to
leave an open door for unusual actions – the system should therefore warn the user, but
not *forbid* any actions explicitly. As emergencies are per definition unforeseeable, the
system has to provide means for taking unforeseeable actions instead of preventing
them.

While such checks may also be hard-coded in the software, it can be beneficial to
perform them based on an ontology, as discussed in Sect. 4.3.2. From an engineering
point of view, delegating consistency checking to an ontology reasoner reduces code
tangling, as consistency checking code may be scattered way across an application.
Furthermore, having all statements about consistency in one ontology eases maintainability and involvement of the end users, and leaves the definition of consistency
statements to the domain expert developing the ontology, instead of the developer
programming the application.

In SoKNOS, the ontology on deployment regulations contains the information
about which operational resource is suitable for which task. Based on this ontology,
a reasoner may check whether the assigned unit is suitable for a task or not. The
domain knowledge involved in this decision can be rather complex; it can, for
example, include information about the devices carried by a tactical unit, the people
operating the unit, the problem that is addressed by the task, and so on.

The implementation is quite straight forward: when the user performs an assignment of a resource to a task, a query is generated and passed to the JQE (see above), which asks whether the resource is suitable for the respective task. Based on the knowledge formalized in the ontology, the reasoner answers the query. The processing time of the query is below one second, so the user can be warned instantly, if required, and is not interrupted in her work.

5.5.5.6 Improved Information Visualization

In a typical IT system landscape, information is contained in different applications. While integrating these applications by facilitating cross-application interaction, finding and aggregating the information needed for a certain purpose in different applications may still be a time consuming task.

In SoKNOS, we have used the semantic annotations that are present for each information object for creating an ontology-based visualization of the data contained in the different systems. This visualization is discussed in more detail in Chap. 10.

5.6 Summary

This chapter has introduced an overall approach of using ontologies and rules for application integration on the user interface level. We have discussed the goals and assumptions of the approach, motivated a set of several design decisions, and sketched where ontologies and rules are used in the framework. The roles and tasks in UI integration have been discussed, and the basic technological architecture of the integration framework has been introduced. In the last section, we have taken a first glance at *SoKNOS*, a prototype from the emergency management domain, which was built on top of the framework developed in this book. This prototype will be used as a running example and a case study throughout the following chapters.

Chapter 6
An Ontology of User Interfaces and Interactions

Abstract This chapter describes the development of a ontology of the user interfaces and interactions domain used for UI integration. As foreseen by most ontology engineering approaches (e.g., Uschold and Grüninger 1996, p. 15, and Fernández, Gómez-Pérez, and Juristo 1997, p. 37), building the ontology was started by collecting the relevant concepts from the domain. To this end, various UI description languages (UIDLs) have been analyzed. Section 6.1 shows a survey of the languages inspected. Based on the concepts identified in this survey, the domain ontology has been built. Section 6.2 describes this ontology with its basic concepts and design patterns.

6.1 Existing User Interface Description Languages

Various languages for describing user interfaces exist. They have been developed with different purposes: for creating more modular and device-independent, portable UIs, for communicating requirements between developers and other stakeholders (Guerrero-Garcia et al, 2009, p. 36), to facilitate rapid development, or to provide a compressed form for transferring the interface to the client in case of limited bandwidth (Abrams et al, 1999, p. 1700).

This section reviews a selection of those languages, identifies their key concepts, and depicts modeling techniques. The results of this section are then used to build a concise and complete domain ontology of user interfaces and interactions.

Surveys on UI description languages haven been given by Souchon and Vander-donckt (2003, pp. 377), (Paternò et al, 2008b, pp. 23) and Guerrero-Garcia et al (2009, pp. 36). Together, they list 20 of such languages. The selection made for this section has been made based on popularity in the literature, relevance with respect to the modeling goals of the ontology, availability of detailed documentation (as the exact set of tags or elements is needed for building the vocabulary), and expressiveness.

To structure the languages analyzed, we follow the Cameleon reference framework, which foresees four levels of models (Calvary et al, 2002, pp. 22):

- The *concepts and tasks model* defines the domain objects that can be manipulated with a user interface (e.g. "enter a person's weight"), and the tasks which can be performed by a user of that interface.
- The *abstract user interface (AUI)* model defines the UI components that are foreseen on an abstract level, without targeting at specific widget types (e.g., "a component to enter a numerical value"). The AUI is independent of a specific modality (Paternò et al, 2008a, p. 238), such as speech or mouse-and-keyboard interaction.
- The *concrete user interface (CUI)* model defines the concrete widgets that fulfil the task, e.g. "a slider widget" or "a validated text input field". The CUI relies on a specific modality (Paternò et al, 2008a, p. 239).
- The *final user interface* is the runnable user interface, which can be directly executed on a computer, either as binary code or in form of an interpreted language, such as HTML.

Figure 6.1 shows the languages examined in this section, classified in the Cameleon reference framework. Since the focus is on the expressivity of the respective languages, the final user interface has been merged with the concrete user interface, since the fact whether a specification is directly executable or not does not necessarily interfere with the expressivity of the underlying language.

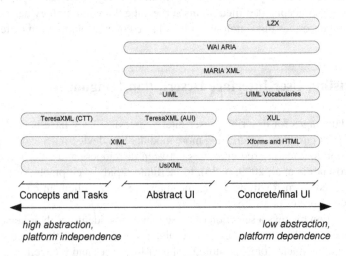

Fig. 6.1: Overview of examined UI description languages

6.1.1 HTML and XForms

HTML is – in the first place – not a language for defining user interfaces, but for *text markup*, i.e., for defining structural blocks in a text and hyperlinks between different texts. In its original form, which dates back to the early 1990s, HTML could be used to define paragraphs, headlines, lists, images in text, and hyperlinks (Berners-Lee and Connolly, 1993).

The original HTML specification has changed in two directions: first, more fine-grained capabilities for controlling the layout of web pages, have emerged, which culminated in the specification of Cascading Style Sheets (CSS) (W3C, 2010a), a layout definition language. Second, with the advent of more complex and interactive web-based applications, reasonable extensions towards describing interactions with web-based applications gained focus in the HTML specification. The currently proposed version of HTML, the working draft of HTML5 (W3C, 2011b), foresees a set of language means for describing interactions.

There are different components for defining *forms* in HTML, which are one of the main mechanisms for creating interactive applications. The central elements of HTML forms are:

`input`   for defining text input fields. There are different content types that can be defined for the input field, such as "date" or "telephone number", as well as ranges for numerical values. Behavioral characteristics such as autocomplete support may also be specified. Input fields for texts with line breaks are defined with `textarea`.

`select`   and other elements are used to define input fields for selecting from a predefined list of values.

`button`   is used to define buttons. There are special buttons for submitting and resetting forms, as well as buttons with user defined behavior. For reasons of backward compatibility, buttons may also be defined with `input`.

Other elements are used to output data, either in textual or in graphical form. There are further elements for specifying interaction, such as the provision of a summary/detail view of the same data, or menus. Besides form elements, HTML defines different types of events that can occur when interacting with a web-based application. Those events encompass

User actions   such as clicking, dragging and dropping, scrolling, hitting the keyboard, etc.

Browser-related events   such as going on line or off line, changing the displayed page, printing the page, etc.

Media events   occurring when showing embedded media, such as playing, pausing, or resuming the media.

Generic events   such as undo and redo.

In total, HTML5 defines 14 different types of (interactive) UI components, and 71 different events that can be raised by those components. It provides only little means to specify the actual behavior, i.e., what is supposed to happen when the user presses a button or submits a form. Furthermore, there is only limited support for describing the state of components, they can only be defined as hidden or visible, and input elements may additionally be defined as enabled or disabled.

With the advent of web-based formats other than HTML, such as *WML* for mobile applications (Wireless Application Protocol Forum, Ltd., 2001) or *VoiceXML* for dialogue-based applications (W3C, 2010c), there has been an effort to factor out some of the form definition part into an abstract, device-independent format of its own, called *XForms* (W3C, 2009e). It allows for defining input fields with value restrictions, as well as processing logic of those forms. XForms has eight different types of (interactive) UI components, and 43 different event types. For developing the ontology, we have concentrated on XForms, which provides a more conceptual view on form based applications than the hypertext-centric HTML does.

6.1.2 XIML

XIML (Puerta and Eisenstein, 2002, pp. 214) provides very high-level means for defining user interfaces. Predefined abstract components in XIML are (Puerta and Eisenstein, 2001, pp. 3):

Task   allows for the definition of user tasks, composed of partial tasks, and their execution order and conditions.

Domain   allows for defining the objects that the user can view and/or manipulate in the user interface.

User   allows for defining different user roles.

Presentation   allows for defining the layout of a user interface.

Dialog   defines the behaviour of the user interface.

Various links can be made between those different models, stating which users perform which tasks, which domain objects are displayed by which presentation elements, and so on (Vanderdonckt, 2000, p. 10).

As XIML is defined at a very abstract level, there are (intentionally) no *concrete* UI elements, events, user roles, etc. defined. The developer has to define those elements all by himself, which one the hand grants a high flexibility, but on the other hand limits the use of the language in terms of development efforts and compatibility of different XIML models (Vanderdonckt, 2000, p. 14). Furthermore, XIML provides numerous extension points which allow the developer to create their own custom models, classes, relations, etc.

As the last update to XIML dates back to 2004, it is not clear whether XIML will be developed any further in the future.

6.1.3 XUL

XUL (Mozilla, 2011b) is an XML-based user interface description language. It is interpreted by Mozilla's Gecko Engine (Mozilla, 2011a). The user interfaces of popular applications like Thunderbird and Firefox are defined in XUL (Feldt, 2007, p. 77).

XUL defines different basic elements, e.g., window types and interactive widgets, general ones such as text input fields as well as specific ones such as date or color pickers, summing up to 83 element types. Furthermore, there are elements for controlling the layout, templates for showing data from data sources, and means to add behavior with JavaScript. In addition, XUL defines 44 event types.

Other features of XUL include the XML Binding Language XBL for defining custom widget types, a mechanism called *overlays* which is used for customization and manipulation of existing XUL UIs (similar to the restructure technique in UIML), a mechanism for invoking components written in other programming languages, and the possibility to create automatic installers for XUL based applications.

6.1.4 TeresaXML and MARIA XML

TeresaXML is a set of two XML schemas: one for describing tasks, and one for describing abstract user interfaces. Together with an authoring platform and a set of transformation mechanisms, they form the Teresa platform (Paternò et al, 2008a, pp. 235). For defining tasks, the ConcurTaskTrees (CTT) method is used (Paternò et al, 1997, pp. 362).

The Teresa toolkit provides editors for both the concepts and tasks models and the AUI model (see figure 6.2). Generators can transform from concepts and tasks to a basic AUI definition, as well as from an AUI to various CUI models, such as desktop applications and speech based UIs.

The AUI language of Teresa facilitates the definition of user interfaces as a set of presentation elements, their visual arrangement (called "composition") and their interactive arrangement (called "connection"). A small set of basic abstract presentation elements is given, such as single and multiple choice inputs, or text outputs.

The successor of Teresa XML is *MARIA* (Model-based lAnguage foR Interactive Applications), which provides a set of enhancements and improvements over Teresa XML, which encompass the possibility to define a data and an event model, dynamic manipulations of UI elements, and continuously updated elements. There are also tools for reverse engineering existing user interfaces, e.g., HTML pages, to MARIA descriptions (Bandelloni et al, 2008, pp. 285).

6.1.5 LZX

LZX is an XML based language used in the open source platform *OpenLaszlo*, which provides a framework for building rich client applications on the web, which can be executed as DHTML (dynamic HTML, i.e., HTML with AJAX) and JavaScript as

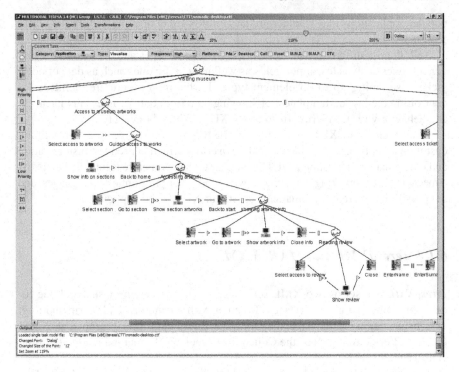

Fig. 6.2: A screenshot of the Teresa toolkit

well as a Flash application (Laszlo Systems, 2006). User interfaces can be written in the declarative LZX language, which is then compiled to DHTML or Flash.

LZX has 54 types of basic components, starting from simple drawing elements up to interactive elements such as buttons or input fields. Furthermore, there are specialized components, e.g., for charting data, showing media, getting pictures from a user's camera, etc.

LZX also supports defining behavior with JavaScript, based on events. There are 15 different predefined event types to capture events from the mouse and the keyboard, as well as other events, e.g., reacting to interactions with the browser the OpenLaszlo application runs in, or to predefined timers. Furthermore, LZX has a basic notion of states an object can have, although the only predefined states are for defining that an object is being dragged or being resized.

Languages similar to LZX are MXML, the language used by Adobe Flex (Adobe Systems Inc., 2011), and XAML developed by Microsoft (Microsoft Corporation, 2011c).

6.1.6 *WAI ARIA*

WAI ARIA (see also Sect. 4.2.3) is an initiative by the W3C for making web applications more accessible (W3C, 2011a). It defines a set of *roles* that a UI element can take. Those annotations can be embedded, e.g., in HTML pages, and may be used to assist users with cognitive disabilities to use web applications by providing additional assistance, e.g., speech output or visual magnification. Those assistive technologies have to rely on some abstract representation of the user interface components. WAI ARIA is also available as an OWL ontology.

Consequently, WAI ARIA defines a hierarchy of UI elements, together with a set of properties and state information. The set of roles is divided into eleven abstract and 60 concrete roles. The class model of WAI ARIA contains some multiple inheritance relations and mixes concerns in some places, such as presentation form and contents. For example, the `section` class contains sibling subclasses `marquee` and `definition` – where one defines a form (i.e., text flying from side to side), while the other defines contents. Furthermore, it is does not follow a rigid ontology engineering approach, but contains some questionable subclass relations. The top level consists of the three categories WINDOW, WIDGET, and STRUCTURE, but there are many categories which are sub categories of more than one of those. For example, ALERT DIALOG is at the same time a sub category of WINDOW and of REGION (a sub category of STRUCTURE), where the latter is explained to be "a large perceivable section of a web page or document", while the former follows the notion of being a browser displaying such web pages and documents. The WAI ARIA ontology is not general, but has a strong bias towards web based user interfaces, which makes it difficult to transfer it to other types of user interfaces. The hardware parts of user interfaces are not contained in WAI ARIA, neither are user interactions.

Furthermore, WAI ARIA defines a set of different states and properties a UI component can have, most of which are orthogonal. Although states and properties are not clearly separated in the WAI ARIA ontology, the documentation states that states are suspect to change during a component's life cycle, while properties are not.

6.1.7 *UIML*

The User Interface Markup Language (OASIS, 2009) is a standard proposed by OASIS, which has been introduced in 1997 and continuously revised ever since. Like XIML, foresees the definition of UI parts, their presentation (e.g., look and feel), and their behavior. Dynamic UIs can be defined by means of restructuring the existing user interface when a certain event occurs. Furthermore, the mapping of the UI model to components in an actual implementation (such as Java Swing widgets) and the wiring of UI components to a business logic API can be specified (Abrams et al, 1999, pp. 1695).

Like XIML, UIML only provides the basic building blocks of user interfaces. The user can define abstract conceptual UI parts and mappings to different technological platforms. Those mappings are based on a *vocabulary* (UIML.org, 2000). Each vocabulary can only be used for one specific target platform, and besides the very abstract model, there is no connection between models for different platforms, and cross-platform development is therefore not directly supported. Behaviors can also be defined based on the events defined in the vocabularies.

To overcome the problem of heterogeneous vocabularies, Simon et al (2004, pp. 434) have proposed a *unified vocabulary* defining the basic building blocks that are common to most user interfaces regardless of their platform, such as input elements or images. They define ten interactive and four non interactive elements.

As the largest of the available (platform specific) UIML vocabularies, the Java Swing vocabulary defines 16 events and corresponding listeners, and 29 component types with different sets of up to 41 properties, which can be used to express the state and behavior of those components. Another large vocabulary reflects the capabilities of HTML, which is described above.

6.1.8 UsiXML

UsiXML is a language developed as a UIDL for defining user interfaces without any assumptions about hardware, platform, or software toolkit they run on. It has been designed since 2003 (Limbourg et al, 2004, pp. 55), the current version is 1.8 from 2007, and there are currently efforts to establish UsiXML as a W3C standard. It provides different levels of abstraction, following the Cameleon unifying reference framework (Calvary et al, 2003, p. 293): with UsiXML, abstract user interfaces (AUI) can be expressed as well as concrete user interfaces (CUI).

While UsiXML's AUI defines only a few core concepts such as input or output elements and some basic relations between them (UsiXML Consortium, 2007, pp. 20), the CUI provides a rich meta model of user interface components (UsiXML Consortium, 2007, pp. 26).

On the CUI level, UsiXML foresees 20 event types, as well as more than 100 component types for describing classic WIMP (window, icon, menu, pointing device) interfaces as well as tangible and speech-based user interfaces (UsiXML Consortium, 2007, p. 50)

6.2 Design and Implementation of the Ontology

For implementing the ontology, we have first collected the concepts which are defined in the different user interface description languages. As shown in figure 6.3 using the example of component types, the different languages are heterogeneous with respect to their scope and contents, i.e., there is a very long tail of concepts contained only in a few languages. This shows that it makes sense to take different languages into account when identifying the core concepts. Furthermore, each user interface description language has a certain bias. Therefore, taking several languages into account for collecting concepts for the ontology helps reducing the bias and ensure generality and thus reusability of the ontology.

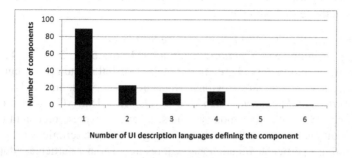

Fig. 6.3: Distribution of UI component definitions across different UI description languages

We have split our ontology into two levels: a top level and a detail level. While the top level defines the basic concepts of user interfaces, such as components and actions, and their relations, the detail level contains detailed categorizations of those concepts, such as a categorization of user interface components.

6.2.1 Typical Queries

In the scenario of application integration, facilitating cross-application interactions is the major rationale for using ontologies. As sketched in Sect. 5.3, that integration is implemented by processing annotated events.

The role of the central event processor, based on an ontology reasoner, is to compute how applications are supposed to react to events issued by other applications. The dominant query therefore is: *Which events are caused by a particular observed event?*

There may be other use cases in which other queries might become important. In Chap. 10, we will introduce the *semantic data explorer*, a tool for visually exploring data contained in the individual integrated applications. For implementing that semantic data explorer, a crucial query is: *How is a particular object related to other objects?*

Another possible use case with another type of relevant query is the automatic explanation of user interfaces (see Sect. 4.3.3). In that context, a typical query would be *What sorts of interaction does a particular application/component support?*

6.2.2 Reused Generic Ontologies

For building the ontology of user interfaces and interactions, we have reused a set of existing ontologies. Figure 6.4 shows those ontologies and their relations.

In detail, the reused ontologies are:

- *DOLCE*, a general top level ontology (see Sect. 3.2).
- *Spatial Relations* and *Temporal Relations* (Masolo et al, 2003, p. 179), two ontologies defining possible relations between spatial and temporal regions and the objects occupying those regions, which are categories defined in DOLCE.
- *Descriptions and Situations* (also known as DOLCE DnS) (Gangemi and Mika, 2003, pp. 689) contains, amongst others, means to express preconditions and postconditions by stating that tasks following a certain descriptions may only be executed in a particular situation and will result in another particular situation.
- While DOLCE only defines general participations of endurants in perdurants, the ontology of *Functional Participation* (Masolo et al, 2003, p. 179) contains more fine grained participation relations, such as objects being an instrument for or a product of performing a process.
- The ontology of *Plans* (Bottazzi et al, 2006, pp. 192) defines tasks, goals, and their relations. It uses the DnS ontology, e.g., to define situations that occur as executions of plans.
- The ontology of *Information Objects* (Gangemi et al, 2005, pp. 80) defines information objects (i.e. objects realizing some information, such as books), their physical and non-phyiscal realizations, and their relations to real world objects and agents interpreting their information. As computer programs mainly consist of such information objects, it is a useful basis for defining computer program related categories.
- The *Core Ontology of Software* (Oberle et al, 2009, pp. 385) contains categories for software and its parts, such as classes, methods, and abstract data. Figure 6.5 depicts the core concepts of the core ontology of software and their alignment with the foundational ontologies it is based on. The *Core Ontology of Software Components* (Oberle et al, 2009, pp. 395) extends the core ontology of software by adding definitions for defining components, the frameworks they are built upon, and their configurations. Other extensions to the core ontology of software, which are not used in this work, encompass licenses, access rights and policies (Oberle et al, 2009, pp. ,392), and web services (Oberle et al, 2006, pp. 163).

Since user interface components are also software components in general, we use the concepts defined in the core ontology of software components as a basis for our ontology on user interfaces and interactions, as well as the other top level ontologies, both implicitly and explicitly.

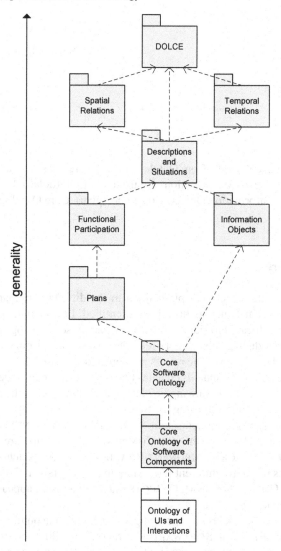

Fig. 6.4: Ontologies reused for building the ontology of user interfaces and interactions, based on Oberle et al (2009, p. 386) and Masolo et al (2003, p. 180).

6.2.3 The Top Level

For defining the top level of our ontology on user interfaces and interactions, we have taken into account five of the user interface standards discussed in section 6.1: The abstract user interface model of UsiXML, XIML, UIML, the abstract levels of WAI-ARIA and MARIA XML. As MARIA XML is the direct successor of Teresa XML, the latter has not been taken into account.

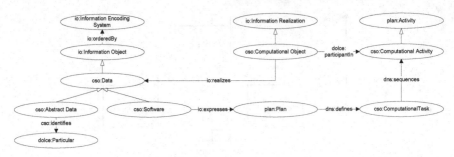

Fig. 6.5: Core concepts of the Core Ontology of Software (Oberle et al, 2009, p. 388). The following namespace conventions are used: DOLCE (dolce), Descriptions and Situations (dns), Information Objects (io), Plans (plan), Core Ontology of Software (cso).

6.2.3.1 Categories

In the first step, the basic concepts defined in the different standards have been collected, and similar concepts have been identified. In a second step, those concepts have been allocated to (i.e., aligned with) the reused ontologies discussed in Sect. 6.2.2 by introducing sub category relations to categories from either the reused ontology or the UI ontology. The results are depicted in table 6.1.

Each of the examined standards contains one or more concepts to define USER IN-TERFACE COMPONENTS. Following Fowler's classic three tier architecture (Fowler, 2003, pp. 19), we divide the category SOFTWARE COMPONENTS from the core ontology of software components into STORAGE COMPONENTS, PROCESSING COMPONENTS, and USER INTERFACE COMPONENTS. The latter are realized at run time by USER INTERFACE COMPONENT REALIZATIONS. As sketched in figure 6.6, such realizations may have different forms, ranging from VISUAL COMPUTATIONAL OBJECTS, i.e., COMPUTATIONAL OBJECTS that have a visual appearance, to TAN-GIBLE HARDWARE OBJECTS.

User interface components have been aligned to the existing ontologies by defining them as a special kind of SOFTWARE COMPONENT, which conforms with the original definition of software components as *classes that conform some framework specification* (Oberle et al, 2009, p. 396), while classes are defined as *pieces of software consisting only of data and methods* (Oberle et al, 2009, p. 389) (and thus go beyond the narrower understanding of a "class", as it is used in object oriented programming).

As user interface components are allowed be part of other user interfaces (see Sect. 6.2.4), it is not necessary to introduce separate categories for composite and elementary user interface components. Instead, they are implicitly defined as user interface components with and without parts, a design pattern often encountered

Category	Super Category	UsiXML AUI	XIML	UIML	WAI-ARIA AUI	MARIA AUI
User Interface Component	cosc: Software Component	Abstract Interaction Object, Abstract Container, Abstract Individual Component	Presentation Element	Part, Structure	Widget, Composite	Presentation
User Interface	User Interface Component	UI Model	Interface	Interface		Interface
Interaction	dns:Plan	Facet	Dialog, Dialog Element	Behavior		Dialog Model, Dialog Expression
Input	dns:Task	Input			Input, Select	Edit, Selection
Range	dolce:Region	Selection Value			Range	Numerical edit range
Output	cos:Computational Task	Output	Response			Output Only
Control		* Dialog > Execution Order				Connection, Control
Condition	dns:Situation					
Event	dolce:event			Event		Event
Navigation	dns:Task	Navigation				Navigator
Style	dolce: Physical Quality		Presentation	Style		
Grouping		* abstract Adjacency				Grouping
Domain Model		Domain Model				Data Model
Data Object	cos:Abstract Data	Domain Element				Data Object

Table 6.1: Concepts from user interface standards and their alignment to the reused ontologies, where applicable. The table contains all concepts that exist in at least *two* of the examined standards. Concepts that are represented as named relations or containment of XML tags are marked with an asterisk, XML tag containment is marked with ">". The following namespace conventions are used for aligned concepts: DOLCE (dolce), Descriptions and Situations (dns), Information Objects (io), Plans (plan), Core Ontology of Software (cos), Core Ontology of Software Components (cosc).

in the DOLCE ontologies[1]. Likewise, user interfaces are defined as a sub category of user interface components. A USER INTERFACE can be seen as the top most user interface component (e.g., an application's window) that has no user interface components it is part of, and that is composed from other user interface components.

In the core ontology of software, as shown in figure 6.5 a SOFTWARE is defined to express a PLAN, which defines what this particular piece of software can do. That plan defines a set of COMPUTATIONAL TASKS, which are carried out as COMPUTATIONAL ACTIVITIES.

While this definition is appropriate for describing merely the computational aspects of software, e.g., business logic components performing storage and calculation tasks, it does not provide sufficient means for defining the *interactive* aspects which are particularly important for user interfaces. Therefore, we have changed that definition by introducing USER TASKS on the same level as COMPUTATIONAL TASKS, which are carried out as USER ACTIVITIES. Plans defining sequences of both computational and user tasks are defined as INTERACTION PLANS. Such interaction plans are present in most of the user interface definition languages, where they are called, e.g. Behavior, Facet, etc.

Several of the examined UI description languages also allow for defining conditions for different interactions. In the Plan ontology, SITUATIONS are used for conditions of plans: a plan can be executed only in certain situations. Post conditions are also defined in that ontology as the situation that the execution of a plan will result in.

The distinction of activities and tasks is essential to the framework of ontologies we use: "tasks are the descriptive counterparts of activities which are actually carried out" (Oberle et al, 2009, p. 388). In the descriptions and situations ontology, a TASK is a concept which defines how ACTIVITIES are sequenced, while those ACTIVITIES are the perdurants which are actually happening. As a task may sequence different activities, activities may be used for more fine-grained definitions than tasks. For user interfaces, a typical task is *select an object*. Corresponding activities for that task can be *click a radio button*, *click on a drop down list* and *click an entry in that list*, *type a shortcut key*, etc.

We found this distinction quite useful, as a task can be sequenced by different activities for different user interface modalities (e.g. speech input and typing can be activities for input). Thus, the task level is a *modality independent* description defining the *purpose* of a UI component, while the activity level is a *modality dependent* description defining the *usage* of a UI component.

Another important in user interfaces is the layout and style of user interface components. Those are properties of the VISUAL COMPUTATIONAL OBJECTS realizing the components. While STYLE is a sub category of PHYSICAL QUALITY, LAYOUT describes with the relative positioning of the SCREEN REGIONS that the objects occupy.

---

[1] Note that the containment of an instance in the set of elementary user interface component can only be computed under closed world semantics (see Sect. 5.2.4).

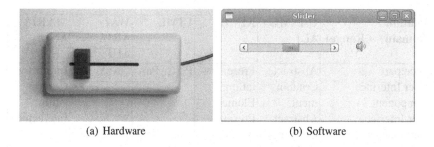

          (a) Hardware   (b) Software

Fig. 6.6: Different realizations of a slider user interface component[2]

Domain objects are reflected by ABSTRACT DATA. In the Core Software Ontology, abstract data objects can identify any kind of object (either a PARTICULAR when using a domain ontology aligned with DOLCE, or a THING in general). As pointed out in Sect. 5.2, we define domain objects in a separate real world domain ontology. Therefore, we use the IDENTIFY relation as a link to that ontology. For the same reason, we do not take into account the possibility to further specify categories from the real world domain, as provided, e.g., by XIML. Another group of elements which are neglected are those whose purpose is to provide language means that are provided by ontologies as well, such as rules in UIML, or relation definitions in XIML.

The Core Ontology of Software already defines USERS as a special kind of ABSTRACT DATA which only IDENTIFIES an AGENT, e.g., a human interacting with the system (Oberle et al, 2009, pp. 399). Furthermore, the Core Ontology of Software also defines HARDWARE, which fits the XIML definitions of workstations and their elements (RedWhale Software, 2000, p. 15).

6.2.3.2 Relations

After defining the core categories of the ontology, relations between those categories can be defined. As most of the UI definition languages used as a basis are present as UML class diagrams or XML schemata, they already define a set of relation (explicitly in the UML class diagrams, implicitly in the XML schemata by the nesting of elements).

Some of the relations defined are already present by the predefined category relations used in DOLCE and the other reused ontologies and only need to be refined, i.e., by imposing further restrictions on the domain and range of those relations. Table 6.2 shows those relations and their equivalent in the reused ontologies.

---

[2]   Image   sources: http://www.flickr.com/photos/anachrocomputer/2574918867/, http://zetcode.com/tutorials/javaswttutorial/widgets/, accessed April 20th, 2011.

Relation (Domain → Range)	UsiXML AUI	XIML	UIML	WAI-ARIA AUI	MARIA AUI
dolce:part (User Interface Component → User Interface Component)	Abstract Containment, Abstract Container> Abstract Interaction Object, UIModel> Abstract Interaction Object	Presentation Element> Presentation Element, Presentation> Presentation Element	Part> Part	Owns	Interactor Composition> Interactor
dolce:part (Interaction Pattern → Interaction Pattern)		Dialog> Dialog Element, Dialog Element> Dialog Element			Dialog Model> Dialog Expression
dolce:part (Hardware → Hardware)		Workstation> Workstation Element, Workstation Element> Workstation Element			
tr:causally follows (Activity → Activity)	spatio-Temporal	Dialog> Execution Order, Dialog Element> Response	Condition> Event	flowto	*Connection
fp:instrument (Activity → User Interface Component Realization)	Facet> Abstract Individual Component	Interaction Technique			Dialog Model> Presentation

fp:use of (User Activity → Computational Object)	manipulates, triggers		Behavior> Call		Activator*, Interactor> Data Object
plan:task-precondition (dns:Task → Situation)		Dialog Element> Condition	Behavior> Condition		Presen-tation> Condi-tional Connec-tion>Cond
plan:task-postcondition (dns:Task → Situation)		Dialog Element> Condition			
plan:component (Task → Task)		Task Model> Task Ele-ment, Task Element> Task Element			
dns:expresses (User Interface Component → Interaction Pattern)	Abstract Individual Compo-nent> Facet		Part> Behavior		Presen-tation> Interactor Composi-tion
dolce:has quality (Visual Realization → Style)			Part> Style		
dns:about (Informative User Interface Component → User Interface Component)				described by, labeled by	

Table 6.2: Relations of the top level ontology already covered by the reused ontologies. The notation X>Y denotes an implicit or unnamed relation in the original model. The notation *X denotes that this relation is implemented as a class in the original model. The following name space conventions are used: DOLCE (dolce), Temporal Relations (tr), Functional Participation (fp), Plans (plan), Descriptions and Situations (dns).

The containment of user interface components is expressed using the DOLCE:PART relation. The same holds for INTERACTION PATTERNS, which can also be part of other patterns.

Orders between activities within a task are expressed using the CAUSALLY FOL-LOWS relation. We do not use the more general FOLLOWS relation, as non-causal (i.e., accidental) sequences are usually not modeled in a UI model, although they may be helpful when using ontologies, e.g., for recording and analyzing streams of events (Anicic and Stojanovic, 2008, pp. 397).

The relation that holds between a user interface component and an activity (i.e., the user performing some activity *with* a certain component, the system doing some output *with* a certain component) is expressed using the INSTRUMENT relation, which "catches the everyday language notion of being the tool, support or devisce [sic] of an action", as the comment of the relation in the ontology states. Note that this relation holds between the ACTIVITY USER INTERFACE COMPONENT *Realization*, not the USER INTERFACE COMPONENT itself, as the user will always interact with a concrete realization. Furthermore, according to the defining ontology, the INSTRUMENT relation cannot hold between an ACTIVITY and an INFORMATION OBJECT.

To define how activities interact with data (e.g., a user entering *a date*, the interface displaying *a value*), we use the USE OF relation, which connects an ACTIVITY to a COMPUTATIONAL OBJECT. Like for user interface components, this relation uses the actual realization of the data, not the abstract description of the data. As a COMPUTATIONAL OBJECT may also REALIZE a piece of software which EXECUTES a COMPUTATIONAL TASK, the USE OF relation may also be used to define the calling of COMPUTATIONAL TASKS via some USER INTERFACE COMPONENT. Likewise, the link between INTERACTIONS and the ACTIVITIES that are part of those interactions is indirectly expressed via TASK.

The execution of tasks may be bound to conditions, which, in DOLCE DnS, are represented as situations (i.e., a task may be executed only in a certain situation). The plan ontology defines the relations TASK-PRECONDITION as well as TASK-POSTCONDITION to express these links.

There were only a few relations that did not have a counterpart in the reused ontologies, as depicted in table 6.3.

UsiXML as well as WAI-ARIA foresee the possibility that one component CON-TROLS another one. This is different from the controlling component being part of the controlled component.

Adjacent or grouped USER INTERFACE COMPONENTS can be defined both in UsiXML and in MARIA. Using the foundational ontologies, it is more precisely stated that the SCREEN REGIONS where the corresponding VISUAL REALIZATIONS are located are adjacent. Therefore, we have introduced the category SCREEN RE-GION as a sub category of PHYSICAL REGION, and defined the ADJACENT relation between those regions.

Likewise, layout constraints, as they can be defined, e.g., in UIML, most often determine the positioning of user interface components relative to each other. Thus, layout constraints are a relation between the occupied SCREEN REGIONS. This also encompasses the `Layout` element defined in UIML.

The contents of (informative) user interface components are defined via the HAS CONTENT relation. This relation links a user interface component to an abstract data object. According to the core ontology of software components, this abstract data object may identify a real world object.

UsiXML, WAI ARIA, and MARIA XML have interactors defining range constrained inputs, e.g., input elements that have numerical bounds, or a finite list of possible values. The means to define such constraints are indirectly present in our ontology: the USER ACTIVITY sequenced by the INPUT TASK uses a COMPUTATIONAL OBJECT, which in turn realizes DATA. As defined in the Core Ontology of Software, that DATA has a data type, which may be a REGION (e.g., a numerical range) as well as another DATA type.

Relation (Domain → Range)	UsiXML AUI	XIML	UIML	WAI-ARIA AUI	MARIA AUI
controls (User Interface Component → User Interface Component)	Aui Dialog Control			Controls	
adjacent (dolce:physical-region → dolce:physical-region)	Abstract Adjacency				*Grouping
relative position (Screen Region → Screen Region)			*Layout		
has content (Informative User Interface Component → cos:Abstract Data)			Part> Content		

Table 6.3: Relations of the top level ontology that have been added. The notation X>Y denotes an implicit or unnamed relation in the original model. The notation *X denotes that this relation is implemented as a class in the original model. The following name space conventions are used: DOLCE (dolce).

6.2.3.3 The Complete Picture

In the integration framework discussed in this book, we use F-Logic as an ontology language, as discussed in Sect. 5.2.4. The ontology of user interfaces and interactions, however, is an artifact which can be potentially used in many other scenarios as well, as the collection of applications in Chap. 4 has shown. Therefore, we have decided to develop the ontology in OWL, which is more prominent as a standard, and convert it to F-Logic for using it in our framework.

The OWL version of the top level ontology consists of 15 classes, two relations, and 75 axioms, not counting the classes, relations, and axioms that have been imported from reused top level ontologies. The top level is shown in Fig. 6.7, using a fourfold separation into things that exist at design time (such as definitions for interactions) and things that exist at run time (such as the actions that are actually carried out by the user or the system), and into components and interactions.

6.2.4 The Detail Level

The top level ontology defines what user interface components, their realizations, user tasks, and user activities are, how they are related, and aligns them to the reused upper level ontologies – the DOLCE family and the software ontologies introduced by Oberle et al (2009). On the detail level, we further break down those basic categories at various points.

First, we provide a deep categorization of user interface components. We have decided to define that categorization on the level of user interface components, not on the level their realizations, i.e., on the design time, not on the run time level. By following the *realizes* relation from a realization to the user interface component, the realizations are also implicitly classified, and redundancies are avoided. For example, a category such as BUTTON REALIZATION (which we omit) could be defined as follows:

$$ButtonRealization(?r) \Leftarrow UserInterfaceComponentRealization(?r)$$
$$\wedge \ realizes(?r, ?c) \wedge Button(?c) \qquad (6.1)$$

Rule 6.1 states that each USERINTERFACECOMPONENTREALIZATION which realizes a BUTTON is a BUTTONREALIZATION. It shows that, if needed, the categorization of a USERINTERFACECOMPONENTREALIZATION can always be derived from the component it realizes. It is thus not necessary to provide a deep categorization of both USERINTERFACECOMPONENTREALIZATION and USERINTERFACE-COMPONENT.

We further categorize user tasks and system tasks, as well as user activities. User and system tasks are on the level of descriptions and depict *what* the user or the system does, while user and system activities are on the run time level and depict *how* the user or the system performs a task. For user interfaces, it is not necessary to further detail system activities, as the particular method of computation in a computational task is not relevant. A categorization of user activities, on the other hand, is highly relevant for the characterization of user interfaces and their usage.

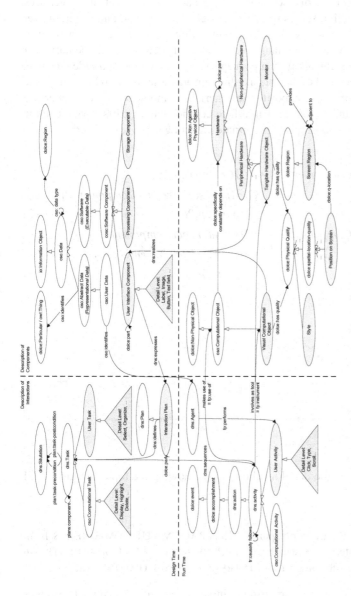

Fig. 6.7: The top level of the ontology of the user interfaces and interactions domain (Paulheim and Probst, 2011). In the upper part, the design time concepts are shown, the lower part contains the run time concepts. The left part deals with interactions, the right part with components. The white ellipses denote concepts from the reused ontologies (with the following namespace conventions: DOLCE (dolce), Information Objects (io), Temporal Relations (tr), Functional Participation (fp), Plans (plan), Descriptions and Situations (dns), Core Software Ontology (cso), Core Ontology of Software Components (cosc)), the grey ellipses denote concepts from the top level ontology of the user interfaces and interactions domain. The gray triangles denote definitions carried out in the detail ontology.

6.2.4.1 UI Components

There are two basic, orthogonal distinctions we have made to classify user interface components. The first is the distinction into elementary and composite user interfaces. Although this distinction seems trivial at first glance, it is not, and different user interface description languages have different notions of what an elementary user interface is. For example, some languages treat a scrollbar as an elementary user interface, while others contain further concepts for describing the movable rectangle and the buttons at each end of the bar, and thus consider a scrollbar to be a composite user interface. By defining composite user interface components as "user interface components which have other user interface components as parts", we leave the degree of freedom of choosing an appropriate modeling depth to the user:

$$
\begin{aligned}
CompositeUIComponent(?c) &\Leftrightarrow UIComponent(?c) \\
&\wedge\ (\exists?p : UserInterfaceComponent(?p) \\
&\quad\wedge part(?p,?c)) \tag{6.2} \\
BasicUIComponent(?c) &\Leftrightarrow UserInterfaceComponent(?c) \\
&\wedge\ \neg(\exists?p : UIComponent(?p) \\
&\quad\wedge part(?p,?c)) \tag{6.3}
\end{aligned}
$$

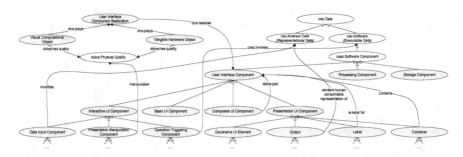

Fig. 6.8: Excerpt from the detail level ontology, showing the top categories of UI components

The other major distinction separates INTERACTIVE UI COMPONENTS from those that are non-interactive, which we call PRESENTATION UI COMPONENTS. We have identified three sub categories of INTERACTIVE UI COMPONENTS:

DATA INPUT COMPONENTS   are used to input and modify domain data, such as customer data. In some cases, they may at the same time output domain data (such as editable text fields which display the current value), while in others, they may not. A key distinction is whether the components provides direct feedback, such as a text field which displays the characters that have been entered or a

selection list where the selected entry is highlighted, or not, such as a speech input
device. DATA INPUT COMPONENTS are directly connected to the ABSTRACT
DATA that is entered. As that ABSTRACT DATA in turn has some data type with a
certain REGION, value restrictions of the DATA INPUT COMPONENT are defined
indirectly.

PRESENTATION MANIPULATION COMPONENTS   are used to alter the way information is presented to the user without changing the information itself. Such a
manipulation may be continuous, such as with a scroll bar or a window resizing
handle, or abrupt, such as with tab activators. Presentation manipuluation components alter PHYSICAL QUALITIES of some USER INTERFACE COMPONENT
REALIZATION, which, in most cases, is not the realization of the PRESENTA-
TION MANIPULATION COMPONENT itself, but some other USER INTERFACE
COMPONENT.

OPERATION TRIGGERING COMPONENTS   activate some system functionality. Operations may be triggered by selecting them from a list, such as in a menu, or
by entering them directly, e.g., via speech or a command line console. The use
of an OPERATION TRIGGERING COMPONENT results in the invocation of some
SOFTWARE.

For PRESENTATION UI COMPONENTS, we have identified four major sub categories:

DECORATIVE UI ELEMENTS   are elements that do neither provide any function
nor present any data, such as blank spaces or separators.

OUTPUTS   render human consumable representations of data. Examples for outputs
are texts on screen, spoken texts, images, or videos.

LABELS   provide a description of other user interfaces. Examples for labels are
static text labels displayed next to interactive UI components, dynamically activated tool tips, or prompts in speech interaction.

CONTAINERS   structure a user interface by grouping other user interface components. There are single purpose containers that may contain only particular
types of user interface components, such as menu bars or tool bars, and universal
containers that do not have such limitations, such as lists or windows.

Below that super categories, the ontology contains 80 different categories of user
interface components in total.

6.2.4.2 User Tasks

When categorizing user tasks, we have identified four different super categories of
user tasks:

INFORMATION CONSUMPTION TASKS   are all tasks where information provided
by a system – typically using an OUTPUT component – is consumed by a user.

INFORMATION INPUT TASKS   are all tasks where information is provided by the
user to the system, typically using some INPUT component. Input tasks can be

performed as unbound input, e.g., entering text into a text field, or as bound input, e.g., by selecting from a list of values. Sorting items, which is equivalent to assigning a position value to each item, are bound input tasks, too, since there is a fixed, limited list of values for each position value.

COMMAND ISSUING TASKS   are all tasks where the user issues a system command, typically using an OPERATION TRIGGERING COMPONENT.

INFORMATION ORGANIZATION TASKS   are performed in order to organize the consumption of information, e.g., by scrolling, following a link in a hypertext document, or fast-forwarding an audio playback.

In total, the ontology encompasses 15 different categories for user tasks.

6.2.4.3 Computational Tasks

For computational tasks, we have identified three different super categories:

INFORMATION ADMINISTRATION TASKS   are all tasks concerned with managing data stored in different media. Typical information administration tasks are loading and saving data.

INFORMATION MANIPULATION TASKS   are concerned with altering information objects, e.g., creating, modifying, and deleting information objects.

INFORMATION PRESENTATION TASKS   are particularly relevant for user interfaces, as they control the presentation of information. We distinguish INFORMATION PRESENTATION INITIALIZATION TASKS, which start the presentation of an information object, such as displaying or printing an information object, and INFORMATION PRESENTATION MODIFICATION TASKS, which influence an already started presentation, e.g., by highlighting or moving a VISUAL COMPUTATIONAL OBJECT.

In total, the ontology encompasses 20 different categories for computational tasks.

6.2.4.4 User Activities

While USER TASKS are conceptual descriptions of tasks that a user may perform, USER ACTIVITIES are the carried out PERDURANTS, i.e., the activities that are actually happening as an event. As the user activities strongly depend on the modalities and devices used, we have used the different modalities as a top level categorization and established links to hardware devices that are used as instruments in those activities, as depicted in figure 6.9. The top categories for user activities in the ontology are:

KEYBOARD ACTIVITIES   which may be typing text or pressing function keys.

MOUSE ACTIVITIES   , such as clicking, scrolling, or making gestures. Note that we have *not* defined a category such as MOUSE MOVE, as moving the mouse is usually just an act of preparing some other activity, such as a click, but not a meaningful activity in itself.

PEN BASED ACTIVITIES involve the use of a digital pen for writing, drawing, or activating functions in a pen-based interaction setup (Igarashi and Zeleznik, 2007, pp. 26).

PERCEPTION ACTIVITIES are the counterpart of information consumption tasks. Depending on the modality, such activities may encompass, e.g., viewing, listening, or feeling.

SPEECH ACTIVITIES are carried out by speaking text into a microphone, e.g., for issuing commands or entering data.

TANGIBLE ACTIVITIES involve the instrumentation of tangible objects, e.g., moving, rotating, or shaking those objects.

TOUCH ACTIVITIES encompass all sorts of activities carried out on touch screens, either small scale (like, e.g., iPhone) or large scale (like, e.g., touch tables or wall sized displays). Those activities may range from simply "clicking" items to performing complex gestures.

In total, the ontology contains 38 categories for user activities. We have intentionally not defined any explicit restrictions on the SEQUENCES relation between USER TASKS and USER ACTIVITIES, as new types of user interfaces may also use unforeseen combinations.

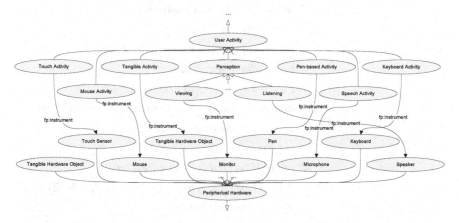

Fig. 6.9: Example for user activities and their mapping to hardware devices

6.3 Integration Rules

Integration rules are the the glue that bind the integrated applications together. Each integration rule facilitates one or more interactions between different applications.

6.3.1 Case Study: Definition of Integration Rules

In the previous chapter, we have used an example from the SoKNOS emergency management system to demonstrate the interaction between integrated applications (see Sect. 5.5.3). This interaction lets the user link resources to measures by dragging and dropping the resource to the measure. The corresponding formal interaction rule looks as follows:

$$\forall ?ua, ?co1, ?d1, ?r, ?m,$$
$$?co2, ?d2, ?vco, ?uic : \quad ui : mouse\_drop\_activity(?ua)$$
$$\land\; cso : computational\_object(?co1)$$
$$\land\; fp : use\_of(?ua, ?co1)$$
$$\land\; cso : data(?d1) \land dns : realizes(?co1, ?d1)$$
$$\land\; domain : resource(?r) \land cso : identifies(?d1, ?r)$$
$$\land\; ui : visual\_computational\_object(?vco)$$
$$\land\; fp : instrument(?ua, ?vco)$$
$$\land\; ui : presentation\_ui\_component(?uic)$$
$$\land\; dns : realizes(?vco, ?uic)$$
$$\land\; cso : computational\_object(?co2)$$
$$\land\; ui : renders(?uic, ?co2)$$
$$\land\; cso : data(?d2) \land dns : realizes(?co2, ?d2)$$
$$\land\; domain : measure(?m) \land cso : identifies(?d2, ?m)$$
$$\Rightarrow \exists ?ca, ?ct \;:\; cso : computational\_activity(?ca)$$
$$\land\; tr : causally\_follows(?ca, ?ua)$$
$$\land\; ui : link(?ct) \land dns : sequences(?ct, ?ca)$$
$$\land\; fp : use\_of(?ca, ?co1) \land fp : use\_of(?ca, ?co2)$$
$$\land\; fp : instrument(?ca, ?vco) \tag{6.4}$$

The rule states that any DROP ACTIVITY performed with a RESOURCE on a VISUAL COMPUTATIONAL OBJECT rendering a MEASURE will cause a SYSTEM ACTIVITY. That activity is sequenced by a LINK TASK the two COMPUTATIONAL OBJECTS identifying the respective RESOURCE and MEASURE.[3]

For being encoded in a rule language such as F-Logic, the existential quantifier in the rule's head has to be transformed using skolem terms (see Sect. 5.2.5):

---

[3] These rule definitions extend the usual predicate logic syntax by using namespaces, following the pattern *namespace : function*. The following namespace abbreviations are used: Core Software Ontology (cso), DOLCE Descriptions and Situations (dns), Real World Domain Ontology (domain), Functional Participation (fp), Temporal Relationships (tr), User Interfaces and Interactions (ui).

$$\forall ?ua, ?co1, ?d1, ?r, ?m,$$

$$?co2, ?d2, ?vco, ?uic: \quad ui: mouse\_drop\_activity(?ua)$$

$$\wedge \; cso: computational\_object(?co1)$$

$$\wedge \; fp: use\_of(?ua, ?co1)$$

$$\wedge \; cso: data(?d1) \wedge dns: realizes(?co1, ?d1)$$

$$\wedge \; domain: resource(?r) \wedge cso: identifies(?d1, ?r)$$

$$\wedge \; ui: visual\_computational\_object(?vco)$$

$$\wedge \; fp: instrument(?ua, ?vco)$$

$$\wedge \; ui: presentation\_ui\_component(?uic)$$

$$\wedge \; dns: realizes(?vco, ?uic)$$

$$\wedge \; cso: computational\_object(?co2)$$

$$\wedge \; ui: renders(?uic, ?co2)$$

$$\wedge \; cso: data(?d2) \wedge dns: realizes(?co2, ?d2)$$

$$\wedge \; domain: measure(?m) \wedge cso: identifies(?d2, ?m)$$

$$\Rightarrow \quad cso: computational\_activity(f_{ca}(?ua))$$

$$\wedge \; tr: causally\_follows(?ca, f_{ca}(?ua))$$

$$\wedge \; ui: link(f_{ct}(?ua))$$

$$\wedge \; dns: sequences(f_{ct}(?ua), f_{ca}(?ua))$$

$$\wedge \; fp: use\_of(f_{ca}(?ua), ?co1)$$

$$\wedge \; fp: use\_of(f_{ca}(?ua), ?co2)$$

$$\wedge \; fp: instrument(?ca, ?vco) \tag{6.5}$$

In that equation, the existential quantifier has been eliminated, and the instances of COMPUTATIONAL ACTIVITY and LINK are identified with a skolem function, which creates a new identifier for each user action triggering the rule.

When an event annotated with the corresponding information is processed, the reasoner will typically query for activities which are CAUSALLY FOLLOWED by the activity the event informs about. Given the instance information about the VISUAL COMPUTATIONAL OBJECTS that exist in the integrated applications, that query will issue the corresponding instances of activities. Those results can then be used to notify the corresponding applications, as discussed in Sect. 5.5.3. Fig. 6.10 shows the statements processed by the reasoner and how they are obtained, and the resulting statements produced, describing the event to be triggered.

Rule (6.4) only uses two categories from the real world domain ontology, i.e., MEASURE and RESOURCE. However, it is possible to use more sophisticated reasoning in the real world domain ontology. A typical example would be the restriction of the interaction to resources that are actually suitable for the respective measure. As discussed in Sect. 5.5.5, computing whether a RESOURCE is suitable for a MEASURE involves complex reasoning.

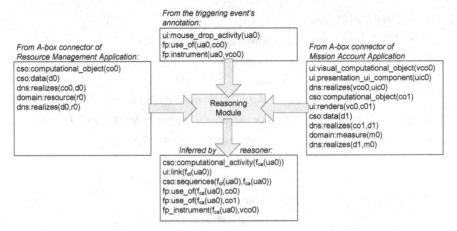

Fig. 6.10: A-Box statements processed by the reasoner

6.3.2 Global Integration Rules

The rule states that any USER ACTIVITY which is sequenced by an ACTIVATE TASK is CAUSALLY FOLLOWED by one SYSTEM ACTIVITY which is sequenced by a HIGHLIGHT TASK per VISUAL COMPUTATIONAL OBJECT which IDENTIFIES the same real world PROBLEM as the COMPUTATIONAL OBJECT which was activated in the user action. The condition is valid for any sort of activation, no matter what particular USER ACTIVITY it is realized with. For being encoded in a rule language such as F-Logic, the existential quantifier in the rule's head has to be transformed into a Skolem term (see Sect. 5.2.5).

Besides integration rules which are responsible for specific interactions between applications, it is also useful to define *global* integration rules. An integration rule is considered *global* if it does not refer to any concepts defined in an application ontology. Global integration rules may be domain specific if they refer to concepts from the real world domain ontology, or domain independent if they do not.

Local (i.e,. non-global) integration rules which are specific for one application can be stored in the respective application ontology, as long as they do not refer to concepts from other application ontologies. Following our initial strict notion of loose coupling (see Sect. 5.1), such integration rules should not contain any references to concepts defined in any other application ontology. Ideally, rules should only contain references to concepts defined in *at most one* application ontology, although there may be special cases where this is not sufficient.

Domain-specific global integration rules can be stored in a single ontology which defines the overall behavior of the application. Domain-independent global integration rules may also be stored in the domain ontology of the user interfaces and interactions domain, as they enable general features in UI integration which are not bound to any real world domain.

The definition of *linked views* (Eick and Wills, 1995, pp. 445), i.e., highlighting the same object in different views when the user selects one instance of that object, is a good candidate for global integration rules. A corresponding interaction rule for objects of the real world domain category PROBLEM may be formulated as follows:[4]

$$
\begin{aligned}
\forall ?ua, ?ut, ?co1, ?d1, ?m, ?co2, ?d2 : \quad & ui : user\_activity(?ua) \\
& \wedge\ ui : activate\_task(?ut) \\
& \wedge\ dns : sequences(?ut, ?ua) \\
& \wedge\ cso : computational\_object(?co1) \\
& \wedge\ fp : use\_of(?ua, ?co1) \\
& \wedge\ cso : data(?d1) \\
& \wedge\ dns : realizes(?co1, ?d1) \\
& \wedge\ domain : measure(?m) \\
& \wedge\ cso : identifies(?d1, ?m) \\
& \wedge\ ui : visual\_computational\_object(?co2) \\
& \wedge\ cso : data(?d2) \\
& \wedge\ dns : realizes(?co2, ?d2) \\
& \wedge\ cso : identifies(?d2, ?m) \\
\Rightarrow \exists ?ca, ?ct : \quad & cso : computational\_activity(?ca) \\
& \wedge\ tr : causally\_follows(?ca, ?ua) \\
& \wedge\ ui : highlight(?ct) \\
& \wedge\ dns : sequences(?ct, ?ca) \\
& \wedge\ fp : use\_of(?ca, ?co2) \qquad (6.6)
\end{aligned}
$$

This rule states that for each ACTIVATE TASK performed with a COMPUTATIONAL OBJECT identifying a MEASURE, all other VISUAL COMPUTATIONAL OBJECTS identifying the same MEASURE are to be highlighted. Such a definition of a linked views integration is domain-specific, as it explicitly refers to the MEASURE category and only works for instances from that category. Linked views, however, may also be defined globally and in a domain-independent fashion:

---

[4] Note that the rule, unlike the example (6.4), uses a *user task*, not a *user activity*, as a criterion to decide whether the interaction should be triggered or not. This reflects that drag and drop, as shown in (6.4), is a modality dependent interaction (it can only be performed with mouse or touch screen displays), while linked views can be principally achieved with any kind of modality.

$\forall ?ua, ?ut, ?co1, ?d1, ?co2, ?d2, ?o : \quad ui : user\_activity(?ua)$

$\qquad\qquad\qquad\qquad\qquad \wedge\ ui : activate\_task(?ut)$

$\qquad\qquad\qquad\qquad\qquad \wedge\ dns : sequences(?ut, ?ua)$

$\qquad\qquad\qquad\qquad\qquad \wedge\ cso : computational\_object(?co1)$

$\qquad\qquad\qquad\qquad\qquad \wedge\ fp : use\_of(?ua, ?co1)$

$\qquad\qquad\qquad\qquad\qquad \wedge\ cso : data(?d1) \wedge dns : realizes(?co1, ?d1)$

$\qquad\qquad\qquad\qquad\qquad \wedge\ ui : visual_computational\_object(?co2)$

$\qquad\qquad\qquad\qquad\qquad \wedge\ cso : data(?d2) \wedge dns : realizes(?co2, ?d2)$

$\qquad\qquad\qquad\qquad\qquad \wedge\ cso : identifies(?d1, ?o)$

$\qquad\qquad\qquad\qquad\qquad \wedge\ cso : identifies(?d2, ?o)$

$\Rightarrow \exists ?ca, ?ct :\quad cso : computational\_activity(?ca)$

$\qquad\qquad\qquad\qquad\qquad \wedge\ tr : causally\_follows(?ca, ?ua)$

$\qquad\qquad\qquad\qquad\qquad \wedge\ ui : highlight(?ct) \wedge dns : sequences(?ct, ?ca)$

$\qquad\qquad\qquad\qquad\qquad \wedge\ fp : use\_of(?ca, ?co2)$ \hfill (6.7)

In contrast to (6.6), this definition omits the variable $?m$ and does not restrict the ranges of the data objects $?d1$ and $?d2$. Therefore, it does not refer to any concepts defined in the real world domain ontology, which makes it domain independent and globally applicable. The rule states that for *any* activated COMPUTATIONAL OBJECT, the other corresponding VISUAL COMPUTATIONAL OBJECTS are to be highlighted. The rule therefore facilitates meaningful between all applications which produce the suitable ACTIVATE_TASK events, consume HIGHLIGHT events, and use the same real world domain ontology for annotating their information objects.

Another example for global integration rules is providing support user for drag and drop by highlighting potential drop locations when a user starts dragging an object. In theory, that support may be provided by the following rule (Paulheim, 2010a, pp. 65):

$\forall ?ua, ?ut, ?co, ?d, ?c:$ $ui : drag\_activity(?ua)$

$\wedge\ ui : user\_task(?ut) \wedge dns : sequences(?ut, ?ua)$

$\wedge\ cso : computational\_object(?co) \wedge fp : use\_of(?ua, ?co)$

$\wedge\ (\exists ?ua_{hyp} : ui : drop\_activity(?ua_{hyp})$

$\wedge\quad fp : use\_of(?ua_{hyp}, ?co)$

$\wedge\quad fp : instrument(?ua_{hyp}, c)$

$\Rightarrow \exists ?a_{hyp} : dns : activity(?a_{hyp})$

$\wedge\quad tr : causally\_follows(?a_{hyp}, ?ua_{hyp}))$

$\Rightarrow \exists ?ca, ?ct\ :\ cso : computational\_activity(?ca)$

$\wedge\ tr : causally\_follows(?ca, ?ua)$

$\wedge\ ui : highlight(?ct) \wedge dns : sequences(?ct, ?ca)$

$\wedge\ fp : use\_of(?ca, ?c)$ (6.8)

This rule states that whenever an object is dragged, then for each component where a drop action with that object would cause an activity to be triggered, this component is to be highlighted. The rule is formulated using a *nested rule* stating that if there a (hypothetical) DROP ACTIVITY $?ua_{hyp}$ using the dragged object on a COMPONENT $?c$ would cause a (hypothetical) ACTIVITY $?a_{hyp}$, then that component should be highlighted upon the DRAG ACTIVITY. If there is another rule stating the results for the drop activity, equation 6.8 can be properly evaluated. Unlike the interactions defined in rule 6.7, this rule uses a restriction on the USER ACTIVITY, not the USER TASK, since it is a specific rule for the mouse input modality.

In many rule definition languages, nested rules such as in equation 6.8 cannot be defined. Thus, for an actual implementation, that rule needs to be broken into different ones. One possible approximation is to separate the statement of existence of the hypothetical DROP ACTIVITY from the rule triggering the actual highlighting:

$\forall ?ua, ?ut, ?co, ?c:$ $ui : drag\_activity(?ua)$

$\wedge\ ui : user\_task(?ut) \wedge dns : sequences(?ut, ?ua)$

$\wedge\ cso : computational\_object(?co) \wedge fp : use\_of(?ua, ?co)$

$\Rightarrow \exists ?ua_{hyp}, ?ut_{hyp}\ :\ ui : drop\_activity(?ua_{hyp}) \wedge hypothetical\_instance(?ua_{hyp})$

$\wedge\ ui : user\_task(?ut_{hyp}) \wedge hypothetical\_instance(?ut_{hyp})$

$\wedge\ dns : sequences(?ut_{hyp}, ?ua_{hyp})$

$\wedge\ fp : use\_of(?da, ?co) \wedge fp : instrument(?da, ?c)$ (6.9)

$$\forall ?ua, ?ut, ?c : \quad ui : drop\_activity(?ua)$$
$$\land ui : user\_task(?ut) \land dns : sequences(?ut, ?ua)$$
$$\land hypothetical\_instance(?ua) \land hypothetical\_instance(?ut)$$
$$\land fp : instrument(?ua, ?c)$$
$$\land (\exists ?a_{hyp} : dns : activity(?a_{hyp})$$
$$\land \quad tr : causally\_follows(?a_{hyp}, ?ua_{hyp}))$$
$$\Rightarrow \exists ?ca, ?ct \ : \ cso : computational\_activity(?ca)$$
$$\land tr : causally\_follows(?ca, ?ua)$$
$$\land ui : highlight(?ct) \land dns : sequences(?ct, ?ca)$$
$$\land fp : use\_of(?ca, ?c) \tag{6.10}$$

Rule (6.9) states that there is a hypothetical DROP ACTIVITY with the dragged object for each COMPONENT, and (6.10)states that for each hypothetical DROP ACTIVITY, if there is a triggered activity, then the COMPONENT INSTRUMENTED BY the hypothetical drop activity shall be highlighted. Introducing hypothetical activities means that the query for processing events has to be adjusted in that only non-hypothetical results are returned, since the hypothetical results are only needed as intermediate results for computation.

Note that the implemented solution for highlighting suitable drop locations does not require any additional type of query. Although a straight forward solution might introduce a new type of query, such as *What are the locations where the dragged object could be dropped?*, the solution sketched above does not introduce any new query types compared to those shown in Sect. 6.2.1. As we will discuss in Chap. 8, it may be difficult to optimize the system's run time performance for different types of queries at the same time. Therefore, it is beneficial to reduce the number of queries as much as possible.

6.4 Summary

In this chapter, we have presented an ontology of the domain of user interfaces and interactions, as well as documented the respective ontology engineering process. Starting from an analysis of popular and well-documented user interface description languages, core concepts have been identified for building the ontology. The ontology itself has been split into a top and a detail level ontology: the top level ontology defines the categories that exist in the domain, such as user interface components and interactions, using a set of upper level ontologies grounded in the formal ontology DOLCE. The detail level ontology contains fine-grained categorizations of components, user tasks, user activities, peripheral hardware items, etc. Based on those ontologies, we have demonstrated how local and global integration rules can be defined which enable a reasoner to process events and thereby facilitate integration of applications.

Chapter 7
Data Object Exchange

Abstract One integral part of application integration is providing a possibility to exchange data. When using ontologies, annotations using concepts defined in those ontologies are commonly used. However, current approaches to annotating class models most often do not respect typical mismatches between those class models and formal ontologies. In Sect. 7.1, we will briefly introduce the state of the art in annotating class models, followed by a set of common problems that cannot be tackled by most of those approaches in Sect. 7.2. Section 7.3 introduces a rule-based solution that can cope with those problems, and Sect. 7.4 shows how annotation of class models was employed in SoKNOS.

7.1 Annotation of Class Models

In Sect. 5.4.2, we have discussed the *linked data provider* component of the framework's containers, which provides an ontology-based representation of the data contained in an integrated application. Such an ontology-based representation is necessary for two purposes: first, it enables a reasoner to derive information from that data. Second, it allows for exchanging data between applications based on a common, formal conceptualization.

Fig. 7.1 shows how a Java class is mapped to an ontology with the framework otm-j (Quasthoff and Meinel, 2009, pp. 443), a typical example for an intrusive programming framework (see section 3.3.3). Java annotations (Sun Microsystems, 2010) are used to define that each instance of the Java class Person belong to the category PERSON in the widely used FOAF (friend of a friend) ontology (Brickley and Miller, 2010). Furthermore, two getter methods of the class are mapped to the data relation NAME and the object relation KNOWS of FOAF. Based on these annotations, each object of the Java class Person can be transferred to an RDF representation obeying the FOAF ontology. Other approaches for working with direct programming models, as those discussed in Sect. 3.3.3, work with very similar mechanisms.

```
@RDF( base=FOAF, uri="Person")
public class Person {

    @RDF("name")
    String getName() {
        ...
    }

    @RDF("knows")
    Collection<Person> getFriends() {
        ...
    }
}
```

Fig. 7.1: Example for mapping a Java class to an ontology with otm-j (Quasthoff and Meinel, 2009, p. 447).

Two important observations can be made with the example. First, the approach is *intrusive*. The Java classes have been altered for facilitating the mapping to the ontology by adding the Java annotations. A non-intrusive-approach, on the other hand, would use, e.g., a separate mapping file. Non-intrusive approaches are more versatile, since they can also be applied in cases where the class model cannot or must not be altered, be it for technical or for legal reasons.

Second, the approach relies on a 1:1 mapping between the class model and the ontology, as each instance of Person is mapped to the same category in the ontology, and each result of a getter call is mapped to the same relation. We will thus call this a *static mapping*.

Where intrusiveness is a problem, an intrusive implementation can be transformed to a non-intrusive one with some software engineering skills. Static mappings are a harder case, since they are grounded in a conceptual problem, not in a technical one. In Sect. 3.1.5, we have pointed out various differences between ontologies and models, such as class models. Due to those differences, the assumption that a 1:1 mapping can always be found is not realistic. However, most approaches tacitly assume the existence of such a mapping. Even for the more versatile approaches such as the framework discussed by Hillairet et al (2008, pp. 5), the authors state that "the domain model should be rather close to the ontology" (Hillairet et al, 2008, p. 8).

A universal approach should thus support arbitrary, dynamic mappings (as opposed to static mappings), and it should be non-intrusive. Such an approach is not covered by the state of the art in mapping class models to ontologies.

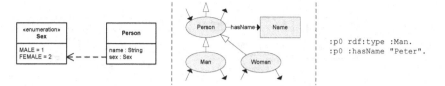

Fig. 7.2: An excerpt from a class model (left), an ontology (middle), and a set desired of example RDF triples to be used for annotation. Multi-purpose classes: the class Person is used to represent instances of both categories MAN and WOMAN. Actual category membership is decided based on a flag. Simply annotating the class with the category PERSON would cause information loss.

7.2 Problems with Static Annotation

The main problem with static semantic annotation approaches is that they assume a 1:1 mapping between a class model and the ontology used for annotating that model. However, many real-world problems suffer from the non-existence of such a mapping. In this section, we introduce a set of canonical examples of such mismatches.

7.2.1 Multi-Purpose and Artificial Classes and Properties

Classes in a programming model may be used for representing information about different things. In Fig. 7.2, a single class Person is used for representing instances of both categories MAN and WOMAN, distinguished by an attribute. Although this class can be mapped to the PERSON category in the ontology, information is lost this way. A static mapping approach cannot evaluate the sex attribute at run time and decide upon its value which annotation to produce, since the mapping is statically defined at design time.

A special case of multi-purpose classes are artificial classes: The class model may also contain classes that do not have any corresponding category in the shared conceptualization, and therefore not in the ontology either. One example is shown in Fig. 7.3: an AdditionalData class is used for storing information both about a person's email address and social security number (SSN). While such a class may be useful for the developer, rigid ontology engineering would avoid categories such as AdditionalData. Thus, objects of that class must be annotated with different ontological categories.

Artificial classes are sometimes used for representing relations. Fig. 7.4 shows such a case: instances of the class PersonRelation are used for representing a relation between two persons. In the ontology-based representation, however, those objects are represented as a set of relations. Thus, that mismatch requires mapping a class to a relation. Such mismatches are also typically for mapping relational data

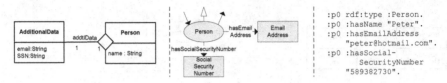

Fig. 7.3: Artificial classes: rigid ontology engineering would avoid categories such as "additional data", although they can be useful in a class model.

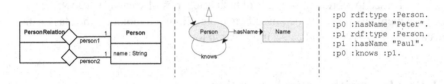

Fig. 7.4: Class for relation: a class is used for representing a relation between two resources.

models following Codd's normal form (Codd, 1985b,a) to ontologies, but also occur when mapping class models to ontologies.

Another special case of multi-purpose classes are classes that are used for both existing and non-existing objects which are kept, e.g., for reasons of traceability. The typical manifestation of that case is a flag indicating that an object has been deleted, while the object is not deleted physically, but only treated as deleted by the program logic. When transforming a set of objects to a set of logical statements according to an ontology, only those objects not bearing the flag should be included in the transformation.

Similarly to using one class for several ontological categories, one relation or attribute in the class model may have different corresponding relations in the ontology. In the example shown in Fig. 7.5, an additional flag attribute is used to determine whether the value of the `contactData` attribute denotes a phone number, a fax number, or an email address.

In worse cases, there might even be no flag attributes determining the actual representation, but only background knowledge held by the developer who uses the class model, as shown in Fig. 7.6. In this example, the same attribute is used to hold information about the phone number and email address, and the program logic distinguishes both cases based on whether the attribute value contains an @ symbol.

7.2.2 Simplified Chains of Relations

For reasons of simplicity, shortcuts are often used in a class model. Such shortcuts may skip some categories when traversing a chain of object relations and move attributes to other categories than in a precise ontology. Fig. 7.7 shows an example:

Fig. 7.5: Multi-purpose relations with a flag: the attribute `contactData` is used to express the relations *hasPhoneNumber*, *hasFaxNumber*, and *hasEmailAddress* (in the class model, only one type of contact information is stored per person). The actual relation is determined based on a flag. Note that the enumeration `ContactType` does not have any corresponding category in the ontology.

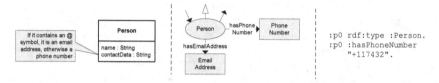

Fig. 7.6: Multi-purpose relations with background knowledge: the attribute `contactData` is used to express the relations *hasPhoneNumber* and *hasEmailAddress*. The actual relation is determined based on the data contained therein.

the `Person` class stores a `postal_code` attribute containing the postal code of the city the person lives in, but there is no direct relation in the ontology, since in a precise formalization, persons do not have postal codes by nature – in the ontology, PERSON and POSTAL CODE are interconnected via the CITY concept, which is omitted in the class model by using a shortcut. Thus, the attribute cannot be directly mapped to one relation in the ontology, but rather to a chain of relations. The intermediate links in the chain – the CITY node in the example – are represented as blank nodes in RDF.

As shown in Fig. 7.8, such shortcuts may also comprise combined chains of object and inheritance relations. In this example, the classes `Professor` and `Student` are modeled as subclasses of `Person` in the class model, while in the ontology, they are modeled as *roles* a person can have – a typical difference between ontological and object-oriented modeling (Guarino and Welty, 2009, pp. 216). In that case, the person and her role become mixed in the class model, i.e. attributes assigned to the ROLE concept in the ontology become attributes of the person.

Shortcuts which encompass only the traversal of the class hierarchy (i.e. the class model leaving out some "intermediate" categories in the ontology) may also occur, but they are not as problematic, because in these cases, a 1:1 mapping between the class model and the ontology still exists, and membership of objects in the non-mapped intermediate categories can be inferred by a reasoner.

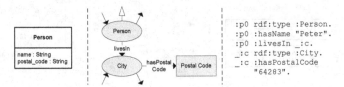

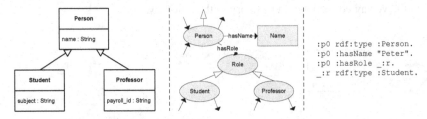

Fig. 7.7: Simplified class model by skipping categories in chains of relations: the postal code of the city a person lives in is stored directly as an attribute of `Person` in the class model, while the path to that postal code is longer in the ontology.

Fig. 7.8: Shortcuts may also include subclass relations, leading to ontologically incorrect subclasses in the class model: here, the role a person plays (`Student` or `Professor`) is modeled as a direct subclass in the class model.

7.2.3 Non-atomic Data Types

Data attributes may often contain non-atomic values, such as a name attribute storing both first and last name (or even worse from an ontologically precise point of view: also an academic degree), dates (consisting of a day, a month, and a year), and so on[1]. Fig. 7.9 illustrates those issues. Furthermore, many data values have a unit, which in most cases is only implicitly known by the developer or written down somewhere in the system specification. Thus, the data type is *incomplete* – without the unit, the number carries no information.

A special kind of non-atomic values are counting attributes, which represent a number of instances. In figure 7.10, the value of the `number_of_children` attribute depicts the number of children a person has, while in the ontology, having children is modeled as a direct relation between persons.

---

[1] Phone numbers, which have been used in various examples in this chapter, are also non-atomic: they consist of a country and an area code, a number, and an extension. The same holds for email and web addresses. However, they are regarded as atomic in most cases.

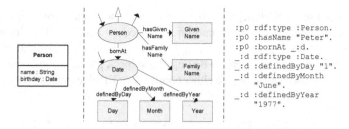

Fig. 7.9: From the values contained in non-atomic data types, several triples have to be generated.

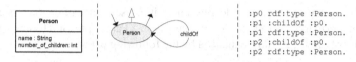

Fig. 7.10: An attribute is used for counting instances. Several triples have to be generated based on the attribute's numerical value.

7.3 Non-Intrusive, Dynamic Annotation of Class Models

The above mismatches demand for a solution allowing for more versatile, non-1:1-mappings between class models and an ontology. We decided for using rules as a mapping mechanism. The implementation is done in a non-intrusive fashion, so that the approach can also be applied to class models which cannot or must not be altered.

7.3.1 Rules for Mapping Class Models to Ontologies

As shown in the examples above, dynamic mappings from class models to ontologies have to take into account instance data of the objects instead of mapping on a class level. Therefore, some language constructs are required for querying object graphs formed by those data objects. There are some approaches for such query mechanisms in the literature, e.g., JQL for Java (Willis et al, 2006, pp. 34), or LINQ for .NET based languages (Meijer et al, 2006, p. 706). In our approach, we decided to use XPath (W3C, 2010d), as it is a standardized, language-independent querying mechanism with implementations, e.g., for Java (Agnew, 2006), .NET (Saxon, 2003), and objects serialized in JSON (Goessner, 2007).

Utilizing such queries, annotations for objects are realized dynamically by creating a representation, e.g., in RDF, as shown in the examples above. Thus, our rules have the following form: the body consists of a test to be performed on an object. The head is a set of RDF triples[2], each consisting of a subject, a predicate, and an object all three of which may depend on the object to annotate. For defining tests and dependent values, we use XPath expressions. If the test is evaluated positively, one or more triples are generated, consisting of a subject, predicate, and object. The subject, predicate, and object may be either constants or XPath expressions as well. Thus, the syntax of our rules looks as follows[3]:

$$\texttt{Rule ::= XPathExpr "}\rightarrow\texttt{" Triple \{"," Triple \} "." ;} \tag{7.1}$$

$$\texttt{Triple ::= 3 * (Constant|XPathExpr) ;} \tag{7.2}$$

In this syntax, `Constant` denotes an arbitrary sequence of characters enclosed in quotation marks, and `XPathExpr` denotes an XPath expression following the XPath standard (W3C, 2010d), enhanced by the following extensions:

- The function `regex()`, called on a Java attribute, evaluates a regular expression (Friedl, 2006) on that object and yields `true` if the regular expression matches the attribute value, false otherwise.
- The function `repeat(XPathExpr)`, called with an XPath expression as an argument in the rule body, causes the rule head to be executed as many times as there are results for the given XPath expression.
- The `%` symbol used in the head refers to the result of the XPath test performed in the body.
- The `.` symbol used in the head refers to the currently serialized object.
- The function `uri()` assigns a unique URI to a Java[4] object. The argument of the function is again an XPath expression, which may also use the `%` and `.` constructs, as described above.

With rules of that kind, RDF representations can be generated from Java objects. An example rule creating part of a semantic annotation for a `Person` object with an `address` attribute may look like that:

$$\texttt{/address} \rightarrow \texttt{uri(.) "<\#hasAddress>" uri(\%) .} \tag{7.3}$$

For a person object p with the unique URI `http://foo.bar#p0`, the rule would be evaluated by retrieving the value of `p.address` (in Java, this typically means calling a getter function). Assuming the result is an address object with the URI `http://foo.bar#a0`, the body is evaluated for generating the corresponding triple, which results in calling the `uri()` function on the object p, producing the constant `<#hasAddress>`, and calling the `uri()` function on the address object

---

[2] For representations other than RDF triples, such as F-Logic expressions, the rule mechanism may be trivially modified.

[3] Notated using the Extended Backus Naur Form (EBNF) (International Organization for Standardization (ISO), 1996)

[4] Although Java is used throughout all the examples, the approach also works for any other object-oriented programming language

identified with the XPath expression of the rule's body (which is referenced to by using the % symbol). Thus, the following triple is generated as an annotation (given `http://foo.bar` is the default namespace):

`<#p0> <#hasAddress> <#a0> .`

Testing attribute values identified by an XPath expression allows for generating triples only if a certain condition is fulfilled. This helps solving the problem of multi-purpose classes:

$$/[sex = "MALE"] \rightarrow uri(.) "<rdf:type>" <\#Man> . \qquad (7.4)$$

According to the XPath syntax, terms in brackets define tests. The corresponding element is only selected in case that the test is evaluated to true. Rule 7.4 thus only fires if the value of the attribute `sex` has the value `"MALE"`, therefore, the corresponding triple is only generated if that condition holds true. The same mechanism can be applied to handle conditional objects with delete flags.

Multi-purpose relations can be handled the same way. If implicit knowledge is involved, e.g. for telling an email address from a phone number, as shown in figure 7.5, additional tests with regular expressions have to be used to make that knowledge explicit:

$$/address[regex(\hat{}.*@.*\$)] \rightarrow uri(.)$$
$$"<rdf:hasEmailAddress>"$$
$$uri(\%) . \qquad (7.5)$$
$$/address[regex(\hat{}[\hat{}@]*\$)] \rightarrow uri(.)$$
$$"<rdf:hasPhoneNumber>"$$
$$uri(\%) . \qquad (7.6)$$

Rule 7.5 fires if the value of the inspected object's address attribute contains an @ symbol, and then produces the corresponding annotation. Rule 7.6 fires in the opposite case.

Artificial classes, as shown in figure 7.3, can also be handled by adding additional triples to the semantic annotation:

$$/addtlData/email \rightarrow uri(.) "<\#hasEmailAddress>" uri(\%) . \qquad (7.7)$$

$$/addtlData/SSN \rightarrow uri(.)$$
$$"<\#hasSocialSecurityNumber>" uri(\%) . \qquad (7.8)$$

Evaluating these rules on a `Person` object, as shown in figure 7.3, the triples are generated if the `AdditionalData` object related to the `Person` object holds a value for `email` or `SSN`, respectively. Thus, all data contained in the `AdditionalData` object are correctly transformed into the RDF representation, although the `AdditionalData` object itself is not mapped to that representation.

Likewise, classes used for relations, as shown in figure 7.4, can be handled:

$$/\rightarrow \texttt{uri(./person1)} \texttt{"<\#knows>"} \texttt{uri(./person2)} . \qquad (7.9)$$

In this rule, no test is used in the rule body, because a triple is generated for *every* instance of `PersonRelation`. An XPath expression is used in the argument of the `uri` function to compute URIs for the two person objects involved.

Like in the examples above, the rules' bodies are fulfilled if the respective attribute of the artificial class exists. If, e.g., the `AdditionalData` object has the `email` attribute set, a respective triple is added to the `Person` object's semantic annotation.

Shortcuts, as shown in figure 7.7 and figure 7.8, are handled by inserting blank nodes (indicated by an underscore):

$$/\texttt{postal\_code} \rightarrow \texttt{uri(.)} \texttt{"<\#livesIn>"} \_\texttt{:city,}$$
$$\_\texttt{:city} \texttt{"<\#hasPostalCode>"} \texttt{uri(\%)} . \qquad (7.10)$$

When the head of rule 7.10 is evaluated, three statements are generated, which are interconnected via one blank node `_:city`, denoting a city that is known to exist, but not further specified. When the results of multiple rule heads are merged, the result of each execution of an individual rule is treated like a separate RDF document, thus, the blank nodes' IDs are renamed to remain unique throughout the merged annotation. Accordingly, the developer of annotation rules has to assure unique names for blank nodes only within one rule, but not across different rules.

Counting attributes can be covered by the repeat function:

$$/\texttt{repeat(number\_of\_children)} \rightarrow \texttt{child} \texttt{"<\#childOf>"} \texttt{uri(.)}.$$
$$(7.11)$$

Rule 7.11 fires if the `number_of_children` attribute is set, and creates n triples with a blank node each for an attribute value of n. The `repeat` function thus is a special construct which directly influences how the rules are processed.

Dealing with other kinds of non-atomic data types, as shown in figure 7.9, can be a more difficult task. In cases where the background knowledge may be formalized, e.g. separating a street name from a house number, regular expressions can be used for implementing dynamic annotation. However, there are numerous cases which cannot be formalized that easily. One typical case is splitting a name into a first name and a last name – even with massive domain knowledge, it is practically impossible to formulate a rule which treats all names in every language correctly (Ley, 2009, p. 1498). This case demonstrates the limitations of automatically annotating objects. Note that this limitation is not a limitation of this particular annotation approach, but a limitation which is due to the fact that some kind of background knowledge can hardly be completely formalized.

For each class, a set of rules is defined. When using inheritance in class models, it is likely that the RDF representation of a sub class is a superset of the representation of the more general classes. Therefore, mapping rules are inherited by default. However, the developer of mapping rules may explicitly overwrite and remove rules defined for a super class.

7.3.2 Rules for Mapping Ontologies to Class Models

For allowing a full round trip object exchange, Java objects have to be created from RDF representations. We again use rules for facilitating that sort of conversion. Assuming that we use RDF as an intermediate format for object annotation, a query language is needed that allows for checking conditions and extracting values from RDF graphs. As discussed in section 3.1.2, SPARQL (W3C, 2008d) is the de facto standard language for querying RDF. Therefore, we use SPARQL for formulating conditions and extracting data.

Typically, objects will be created when a condition is fulfilled, and values are set in these objects. This leads to the following rule syntax for mapping rules from ontologies to class models:

$$
\begin{array}{rll}
\text{Rule} & ::= & \text{SPARQLExpr "$\rightarrow$" ObjFunction} \\
& & \{ \text{ "/" SetObjValue} \} \text{ "." ;} & (7.12) \\
\text{ObjFunction} & ::= & \text{"getObject("SPARQLVariable} \\
& & \{\text{,SPARQLVariable}\} \\
& & \text{"," ClassName ")" ;} & (7.13) \\
\text{SetObjValue} & ::= & \text{XPathExpr "=(ObjFunction} \\
& & \text{| ValueFunction | Constant) ;} & (7.14) \\
\text{ValueFunction} & ::= & \text{"getValue(" (SPARQLVariable} \\
& & \text{| BuiltinFunction)} \\
& & \text{"," ClassName ")" ;} & (7.15) \\
\text{BuiltinFunction} & ::= & \text{"count("SPARQLVariable")"} \\
& & \text{| "concat("SPARQLVariable,} \\
& & \{\text{SPARQLVariable}\}")" ;} & (7.16) \\
\end{array}
$$

Like in the rules for annotating objects with RDF, XPathExpr denotes an XPath expression. SPARQLExpr denotes the WHERE part of a SPARQL expression, and SPARQLVariable denotes a variable defined in that WHERE part and is used for referencing the query's results. ClassName is the name of a Java class which is used when creating objects and object values (for handling primitive types, the corresponding wrapper classes are used as a class name). The built-in functions count and concat are used for counting results and concatenating strings, respectively. Both functions are on the feature list for the next version of SPARQL (W3C, 2009d), thus, those functions may be removed from the rule language once that new version becomes a standard with adequate tool and API support.

The following rule shows a minimal example for creating an object from an RDF graph:

$$\{?.\ :\text{address}\ ?a\} \rightarrow \text{getObject}(?.,\text{foo.bar.Person})/\text{address}$$
$$= \text{getValue}(?a,\text{foo.bar.Address}).\quad (7.17)$$

This rule, applied to an instance of `foaf:Person`, creates a new object of type `foo.bar.Person`, and sets its `address` attribute to the corresponding value. The `getObject` function is used for creating objects, where the first variable is a list of URIs which are used as a key for creating the object. If the function is called with a list of URIs for which an object of that class has already been created, the already created object is returned.

Like for creating annotations, rule sets will invoke each other recursively. In the example given in equation 7.18, the RDF instance of the person's address is processed with its own rule set, thus allowing for setting the `foo.bar.Address` object's values when creating the `foo.bar.Person` object.

When creating object instances of multi-purpose classes, such as shown in figure 7.2, a combination of creating an object and setting a value is used:

$$\{?.\ \text{rdf:type}\ :\text{Man}\} \rightarrow \text{getObject}(?.,\text{foo.bar.Person})/\text{sex}$$
$$= \text{getValue}(``\text{MALE}\,'',\text{foo.bar.Sex}).$$
$$(7.18)$$

The `getValue` function creates an instance of the `foo.bar.Sex` enumeration. Multi-purpose relations, as shown in figures 7.5 and 7.6 are treated the same way. Artificial classes can be created when needed:

$$\{?.\ :\text{hasEmailAddress}\ ?p\}$$
$$\rightarrow \text{getObject}(?.,\text{foo.bar.Person})/\text{addtlData}$$
$$= \text{getObject}(?.,\text{foo.bar.AdditionalData}).\quad (7.19)$$
$$\{?.\ :\text{hasEmailAddress}\ ?p\}$$
$$\rightarrow \text{getObject}(?.,\text{foo.bar.AdditionalData})/\text{email}$$
$$= \text{getValue}(?p).\quad (7.20)$$

Since in the example in figure 7.3, `Email Address` is a data property and hence has no URI, we have used the URI of the corresponding `Person` instance as a key for creating the `foo.bar.AdditionalData` object. These rules create one object of the class `AdditionalData`, connect it to the `Person` object, and set the corresponding value for `email`.

For handling shortcuts, more complex SPARQL expressions are required, as for the example shown in figure 7.7:

$$\{?p \ :livesIn \ ?c, \ ?c \ :hasPostalCode \ ?z\}$$
$$\rightarrow getObject(?.,foo.bar.Person)/postal\_code$$
$$= getValue(?z). \tag{7.21}$$

When executing the SPARQL query, the variable ?c is bound to the blank node depicting the city, as shown in figure 7.7. As there is no corresponding City object in the class model, the variable is not used in the rule head.

There may be cases where a relation in the ontology has to be mapped to a class in the class model, e.g., a KNOWS relation in the ontology being mapped to a PersonRelation class in Java. A corresponding set of rules may look as follows:

$$\{?p0 \ :knows \ ?p1\}$$
$$\rightarrow getObject(?p0,?p1,foo.bar.PersonRelation)/person1$$
$$= getValue(?p0) \ . \tag{7.22}$$
$$\{?p0 \ :knows \ ?p1\}$$
$$\rightarrow getObject(?p0,?p1,foo.bar.PersonRelation)/person2$$
$$= getValue(?p1) \ . \tag{7.23}$$

In that case, a compound key is used for the getObject function, i.e., ?p0, ?p1. The reason is that one PersonRelation object has to be created for each couple of persons being connected by a KNOWS relation.

For creating objects containing non-atomic values, the concat function can be used:

$$\{?. \ :hasZIP \ ?zip, \ ?. \ :hasCity \ ?city\}$$
$$\rightarrow getObject(?.,foo.bar.Person)/address$$
$$= concat(?zip," \ ",?city). \tag{7.24}$$

The address attribute is thus filled with a concatenation of zip and city. Likewise, the count function is used for dealing with counting attributes:

$$\{?c \ :childOf \ ?.\}$$
$$\rightarrow getObject(?.,foo.bar.Person)/number\_of\_children$$
$$= count(?c). \tag{7.25}$$

This rule fills the number_of_children attribute with the number of nodes found which are in a childOf relation to the person[5].

The concat and count built-in function are used for working with non-atomic data types. More specific problems, such as unit conversions, could be solved by adding new built-ins, e.g., for arithmetic operations.

---

[5] Note that this rule makes sense only if assuming that all children are contained in the RDF graph, i.e., the open world assumption is omitted at that place.

Like for the mapping rules from class models to ontologies, rules are defined per category in the ontology and inherited along sub category relations in the ontology, and the developer can overwrite and remove rules defined for a super category.

When creating an object graph from a set of RDF statements, the rule sets for different categories may contain statements leading to the creation of objects. If those rule sets are merged due to an sub category relation between categories, the merged rule sets may contain a number of object creation statements, not all of which may be desired (e.g., a `Vehicle` and a more special `Car` object are created, but only the `Car` object is wanted). To avoid such a creation of unwanted objects, object creation rules are sorted in a way that more specialized objects are created first, and those instances are then reused for less specialized ones instead of creating fresh objects.

To illustrate the problem, consider the following rules defined for the ontology category VEHICLE:

$$?. \ \text{rdf:type Vehicle} \rightarrow \ \text{getObject}(?.,\text{foo.bar.Vehicle}). \tag{7.26}$$

$$?. \ :\text{hasSpeed ?s} \ \rightarrow \ \text{getObject}(?.,\text{foo.bar.Vehicle})$$
$$/\text{speed} = \text{getValue}(?s). \tag{7.27}$$

Further, the following rules are defined for the ontology category CAR, which is a sub category of VEHICLE:

$$?. \ \text{rdf:type Car} \rightarrow \ \text{getObject}(?.,\text{foo.bar.Car}). \tag{7.28}$$

$$?. \ :\text{hasPlate ?p} \rightarrow \ \text{getObject}(?.,\text{foo.bar.Car})$$
$$/\text{licensePlate} = \text{getValue}(?p). \tag{7.29}$$

Given an RDF instance of CAR, working through the rules from top to bottom, an instance of `Vehicle` would be created, and the value for `speed` set on that object, and another instance of `Car`, with the value for `licensePlate` set. However, the developer intends to have one instance of `Car` with both the `speed` and `licensePlate` values set. By sorting the rule set so that 7.28 is executed before 7.26, the object factory will notice upon the execution of 7.26 that an instance of `Car` has already been created for the given RDF instance, and return that object instead of creating a new `Vehicle` instance.

7.3.3 Object Exchange with Template-based Filtering

The rules discussed above are typically evaluated in a recursive manner. When creating the annotation for an object, each object that is encountered underway is queued and processed. For very large object graphs, this means that the resulting annotation can grow unwantedly large. Especially when using the annotation for data exchange between applications where the resulting RDF data may be used as an exchange format, such large annotations are undesirable for reasons of performance.

Consider the class model given in figure 7.11. In this model, persons are employed by companies, and both persons and companies have addresses. When transferring a `Person` object, a desirable annotation may consist of the person's name, her address, and her employer, not including that employer's address. When transferring a `Company` object, on the other hand, the annotation in should contain the company's address, but not every employee.

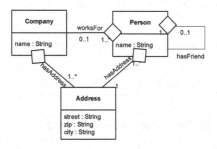

Fig. 7.11: Example class model that can lead to very large annotations

Due to the recursive nature of rule processing, such a behavior cannot be achieved only with the mechanisms sketched above. The rule set for the class `Company` can only state to include the address in the annotation, or it cannot. What is needed is a means to exclude some information dynamically.

A straight forward way would be defining different rule sets for each class, depending on which kind of object is currently serialized. Such a solution would lead to n^2 rule sets for n classes and thus be rather costly. If we would want to take arbitrary paths into account (e.g., include the address of a person's employer into the annotation, but not the addresses of that person's friends' employers), the complexity would even be exponential.

A better alternative is to use *templates* which define the subset of possible annotations that are to be generated for an object of a certain class. While rules define *all* possible annotations that can be produced for an object and are thus universal, templates specifically restrict the set of annotations. For defining templates, we use plain RDF, with blank nodes representing the annotations to be generated. Each blank node can be instantiated multiple times. The "root" object, i.e., the object that the annotation is generated for, is referred to as _:_.

Figure 7.12 shows an example template. In this example, a person's name and address are included in the annotation, as well as her employer's name and address, and her friends and their employers. It does, however, not include her employer's employees and her friends' friends, thus avoiding endless recursion. The example shows that the template approach allows for very fine grained control of annotations, but at a very low complexity: only one template and one rule set is needed per class, thus leading to an overall complexity of $O(n)$ for n classes.

The use of templates has another advantage: while the rule sets remain constant, different templates may be used for different use cases. For example, for informa-

```
_:_  domain : hasName   _: personName .
_:_  domain : worksFor  _: personEmployer .
_:_  domain : hasAddress  _: personAddress .
_:_  domain : hasFriend  _: personFriend .

_: employer  domain : hasName   _: name .
_: employer  domain : hasAddress  _: employerAddress .

_: personAddress  domain : hasStreet  _: personStreet .
...

_: employerAddress  domain : hasStreet  _: employerStreet .
...

_: personFriend  domain : worksFor  _: friendEmployer .
```

Fig. 7.12: Example for a template for restricting an object's annotation

tion exchange between systems within an organization, the exchanged data may include more details than for exchange between organizations. Such a scenario would only require another set of templates, while the rule sets could be reused without modification.

For the reverse direction, i.e., constructing Java objects from RDF, we have not foreseen a template mechanism, since it is assumed that in a data exchange scenario, the incoming RDF representation is limited by nature. In that direction, every possible object is created, and can be left to the further processing logic to ignore or explicitly discard anything that is not required.

7.3.4 Non-intrusive Implementation

To allow for using the annotation mechanisms with arbitrary applications, it is necessary that the annotation works in a non-intrusive way, i.e., that the class models which are to be annotated do not have to be adapted. For this reason, all rules are stored in separate rule files which contain references to the class models and the ontologies used for annotation, but not vice versa. The same holds for the template files used for transmission of RDF data. Thus, the implementation is non-intrusive with respect to both the integrated application and the ontologies used.

Figure 7.13 shows the high-level view on object exchange between applications, where the applications exchange RDF annotation of objects and re-create objects following their own class models from those annotations.

When an object "leaves" an application through that application's API, the object exchange component uses the *mapping engine* for creating the annotation. That mapping engine has four main conceptual building blocks:

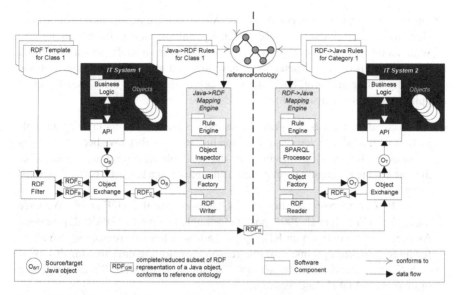

Fig. 7.13: Architecture diagram of object exchange between applications via dynamic annotation (Paulheim et al, 2011b, p. 204). The figure shows the components involved in transferring an object from IT system 1 to IT system 2. For the reverse direction, the respective units are involved on the opposite side (i.e., an RDF filter on the side of IT system 2, etc.). Those have been omitted in the figure for reasons of simplicity.

- The *rule engine* is responsible for loading and executing the appropriate rule sets, including the management of overridden rules, and the ordering of rules. In our approach, this includes keeping track of the objects to annotate, i.e., maintaining a queue of objects whose rule sets have to be invoked recursively. In our prototype implementation, part of the rule engine has been generated by using *JavaCC* (Kodaganallur, 2004, pp. 70).
- The *object inspector* executes expressions for testing conditions on and extracting values from objects. In our prototype implementation, we use JXPath (Agnew, 2006) for executing XPath expressions on a set of Java objects.
- The *URI factory* is used each time the uri function is executed in a rule. It keeps track of unambiguous and unique URIs for each annotated object. In our application integration framework, uniqueness is ensured by assigning each container a unique base URI from which the object's URIs are derived.
- The *RDF writer* takes the results of the rule executions and creates RDF graphs used for annotation. In particular, the RDF writer monitors the uniqueness of identifiers for blank nodes created by rules and renames them, where needed.

The *RDF Filter* component is responsible for reducing the RDF created from an object when transmitting the annotation, as discussed above. For using a linked data provider, like in our framework, it makes sense to use a default filter which only retains references to the connected objects. A consumer, e.g., an ontology reasoner, can then retrieve detail data on those objects by multiple calls to the provider.

With another set of rules, objects can be re-created from RDF annotations. In UI integration, this is relevant when objects have to be exchanged between applications, e.g., during a drag and drop interaction. As depicted in figure 7.13, the respective mapping engine also consists of four parts:

- As for creating annotations, a *rule engine* processes the rules for creating Java objects. It is in particular responsible for loading rule sets that have been recursively invoked, and for ordering rules in a way that no duplicate objects are created. Like the rule engine for creating annotations, this rule engine has been partly generated using *JavaCC*.
- A *SPARQL processor* executes SPARQL queries on the RDF graph. We have used *JENA* (Carroll et al, 2004, pp. 74) for implementing the SPARQL processor. As executing a query on an RDF graph can include some reasoning, we allow for three different options: a simple reasoner exploiting only the transitivity of subClassOf and subPropertyOf relations, a full RDF-S reasoner, and a more powerful OWL Lite reasoner.
- The *object factory* is responsible of creating objects. It is invoked by the getObject and getValue function. The object factory keeps track of objects that have already been created and maps them to their keys.
- The *RDF reader* processes the received annotation and provides it to the SPARQL processor. Like the SPARQL processor, we have used JENA as an RDF reader.

Together, the two mapping engines allow for full round-trip object exchange between applications using only RDF annotations obeying a common ontology.

7.4 Case Study: Annotating the SoKNOS Class Model with the SoKNOS Domain Ontology

Although in SoKNOS, many of the applications integrated have been exclusively developed in the project and hence shared the same class model, semantic annotation was nevertheless an integral part of integrating those applications, since the integration framework demands that the reasoner can use information from the running applications, and domain specific integration rules were used throughout the whole prototype. Since the domain ontology was developed using strict ontology engineering approaches, while the class model was developed separately by software engineers, bridging heterogeneities between the two was essentially required.

7.4.1 Annotation in SoKNOS

The common SoKNOS class model consists of 58 classes with 30 attributes as 25 relations. It has been used as a common subset of applications for allowing them to share basic data.

In addition to the class model, a concise domain ontology was developed (Babitski et al, 2009b), consisting of 156 categories and 136 relations. As discussed in Sect. 5.5.5, the ontology was developed using a rigid ontology engineering approach and grounded in formal top level ontologies. Therefore, many of the mismatches discussed in this chapter could be observed when annotating the common SoKNOS class model with the SoKNOS domain ontology. Fig. 7.14 depicts an excerpt of both the class model and the ontology and shows some simple example mappings.

7.4.2 Mismatches in SoKNOS

A typical mismatch in SoKNOS is a multi-purpose class concerned with measures for fighting fires etc. One class Measure is used to model both planned measures as well as measures that are actually carried out. As they share most of the attribute, only one class is used for both categories, distinguished by a flag. This implementation allows for easy programming, as starting to carry out a planned measure only requires changing the flag in the system. In the ontology, however, both categories are essentially different: a PLANNED MEASURE is a sub category of PLAN, which is a NON-PHYSICAL ENDURANT in DOLCE, while a MEASURE is a sub category of PERDURANT in DOLCE. Thus, there is not even a meaningful super class.

Object counting occurs in SoKNOS, for example, when storing the number of injured people for a particular damage, as it makes no sense at all to create one Java object per injured person.

Deviation type	No. of Occurrences
Multi purpose class	3
Multi purpose relation	2
Artificial class	0
Relation class	1
Shortcuts	3
Conditional objects	2
Object counting	3
Non atomic attributes	4

Table 7.1: Mismatches observed between the common SoKNOS class model and the SoKNOS domain ontology.

Table 7.1 shows the number of observed mismatches between the common So-KNOS class model and the SoKNOS domain ontology. These figures show that about

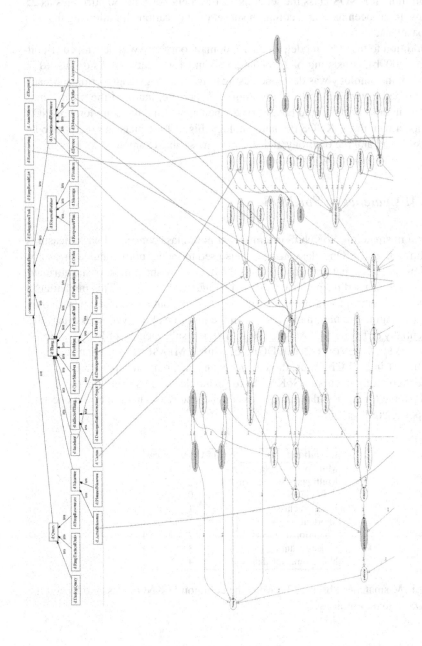

Fig. 7.14: Excerpt from the common SoKNOS class model (top and bottom) and the SoKNOS domain ontology (middle), depicting some simple mappings between the two (Babitski et al, 2009c, p. 45).

16% of all model elements (classes, attributes, and relations) and 6% of all ontology elements (categories and relations) are involved in some of the deviations.

In total, 60 mapping rules were used in SoKNOS to map the class model to the ontology. This number reflects that only a partial mapping was implemented, since objects of some classes were never involved in a cross-application interaction and therefore did not require semantic annotation.

7.4.3 Example Object Exchange in SoKNOS

To illustrate how rule-based object exchange is implemented in SoKNOS, we will use the example of brushing and linking between the mission account application and the geographic information application. When the user selects an object – in this example: a measure addressing a problem – in the mission account application, it is displayed in the geographic information application, using a green marker symbol. To implement this interaction, the relevant information has to be transferred from the mission account application to the geographic information application.

As discussed in Sect. 5.5, the geographic information application is built on top of *ArcGIS* (ESRI Inc., 2010), which uses the *ArcObjects API* (ESRI Inc., 2011) for representing objects, while the mission account application, which is an application developed on purpose for SoKNOS, uses the SoKNOS class model. Therefore, the interaction in this example requires transforming an object from the SoKNOS class model to the ArcObjects class model using the intermediate SoKNOS domain ontology. Fig. 7.15 shows the relevant parts of the two class models, as well as an excerpt of the domain ontology used in between.

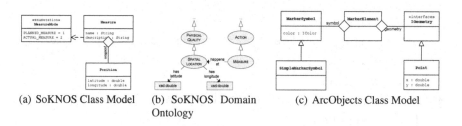

(a) SoKNOS Class Model   (b) SoKNOS Domain Ontology   (c) ArcObjects Class Model

Fig. 7.15: Excerpts from two class models and the corresponding part in the SoKNOS domain ontology

The following set of rules is used to create an RDF representation of a `Measure` object:

```
    /[measureMode="ACTUAL_MEASURE"  ]
→ uri(.) rdf:type :Measure.                          (7.30)
    /position
→ uri(.) :happensAt uri(%),
    uri(%) rdf:type :SpatialLocation,
    uri(%) :hasLatitude %/latitude,
    uri(%) :hasLongitude %/longitude.               (7.31)
```

Rule 7.30 handles the multi-purpose class Measure shown in Fig. 7.15(a). Rule
7.31 creates the triples for the position information. Together, these rules create
five triples describing a Measure object (which is a simplification for illustration
purposes):

```
:m0 rdf:type :Measure.
:m0 :happensAt :s0.
:s0 rdf:type :SpatialLocation,
    :hasLatitude "25.034",
    :hasLongitutde "-84.487".
```

This set of statements is used both for reasoning and evaluating the corresponding
interaction rule, as well as for creating the required set of objects in the geographic
information application in the next step.

When creating a set of Java objects in the geographic information application, a
lot of artificial classes have to be created – in fact, apart from Point, all classes are
artificial, since they represent concepts that only exist for computational purposes,
but not in the real world. The following set of rules creates the appropriate set of
objects:

```
  { ?. :happensAt ?l }
→ getObject(?.,com.esri.arcgis.display.MarkerElement)
   /symbol
   = getObject(?.,
   com.esri.arcgis.display.SimpleMarkerSymbol).    (7.32)
   { ?. :happensAt ?l }
→ getObject(?.,
   com.esri.arcgis.display.SimpleMarkerSymbol)/color
   = getObject(?.,com.esri.arcgis.display.RgbColor).
                                                      (7.33)
   { ?. :happensAt ?l }
→ getObject(?.,com.esri.arcgis.display.RgbColor)
   /green = getValue("255",java.lang.Integer).     (7.34)
```

```
  { ?. :happensAt ?l }
→ getObject(?.,com.esri.arcgis.display.RgbColor)
  /red = getValue("0",java.lang.Integer).               (7.35)
  { ?. :happensAt ?l }
→ getObject(?.,com.esri.arcgis.display.RgbColor)
  /blue = getValue("0",java.lang.Integer).              (7.36)
  { ?. :happensAt ?l }
→ getObject(?.,com.esri.arcgis.display.MarkerElement)
  /geometry
  = getObject(?l,com.esri.arcgis.geometry.Point).  (7.37)
  { ?. :happensAt ?l . ?l :hasLatitude ?x }
→ getObject(?l,com.esri.arcgis.geometry.Point)
  /x = getValue(?x,java.lang,Double).                   (7.38)
  { ?. :happensAt ?l . ?l :hasLongitude ?y }
→ getObject(?l,com.esri.arcgis.geometry.Point)
  /y = getValue(?y,java.lang,Double).                   (7.39)
```

These rules create an instance each of `MarkerElement`, `SimpleMarkerSymbol`, `RbgColor` for the MEASURE RDF element, and an instance of `Point` for the SPATIALLOCATION RDF element. The color value is set constantly, as each MEASURE is represented by a green symbol.

This walk-through example shows how objects are transformed across different class models, using an intermediate domain ontology for representation. Other interactions in SoKNOS use similar transformation if different class models are used. For interactions between applications using the same class model, such as the shared SoKNOS class model, transformations are not necessary. If different technologies are involved, as Chap. 9 will discuss, the transformation steps are not limited to transforming Java objects to RDF and back, but also objects in other programming language, using the same rule mechanism with a different rule interpretation engine.

7.4.4 Performance Evaluation

Since performance is an important issue in user interface development in general (see also Chap. 8), as well as for SoKNOS in particular, we have evaluated our approach with respect to performance. To that end, we have processed different, artificially created sets of objects from 10 to 10000 connected objects in order to test the performance and scalability of our approach.

Figure 7.16 shows the runtime behavior of creating annotations for Java objects; Fig. 7.17 shows the runtime behavior of creating Java objects from annotations. The figures show that in both cases, the run times scale linearly with a growing number of objects (and size of annotation).

For creating annotations, the time for processing a Java object is below one millisecond. For creating Java objects from annotations, the time for processing a Java object is below ten millisecond for the simple transitivity reasoner and the RDF-S reasoner, and slightly larger for the OWL Lite reasoner. Using a more powerful reasoner allows for simpler definitions for rules (e.g., there is no need for defining explicit rules for super categories if a reasoner can compute the category membership) at the price of processing time.

Figs. 7.16 and 7.17 also demonstrate the impact of the template-based filtering mechanism on performance: while applying the template during the serializing step does not lead to a significant performance impact, smaller RDF structures may be deserialized much faster than larger ones. Thus, it is beneficial to reduce the RDF structures to transfer to another system as far as possible. For example, if the RDF structure to be transferred can be reduced by 50%, the total processing time is also decreased by 50%, as the time for creating Java objects from RDF decreases linearly, while there is no overhead in applying the filter.

These results show that the run times do not create a significant overhead and thus, the approach can be applied in a performance critical field like user interface integration.

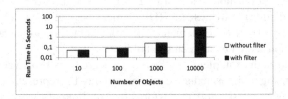

Fig. 7.16: Runtime behavior of creating annotations for Java objects

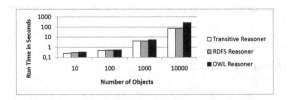

Fig. 7.17: Runtime behavior of creating Java objects from annotations

7.5 Summary

In this section, we have shown how object exchange has been designed and implemented in the integration framework. As most state of the art tools for annotating class models cannot cope with typical mismatches between class models and ontologies, those tools are not suitable for the problem in general. Therefore, we have developed a more versatile approach using rules and templates, which is implemented in a non-intrusive way.

The running case study has shown that the mismatches discussed do in fact occur in real life software projects. With a set of performance measures, we could show that although our approach is fairly powerful, the run-time overhead it creates can be neglected, even in a performance critical use case such as UI integration.

Chapter 8
Efficient Semantic Event Processing

Abstract For user interfaces, a non-efficient implementation can be a show stopper – applications which are perceivably slow will almost always lack acceptance by the end users. On the other hand, using ontologies and reasoning can create a massive overhead which is difficult to handle and conflicts with scalability. After a short review of the state of the art in semantic event processing in Sect. 8.2, this chapter discusses different implementation alternatives and evaluates their effect on performance in Sect. 8.3. Section 8.4 sheds more light on the generalized problem of reasoning on data from running applications. Section 8.5 shows how semantic event processing was implemented in an efficient way in the SoKNOS system.

8.1 Why Efficiency is Important

System performance and reactivity is a major factor influencing the end users' satisfaction. The classic HCI literature defines two seconds as an upper limit for reaction times, as stated by Miller (1968, pp. 270) and (Shneiderman, 1984, pp. 271). Although computers have become much faster during the years, the performance of applications has not increased at the same pace – a phenomenon known as *Wirth's law* (Ross, 2005, p. 35). Thus, we can expect that these limits still apply.

Semantic web based applications, on the other hand, often suffer from poor performance, which can be a major obstacle for successfully applying semantic web technologies in real scenarios, as discussed, e.g., by Hepp (2007, p. 18) and Coskun et al (2009, pp. 605).

In the framework developed in this book, *semantic event processing* is a core part, which is also the most complex one with respect to computation times: for each event, a reasoner is invoked for computing the reactions to that event, which in general is a costly operation. Thus, this event processing step should be considered with great care when designing and implementing the framework.

There are several factors which influence the performance of the event processing step. The number of integration rules increase the complexity for the computation of

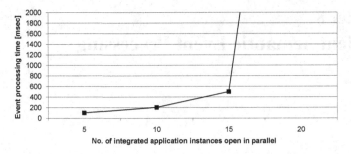

Fig. 8.1: Performance of a naive implementation of semantic event processing, using 10 integration rules per application and 10 data updates per second.

an event's effects. The number of integrated applications that are opened in parallel have an influence on the amount of instance data – components, data objects, state information, etc. – that the reasoner has to take into account. Furthermore, the frequency at which that instance data changes may also have an influence on the reasoner's performance.

Figure 8.1 shows the performance of a naive implementation for semantic event processing, which was used in an early prototype stage of the framework discussed in this book. It shows that for more than 10 integrated applications opened in parallel, the performance increases way beyond the two limits stage – in fact, reaction times of more than 30 seconds could be perceived with that prototype, which is a complete show stopper for applications built upon that framework. This demonstrates the need for more high-performance and scalable solutions.

8.2 State of the Art in Semantic Event Processing

Following the survey by Schmidt et al (2008a, pp. 3), event-driven approaches can be roughly categorized in *event detection* (dealing with the detection and creation of events) and *event processing* (dealing with reacting to those events, e.g. by creating new events and/or changing a system's state). Furthermore, *logic-based* and *non-logic-based* approaches can be distinguished, where the former incorporate formal logic to detect or process events, while the latter do not. Following this categorization, the approach presented in this book uses a logic-based approach to event processing.

The term *semantic event processing* denotes the processing of events based on information on the semantics of that event (Teymourian and Paschke, 2009, p. 1). The decisions in event processing may range from filtering and routing of events to the production of new events from the detected ones. An events' semantics may be comprised of information about the actor who caused the event, the objects with which the event was performed, and many more. Westermann and Jain (2007, pp. 19) propose a six-dimensional common event model, including temporal and spatial aspects as well as information about the involved actors and information objects, as discussed in Sect. 5.3. As semantics can be described by using ontologies based on formal logics, semantic event processing is a subset of logic-based event processing.

One simple form of event processing systems are *publish-subscribe-systems*. Here, clients subscribe to events which deal with a certain topic or, more general, fulfill a certain set of conditions. Ontologies may be used to provide a hierarchy of topics, in the simplest case. Sophisticated approaches can use more complex annotations of events and allow subscription not only on topics, but also on subgraphs of the annotations, e.g. by using SPARQL queries, such as in the approaches discussed by Wang et al (2004, pp. 235), Skovronski and Chiu (2006, pp. 3), and Murth and Kühn (2009, pp. 1375).

More advanced approaches of event processing do not only forward or discard events, but may also create new events or allow the triggering of actions if events occur under certain conditions, an approach known as *event-condition-action* (ECA) rules. There are several approaches to implementing event-driven systems based on ECA rules, e.g. in Datalog (Anicic and Stojanovic, 2008, pp. 395), RuleML (Paschke et al, 2007, pp. 2), or F-Logic , such as in the framework discussed in this book.

Few works exist which inspect the efficiency and scalability issues of using semantic events. In the field of *event detection*, the approach described in (Teymourian and Paschke, 2009, p. 2) uses modular event ontologies for different domains to enable more sophisticated semantic event processing mechanisms based on ECA rules. The authors propose to use reasoning to detect more complex event patterns in a stream of events described by ontologies, and to tell important events from non-important ones. The authors name scalability and real time processing as challenges, although no actual performance figures are presented.

The idea of modular event ontologies is further carried out in (Alferes et al, 2009, pp. 167) and (Behrends et al, 2006, pp. 30). The authors propose a modular approach where not only different ontologies, but also different languages can be used for individual parts of ECA rules. In this very versatile approach, applications on the semantic web can register their rules as well as the corresponding processing units. Annotated events are then processed in a distributed fashion by dynamically calling the registered processing units. As such an approach involves (possibly remote) method calls during the event processing procedure, it may not be suitable in applications with real-time requirements.

The work discussed in (Aasman, 2008, pp. 140) also uses events described with ontologies. The authors focus on mining information from a large database of events, allowing queries about characteristics such as the social relationships between the actors involved in events as well as the temporal and spatial relationships between events. Although real-time processing is not a necessary property in this case, the authors discuss the use of high-performance triple stores to allow fast query answering. A similar approach is described in (Rafatirad et al, 2009, pp. 67), where operators for detecting complex events from a database of atomic events are introduced, based on the model by Westermann and Jain mentioned above.

In the field of *event processing*, there are a few examples of using semantic event processing in the user interface area. One approach is described by Stühmer et al (2009, pp. 894). Web pages annotated with RDFa can be used to create events that also carry information about the semantics of the involved objects. The authors present an approach for producing, processing, and consuming those events, and for constructing complex events from atomic ones. In their approach, the annotations may be used to formulate rules, but no reasoning is applied in processing the events. The approach is evaluated with respect to performance (although no variants are discussed) by means of the example of context-sensitve advertising, and it proves high scalability, but at the price of not incorporating domain knowledge and reasoning in the event processing mechanism at all (and thus not facilitating semantic event processing as defined above).

Another application of semantic event processing in the user interface area is shown by Schmidt et al (2008b, pp. 737). Here, it is employed for run time adaptation of user interfaces, allowing the incorporation of domain knowledge in the reasoning process. The authors present an e-government portal and show the use case of presenting appropriate content based on the users context, and evaluate their approach with regard to run time, reporting event processing times between a few and a few thousand milliseconds, depending on the number of rules and the number of instances that are used to answer a query. The authors present performance measures that allow a direct comparison to our work: While the performance marks are about the same, the framework introduced in this book allows for formulating arbitrary rules on the ontologies, as discussed in Sect. 6.3.1, the approach presented in that paper allows only the use of the class hierarchy.

8.3 Implementation Variants and Evaluation

In order to guarantee efficient computation in our framework, we have implemented and evaluated several variants: processing events locally in a distributed fashion, or globally with a central event processor; maintaining a redundant A-Box, or pulling instance data on demand; caching instance data locally; and designing wrapper rules in different styles. This section depicts those variants as well as experimental results with respect to performance[1].

8.3.1 Local vs. Global Event Processing

Semantic event processing involves operations such as event filtering or the creation of new events from those that are already known, as in our approach. Such operations may be performed either by one central unit, or in a decentralized way by each participant involved in the event exchange, as discussed in Sect. 5.2.2. The two variants are depicted in Fig. 8.2.

---

[1] The performance evaluations have been carried out on a Windows XP 64Bit PC with an Intel Core Duo 3.00GHz processor and 4GB of RAM, using Java 1.6 and OntoBroker 5.3.

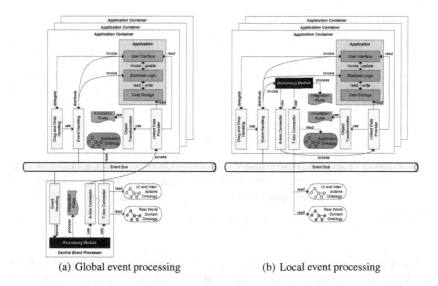

(a) Global event processing   (b) Local event processing

Fig. 8.2: Framework architecture using global vs. local event processing, following Paulheim (2010a, p. 68). The global variant uses one central reasoning and rule engine which processes all domain and *all* application ontologies. The local variant uses several reasoning and rule engines which each process all domain ontologies and *only one* application ontology.

Both approaches have advantages and drawbacks. A centralized event processing unit needs to know about each application ontology, instance information from all applications, as well as the complete set of event processing rules (see Fig. 8.2(a)), thus leading to a large number of rules and axioms to be processed by one unit. This unit may become a bottleneck, and cross-dependencies between rules can slow the whole process down.

For decentralized event processing, there are two options: events are analyzed when they are raised by an application, or when they are received. The first variant requires the whole set of integration rules from all reacting applications as well as the whole set of instances, it is thus equivalent to global event processing. With the second variant, each event has to be analyzed and processed once per application, even if the result of such processing is that the event is discarded in most cases, as only a fraction of all applications will typically react to an event. Furthermore, common domain knowledge, which is an essential ingredient of semantic event processing, has to be replicated and taken into the processing process each time (see Fig. 8.2(b)). Those operations can also have negative impact on the overall event processing performance. On the other hand, only a subset of the integration rules are needed at each local event processor, and in some cases, even only a subset of local instance data may be sufficient to process the event.

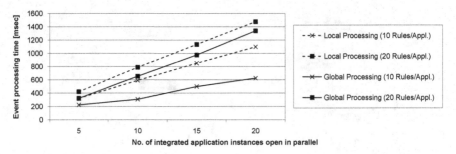

Fig. 8.3: Event processing performance comparison between using global and local processing (Paulheim, 2010a, p. 69). Event processing time has been measured for 5 to 20 instances of integrated applications used in parallel, with 10 and 20 integration rules each.

The measurements depicted in Fig. 8.3 reflect these mixed findings. Both approaches scale about equally well to larger numbers of integrated applications (and thus, larger total numbers of integration rules). For integrated applications with a smaller number of integration rules per application, global processing is about 40% faster than local processing; with a growing number of integration rules per application, the difference is not as significant, but global processing is still slightly faster.

The main reason why global event processing turns out to be faster is that each event has to be processed only once, not once per receiving application – this advantage is not trumped by the larger number of rules in a centralized approach. Furthermore, having several reasoners run in parallel on the same processor (since the different integrated applications are instantiated on one machine) can eventually slow down the whole machine. All the following performance optimizations are therefore implemented and evaluated based on global event processing.

8.3.2 Pushing vs. Pulling of Instance Data

As discussed in Sect. 3.1, ontologies consist of two parts, a T-Box, which contains the definitions of classes and relations, and an A-Box, which contains the information about instances of those classes. Reasoning about an integrated UI and events requires information about the system at run time, such as the application instances that are currently open, the components that constitute them, and the information objects they currently process. This kind of information is stored in the ontologies' A-Boxes. While the T-Boxes remain constant over time, the axioms in the A-Boxes usually change.

In our framework, A-Box data is retrieved through the A-Box connectors (see Sect. 5.4.2). There are two possible ways of implementing this A-Box. A straight forward approach is to use an instance store for the instance data (see Fig. 8.4(a)).

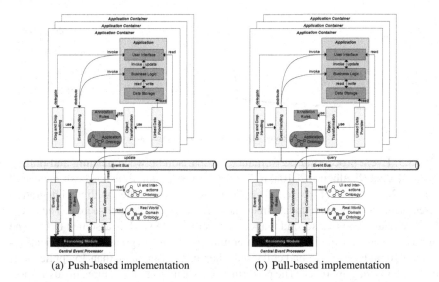

(a) Push-based implementation   (b) Pull-based implementation

Fig. 8.4: Framework architecture using a push-based vs. a pull-based approach, following Paulheim (2010a, p.70). Both variants are demonstrated in an implementation combined with global event processing.

In this approach, integrated applications are responsible for sending (i.e. *pushing*) regular updates to assure that the instance store is always synchronized with the system its instances represent.

Another approach is to use the integrated system itself as an instance store. In this approach, an A-Box connector is used to answer the reasoner's queries when needed. When called upon a query, it passes the query to the applications, collects (i.e. *pulls*) their answers and returns the instance data to the reasoner (see Fig. 8.4(b)).

To make the reasoner invoke a connector, a rule is needed whose head indicates the type of information the wrapper will deliver, and whose body contains a statement for actually calling that wrapper. Technically, a connector is wired to the reasoner with a predicate. For example, a connector providing instance data for an object can be included as follows[2]:

$$instance\_connector(?I, ?C) \Rightarrow ?C(?I). \tag{8.1}$$

This rule states that whenever `instance_connector(?I, ?C)` holds true, `?I` is an instance of `?C`. The reasoning framework, OntoBroker in the case of our framework prototype, is responsible for dispatching the use of the predicate

---

[2] For reasons of understandability, we will use the widely known SWRL human readable syntax for rules, although in SWRL, variables are not allowed for predicates. In our prototype implementation, we have used F-Logic, where variables are possible, at least for predicates defining the class of an instance.

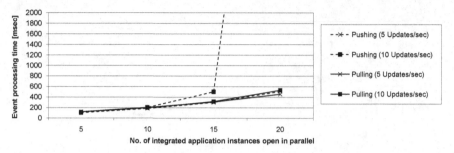

Fig. 8.5: Event processing performance comparison between pushing and pulling instance data (Paulheim, 2010a, p. 71). Event processing time has been measured for 5 to 20 instances of integrated applications used in parallel, with ten integration rules each, working at an update frequency of 5 to 10 updates per second. The figure has been cut at the two second mark where reasonable work is assumed to become impossible, as indicated in the HCI literature. Systems integrated from applications issuing 10 updates per second collapsed when integrating more than 15 applications using the pushing approach. The performance measures in this picture already respect various optimizations, such as caches and rule design .

instance_connector to an implementation of that connector, i.e., a Java method. This method then provides a set of bindings for the variables (in this case: $?I$ and $?C$). If some of the variables are already bound, the contract is that the method returns the valid bindings for the unbound variables which yield a true statement given the already bound ones.

Both approaches have their advantages and drawbacks. Pushing instance data into an instance store causes redundancy, since the data contained in the instance store is also contained in the integrated system itself. Furthermore, to make sure that each query is answered correctly, the updates sent by the applications and the queries issued by the reasoner need to be properly serialized. This may result in slower query execution if a larger number of updates is queued before the query. These problems are avoided when using a pull-based approach.

On the other hand, a pull-based approach includes that instance data is retrieved from external systems while a query is processed. Depending on the reactivity of those systems, the overall query processing time might also increase.

A comparison of both implementations is shown in Fig. 8.5, using applications with ten integration rules each, and varying the number of applications that are integrated at the same time. For applications issuing five updates per second on average, both approaches scale equally well. For applications issuing ten updates per second, the pushing approach does not scale anymore, leading to event processing times of ten seconds or more.

With a pushing approach, the updates from the individual applications form an ever growing queue, slowing down the whole system until a total collapse. This behavior will occur with every reasoning system as soon as the frequency of updates exceeds the inverse of the time it takes to process an update. Thus, only approaches

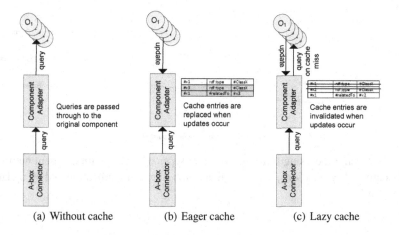

Fig. 8.6: Different variants for using caches

using the pulling approach scale up to larger integrated systems. Therefore, the following considerations are only based on the pulling variant.

8.3.3 Local Caching of Instance Data

While using connector for instance data instead of a redundant A-Box significantly increases the performance, there is still room for improvement. In a straight forward solutions, a representation of the instance data which can be processed by the reasoner (e.g., a set of RDF triples or F-Logic statements) has to be created when the reasoner has to access the instance data. Creating those representations, again, is a costly operation which can be avoided.

To speed up the answer of the A-Box connector, partly caching instance data in the connector is a good strategy (Wiederhold and Genesereth, 1997, p. 44), although it slightly contradicts to the idea of avoiding double bookkeeping – it is the classical trade-off of redundancy vs. performance. We have analyzed three different variants: using no caches at all, i.e., each query for instance data is directly passed to the underlying objects, and statements are assembled at query time (see Fig. 8.6(a)); and using *eager* and *lazy* caching. While the eager cache updates the required statements for each object when that object changes (see Fig. 8.6(b)), the lazy cache flags statements as invalid upon change of the represented object, and re-creates them only if they are requested (see Fig. 8.6(c)).

While using no caches at all avoids unnecessary workload when an update occurs, eager caches are supposed to be the fastest to respond to queries, since all required representations are present when the A-Box wrapper has to access them. Lazy caches

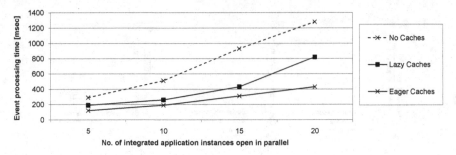

Fig. 8.7: Event processing times for different types of caches with different numbers of instantiated applications, using 10 integration rules per application and 50 updates per second.

can provide a compromise between the two, allowing fast responses to queries as well as avoiding unnecessary workload.

Figure 8.7 shows the performance figures for using wrappers with different types of caches. A significant speedup can be perceived when caches are used, with eager caches being faster than lazy caches.

8.3.4 Design of Connector Rules

To make the reasoner invoke a connector, a rule is needed whose head indicates the type of information the connector will deliver, and whose body contains a statement for actually calling that connector. Technically, a connector is wired to the reasoner with a predicate. The simplest rule for invoking a wrapper delivering instance data has already been depicted in equation 8.1:

$$instance\_connector(?I, ?C) \Rightarrow ?C(?I).$$

This mechanism is the most basic way of integrating a connector which delivers information about instances and the classes they belong to. As it has to be evaluated in each condition in a rule's body where statements like $?C(?I)$ occur (either unbound or with one or both of the variables bound), the connector is invoked. As invoking a connector via such a *generic rule*, can be a relatively costly operation (even with caches involved), this is a solution which may imply some performance issues.

A possible refinement is the use of additional constraints. The idea is that for each integrated application, the set of possible ontology categories that the application's data objects may belong to is known. Given that the union of those sets over all components is #Class1 through #ClassN, the above rule can be refined to an *extended rule* of the following form:

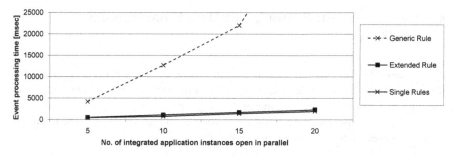

Fig. 8.8: Performance evaluation of different designs of connector rules, using 10 integration rules per application. No caches were used for this evaluation.

$$(equal(?C, \#Class1) \vee equal(?C, \#Class2)... \vee equal(?C, \#ClassN))$$
$$\wedge \; instance\_connector(?I, ?C)$$
$$\Rightarrow ?C(?I) \tag{8.2}$$

Assuming a left to right order of evaluation of the rule's body, the connector is now only invoked in cases where the variable $?C$ is bound to one of the given values. Therefore, the number of the connector's invocations can be drastically reduced.

A variant of that solution is the use of *single rules* instead of one large rule:

$$instance\_connector(?I, \#Class1) \Rightarrow \#Class1(?I)$$
$$instance\_connector(?I, \#Class2) \Rightarrow \#Class2(?I)$$
$$...$$
$$instance\_connector(?I, \#ClassN) \Rightarrow \#ClassN(?I) \tag{8.3}$$

In that case, the connector is not always invoked when evaluating a statement of type $?C(?I)$. Instead, each rule is only invoked for exactly one binding of $?C$. When querying for instances of #Class1, for example, only the first rule's body would be evaluated at all, invoking the wrapper once with one bound variable. On the other hand, the number of rules the reasoner has to evaluate for answering a query is increased.

The above example rules show how to invoke the *instance_connector* predicate, which returns statements about category membership of instances. The other important is *relation_connector*$(?X, ?R, ?Y)$, which has three variables. It returns the set of all triples where object $?X$ is in relation $?R$ with object Y. As for the *instance_connector* predicate, the corresponding types of invocation rules exist.

We have analyzed the performance impact of all three rule types on event processing: the generic rule (8.1), the use of an extended rule (8.2), and the use of single rules (8.3). Figure 8.8 depicts the results.

In summary, the best performance in event processing could be achieved by combining central reasoning with a pulling approach using eager caches, and by using single rules for invoking the connector.

8.4 Generalization: Reasoning on Data From Running Applications

As discussed in this chapter, semantic event processing in integrated applications requires some reasoning on data from those running applications. It is, however, not the only use case where such a reasoning may make sense. In Chap. 4, we have sketched various use cases for applying ontologies in user interfaces. For many of those use cases, such a reasoning makes sense:

- On a semantic desktop, novel ways of searching for data in applications are made possible by extracting semantically annotated information from applications, as discussed, e.g., by Cheyer et al (2005) and Sauermann et al (2005).
- User interfaces can be automatically adapted according to the users' needs by having a reasoner analyze the UI components, the data they contain, and the user's needs (Karim and Tjoa, 2006, pp. 80).
- Help on applications can be provided at run-time, adapted according to the system's current state and/or a user model, as suggested, e.g., by Gribova (2007, pp. 417) and Kohlhase and Kohlhase (2009, pp. 89).

In all of those cases, the information is contained in *running* applications, which means that it is highly dynamic and thus needs to be integrated at run-time. At the same time, user interaction is involved all of the cases, which imposes strict requirements in terms of performance. Thus, high performance integration mechanisms for dynamic data from running applications are needed, also beyond the field of application integration and semantic event processing. However, none of the papers cited above explicitly addresses the performance aspect, although it is sometimes noted as an item for future work.

8.4.1 Generalized Architecture

From our findings in the context of semantic event processing, we have derived a generalized architecture for reasoning on data from running software applications. A central reasoner answers queries about that data and offers some sort of client interface, e.g., using SPARQL or F-Logic. Client components may be, e.g., internal components, such as an event processing logic, or a graphical user interface providing an endpoint for querying the system, as discussed in Chap. 10. An A-Box connector passes queries to the individual application containers. Those containers provide data in

the generalized architecture.

In the figure, a number of integrated applications shown. Each application is encapsulated in a container, which provides an adapter to the reasoner. The adapter consists of four essential parts:

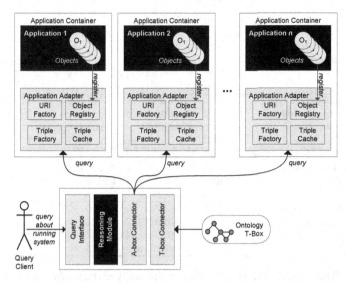

Fig. 8.9: Generalized architecture for reasoning about data from running applications

- Integrated application create and hold objects, which they register at the adapter's *object registry* to reveal them to the reasoner. There are different possible strategies of informing the registry of updates of the registered objects (e.g., using the observer pattern or change listeners); in our current implementation, the application actively sends updates to the object registry.
- From those objects, a *triple factory* creates data that is usable by the reasoner, i.e., RDF triples. The triple factory is also responsible for processing a mapping between the component's class model and the ontology used for information exchange. In the simplest version, this mapping is represented as a table assigning categories in the ontology to classes in the class model. A more sophisticated mapping mechanism has been described in Chap. 7.
- To create such triples, a URI is needed for each object. The *URI factory* is responsible for creating such URIs which are unambiguous and unique throughout the whole integrated system (see Sect. 7.3).
- To improve performance, caches are introduced, as discussed in Sect. 8.3.3.

These adapters are used by the reasoner's A-Box connector to dynamically resolve queries. In addition to that A-Box connector, a T-Box connector provides the T-Box part of the ontology (i.e., the definition of classes and relations) used as a common ground for integrating information from the different components. In contrast to the A-Box, the T-Box is considered as static, and the T-Box connector loads it once when the system starts.

When a query runs, the results of that query have to be consistent. Thus, updates occurring between the start of a query and its end should not be considered when computing the result. To provide such a consistent query answering mechanism, the reasoner sends a lock signal to the application containers when a query is started.

	Description	Query in SPARQL
1	Get all objects of type C	`SELECT ?I WHERE {?I rdf:type C.}`
2a	Get all objects of type C	`SELECT ?I WHERE {?I rdf:type C. ?I R O.}`
2b	in a relation R with	`SELECT ?I WHERE {?I rdf:type C. O R ?I.}`
2a+b	object O	`SELECT ?I WHERE {{?I rdf:type C. ?I R O.}`
		`UNION {?I rdf:type C. O R ?I.}}`
3a	Get all objects of type C	`SELECT ?I WHERE {?I rdf:type C. ?I ?R O.}`
3b	in *any* relation with	`SELECT ?I WHERE {?I rdf:type C. O ?R ?I.}`
3a+b	object O	`SELECT ?I WHERE {{?I rdf:type C. ?I ?R O.}`
		`UNION {?I rdf:type C. O ?R ?I.}}`
4a	Get all objects of *any* type	`SELECT ?I WHERE {?I R O.}`
4b	in a relation R with	`SELECT ?I WHERE {O R ?I.}`
4a+b	object O	`SELECT ?I WHERE {{?I R O.}`
		`UNION {O R ?I.}}`
5a	Get all objects of *any* type	`SELECT ?I WHERE {?I ?R O.}`
5b	in *any* relation with	`SELECT ?I WHERE {O ?R ?I.}`
5a+b	object O	`SELECT ?I WHERE {{?I ?R O.}`
		`UNION {O ?R ?I.}}`

Table 8.1: The different query types we used to analyze the performance impact of different variants, and their SPARQL representation.

Updates coming from the application are then queued until the reasoner notifies the application that the query has been finished.

8.4.2 Performance Evaluations

As that combination proved beneficial for high performance, we have chosen to use A-Box connectors and a centralized architecture, as discussed in Sect. 8.3, and we have analyzed the impact of the different caching variants and connector rules in further detail. Unlike with semantic event processing, where the queries are always similar (see Sect. 6.2.1), the general case allows for arbitrary queries, which may behave differently with respect to performance. Therefore, we have analyzed a larger number of queries, as shown in table 8.1.

The variables in our evaluation are the number of software applications (5, 10, and 20) and the number of object instances maintained by each application (250 and 500, randomly distributed over 10 classes per application). Furthermore, we have varied the average update frequency at which objects were changed (25 and 50 updates per second). Each instance has been given 5 relations to other instances. Thus, our maximum test set has 10000 object instances with 50000 relations.

In Fig. 8.10, we show the results of selected typical queries, which illustrate the main findings of our analysis. Type 1 queries are not shown; they are generally answered very quickly, and there are no significant differences between the approaches. While the figure depicts the results for the $a + b$ flavor of each query type (see table 8.1), the results for the a and b flavor are similar.

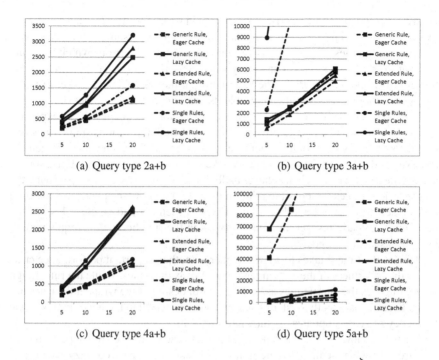

(a) Query type 2a+b

(b) Query type 3a+b

(c) Query type 4a+b

(d) Query type 5a+b

Fig. 8.10: Query times for selected query types, each for 500 object instances per application, and 50 updates per second. The x axis shows the number of components (there have been no explicit measurements for 15 applications), and the y axis shows the query time in seconds.

Generally, the query times using eager caching are faster than those using lazy caching. The actual factor between the two ranges from double speed (e.g., in case of type 4 queries) to only marginal improvements (e.g., in case of type 3 queries). Since lazy caches have to re-create the invalidated triples to answer a query, eager caches can always serve the requested triples directly. Therefore, the latter can answer queries faster.

When looking at scalability, it can be observed that doubling the number of integrated components (which also doubles the number of A-Box instances) about doubles the query answer time in most cases, thus, there is a linear growth of complexity in most cases.

Multiple observations can be made when looking at the individual results regarding different queries. For type 3 queries, it is single rules which produce significant outliers (see figure 8.10(b)), while for type 5 queries, it is generic rules (see figure 8.10(d)). Thus, only only extended rules guarantee reasonable response times in all cases without any outliers, although they are outperformed by generic rules in type 2 and 4 queries.

In case of type 1, 2 and 4 queries, the relation in which the objects sought is already fixed (e.g., "find all persons which *are married to* another person"), while the case of type 3 and 5 queries, the relation is variable (e.g., "find all persons which have *any relation* to another person"). The first type of query is rather *target-oriented*, while the latter is rather *explorative*. The key finding of the results is that target-oriented queries do not pose any significant problems, while explorative queries do.

The bad behavior of single rules in the case of explorative queries can be explained by the fact that when an explorative query is answered, the various single rules fire, thus causing many potentially expensive invocations of the connector. The generic and extended rules, on the other hand, invoke the connector less often. For a similar reason, the generic rule variant behaves badly for the explorative query types: here, the reasoner determines the possible relation types by invoking the connector multiple times, each time trying another relation type. Extended and single rules, on the other hand, already restrict the relation types in the rule body, thus requiring less invocations of the connector.

Besides the time it takes to answer a query, another important performance criterion is the robustness of the system regarding A-Box dynamics. While the rule design only influences the query times as such, a careful design of the wrappers' caches has a significant impact on the system's scalability with respect to the maximum possible frequency of A-Box updates, as shown in Fig. 8.11.

The figure shows that while both eager and lazy caches do not drop in performance too strongly when scaling up the number of instances involved, lazy caching is drastically more robust regarding A-Box dynamics. While several thousand updates per second on the A-Box are possible with lazy caching, eager caching allows for less than 100. As assumed, lazy caches thus scale up much better regarding A-Box dynamics, but at the trade-off of longer query response times.

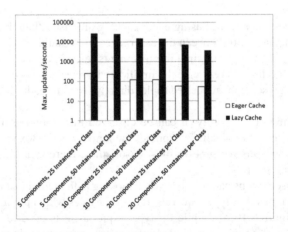

Fig. 8.11: Evaluation of robustness of different caching approaches regarding A-Box dynamics. The graph shows the maximum number of updates per second that the system can process. Note that the y-axis has a logarithmic scale.

8.5 Case Study: Performance in SoKNOS

During the development of the SoKNOS system, performance has always been a major issue. Even the first prototypes have been used for running live demonstrations and conducting user studies, so that reasonable performance was a key requirement. Thus, the introduction of reasoning and semantic event processing had to be done with great care.

All of the optimization strategies discussed above – global vs. local event processing, pushing vs. pulling of instance data, caches, and wrapper invocation rules – have been implemented in the framework and can be parameterized when developing an actual system. Therefore, there were lots of degrees of freedom for building the SoKNOS system.

As global reasoning proved to be faster than local reasoning, we used one central reasoning and event processing instance in SoKNOS. A combination of pulling instance data with eager caching was used, since the frequency of data updates in the applications was rather low. Thus, eager caching was in favor of lazy caching. We have used extended rules, since they proved faster in event processing and in goal-directed queries, which are used in event processing.

Some additional tweaks to improve performance were done in SoKNOS. In Sect. 5.5.4, the toolbox was mentioned, which is a central unit in the SoKNOS user interface. Certain operations with the toolbox which were quite frequent, such as docking the toolbox to an application container as a preparation for interacting with an application. When docking the toolbox to a container, the set of tools to activate is computed by the reasoner. As this set does not change over time, we have pre-computed that set upon system startup and used the pre-computed values to speed up interaction with the toolbox.

Another improvement was targeted at displaying tool tips, e.g., when dragging and dropping objects, or when hovering the mouse over a tool in the toolbox. Those tool tips were also generated from the ontology using the labels of the respective categories of system actions and domain objects involved, such as "Delete order", where "delete" is the label of a system action, and "order" is the label of a domain concept. Those labels have been cached at the first time they were computed, and reused from that point on.

In summary, the SoKNOS system used up to 20 applications in parallel when run on a large, wall-sized screen, connected by 180 integration rules. The reaction time could be kept below one second. In our user studies (see Sect. 12.2), users always reported satisfactory reaction times and system performance.

8.6 Summary

In this chapter, we have shown how the performance of semantic event processing, which is a central part of the application integration framework discussed in this book, can be significantly improved. While the evaluation results for semantic event processing showed that there are some alternatives that are clearly superior to others, the picture is not that clear when generalizing to reasoning on data from running applications in general. Here, some alternatives work better for goal-directed queries, other work better for explorative queries. The selection of a cache implementation strongly depends on the update frequency of the underlying data: for low update frequencies, eager caches should be preferred, high update frequencies are better addressed with lazy caches.

The SoKNOS emergency management prototype, which has been built using the framework discussed in this book, has profited massively from the availability of those alternatives. With a suitable configuration, the event processing times in SoKNOS could be kept below one second, and various user studies showed that the participants were satisfied with the system's performance.

Chapter 9
Crossing Technological Borders

Abstract Integrating user interface components is particularly difficult when heterogeneous user interfaces are involved. While Chap. 7 has dealt with *conceptual heterogeneity*, this chapter addresses *technological heterogeneity*. Different technological platforms have their own programming languages, event processing mechanisms, and so on. This chapter shows the problems with cross-technological UI integration and discusses how the framework introduced in this book can be extended to support heterogeneous technologies. As discussed in Chap. 2, only a few approaches support the integration of heterogeneous UI technologies. Section 9.1 discusses the necessary extensions to the architecture introduced in Chap. 5, and Sect. 9.2 shows how the approach was applied in SoKNOS to integrate applications developed in Java and Flex.

9.1 Architecture for Cross-Technological User Interface Integration

So far, the architecture discussed only addressed containers for Java, or, more generally, technologically homogeneous components. There are several issues to address when stepping from Java-only to multi-technology integration. Table 9.1 lists those issues.

9.1.1 Extending Containers

As discussed in Sect. 5.4.2, containers provide different basic services to the developer. First of all, they are responsible for invoking the application they encapsulate, and for displaying it on screen. While containers for Java components can instantiate those components directly, containers for other technologies need a wrapper that provides a Java interface to another component. Typically, such an interface provides

	Java Only	Multi Technology
Registering and monitoring components	Java components can be directly registered with ontology concepts and monitored with Java event listeners	Different registration and monitoring techniques are required
Reacting to UI events	Java events can be directly caught and distributed	Events have to be collected from and distributed to different technological platforms, typically involving various transformations
Drag and drop	The drag and drop mechanism from Java can be extended directly	Drag and drop may take place between heterogeneous components. Thus, the Java drag and drop mechanism cannot be used directly
Object exchange	Java objects can be directly sent along with events	Objects have to be transformed between technologies.

Table 9.1: Issues to address when stepping from Java-only to multi-technology integration.

a Java user interface component which can be used as a proxy for the respective application.

Another responsibility of the container is to process events. For a non-Java container, this means that events raised in the encapsulated applications need to be caught and processed as Java events. Therefore, the container provides a callback interface for events from the original application. Likewise, methods on the application have to be invoked when an event arrives. As discussed in Sect. 5.4.2, events notify an application about an action that it is supposed to perform. Thus, each incoming event typically corresponds to an action or a method that can be invoked on the encapsulated application. The developer has to provide that wiring in the container. For that reason, the Java interface has to provide means both for informing the Java environment about raised events, as well as for invoking methods on the encapsulated application. Drag and drop is a special case of event handling. This particularly challenging case is described in the next section.

The third service provided by a container is to grant access to the application's objects and components, as well as their states. While containers for Java applications can simply hold a collection of pointers to all registered objects, the matters are not that simple for non-Java applications. Objects have to be exchanged between the encapsulated application and the Java framework using some serialization, e.g., XML (W3C, 2008b) or JSON (json org, 2011). The serialized objects are then used by the container instead of the original Java objects.

9.1.2 Handling Drag and Drop

Most of the interactions supported by the framework discussed in this book follow the same pattern: an event is raised in one application, a reaction is computed, and another application reacts to that event. The event triggering the reaction and the reaction itself are completely decoupled.

Drag and drop is a different case, as it requires the support of a continuous interaction starting in one application (with the drag action) and ending up in another one (with the drop action). The whole action is supposed to be supported by visual feedback, such as a changing mouse cursor (Wagner et al, 1995, pp. 255). Thus, a special solution is required for this kind of interaction.

Basically, two implementation variants can be thought of:

1. The drag and drop mechanism is built from scratch in a way that it supports arbitrary drag sources and drop targets.
2. The drag and drop mechanism of one existing UI toolkit, e.g. Java Swing, is used, and events from other technological platforms are translated to emulated events in that toolkit.

As the framework to extend is implemented in Java, which comes with a flexible and extensible drag and drop mechanism (Oracle Corporation, 2010), the second option was selected in order to minimize the development efforts.

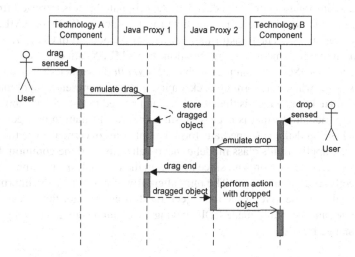

Fig. 9.1: Drag and drop across heterogeneous components using Java proxies (following Paulheim and Erdogan, 2010, p. 305).

To implement cross-technology drag and drop with the Java drag and drop mechanism, *Java proxies* are introduced. Figure 9.1 shows how Java proxies are used to handle drag and drop: when a drag event is sensed on a non-Java component, the corresponding proxy is used to emulate a Java drag event. Furthermore, a pointer to the dragged object is stored. If a drop event is sensed on another component later, the respective proxy emulates a Java drop event. It requests the dragged object from the drag source's proxy and invokes a respective action on the component which registered the drop event.

If drag and drop is performed between a Java and a non-Java component, the respective operations only involve one proxy, i.e., they take place between a Java component and a Java proxy. Likewise, Java-to-Java drag and drop is performed without any proxies.

9.1.3 Extending Information Objects

In a Java-only implementation, objects may be transferred directly between applications, although transformations between different class models may be necessary, as discussed in Chap. 7. For heterogeneous applications, this is not trivially possible.

As discussed in Sect. 5.3.1, the events exchanged contain a pointer to the original object. In a non-Java world, this means that such a pointer points into a different system. Information objects for non-Java objects thus consist of an annotation, an origin (i.e., a pointer to the container which created them), and an object identifier, which can be an arbitrary string.

When an information object is decoded, the original object is retrieved from the contained application in some intermediate format, such as JSON or XML, using the object's identifier. The transformation rules, as introduced in Chap. 7, are then executed on that intermediate representation. For XML, XPath expressions can be used directly, for JSON, techniques such as *JSONPath* (Goessner, 2007) have to be used. Likewise, when transforming back, an intermediate representation of the target object is created first, which is then serialized and passed to the original application.

The intermediate format is necessary since the transformation between the exchanged RDF and the intermediate format is also a conceptual one, mediating between the application's class model conceptualization and the common domain ontology conceptualization, and since objects in the original format cannot be handled directly in the framework. The only alternative for omitting the intermediate format would thus be to replicate the object transformation algorithm in each of the technologies and use ready-made RDF obeying the common domain ontology as the only exchange format.

9.1.4 Combining Heterogeneous Applications with A-Box Connectors and Caches

In Sect. 8.3, we have introduced several techniques for improving the performance for semantic event processing in the framework, and for reasoning on data from running applications in general. These improvements can be transferred to heterogeneous applications as well.

Using an A-Box connector requires that the objects which have to be made known to the reasoner can be accessed from the Java container. Thus, the container has to provide a registry callback method that the contained application may use for registering its objects. Furthermore, an additional callback method is needed for notifying the container about updates on the registered objects. Likewise, the container has to be able to access particular objects based on their identifier; therefore, the application has to provide a respective method.

If those three methods are served by the encapsulated application, all mechanisms for connecting the reasoner to the application discussed in Sect. 8.3 can be implemented: pushing data to the reasoner's A-Box, pulling without caches, as well as with lazy and eager caches.

9.2 Case Study: Integrating Java and Flex User Interface components in SoKNOS

In the SoKNOS project, two main technologies prevailed on the user interface layer: while most of the user interface was written in Java using Swing, some components were developed with Adobe Flex. To integrate those user interface components, the framework had to be enhanced in order to support both Java and Flex based UI components, as well as facilitate integration of both.

9.2.1 Scenario

Adobe Flex (Adobe Systems Inc., 2011), started as Flash by Macromedia in the 90s, was originally designed as a technology for providing animations on web pages, and has since developed into a versatile technology for creating rich user interfaces with sophisticated visualization capabilities, most often in web-based applications (Murugesan, 2007).

This section demonstrates the integration of two heterogeneous applications in SoKNOS, shown in Fig. 9.2. The first application is a *resource management application*, which is used for browsing the resources that are available from one or more organizations, e.g. the fire brigade cars operated by one fire brigade. The resource management application is implemented in Flex.

The second application is the *mission account application*, which is used for managing current and predicted problems, as well as for planning tasks and measures to address those problems. The mission account application is implemented in Java.

Two sorts of interactions are required to support meaningful interaction with those two applications:

1. The assignment of resources to tasks should be done via *drag and drop*. Dragging and dropping a resource to a measure is used to allocate a resource to a measure. Dragging and dropping a resource back from the mission account application to the resource management application deallocates the resource.

2. As in the whole SoKNOS system, brushing and linking (Eick and Wills, 1995) should be used to highlight related information. In this particular scenario, selecting a resource in the resource management application should lead to highlighting the resource and the measure it has been assigned to in the resource management application, and vice versa.

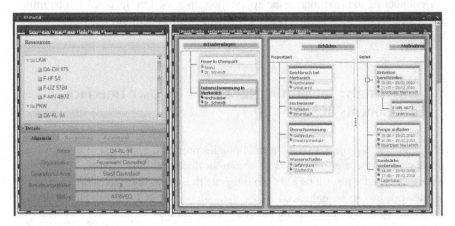

Fig. 9.2: Two heterogeneous, integrated UIs: A resource management application (left, implemented in Flex) and a mission account application (right, implemented in Java). The dashed lines show the original applications running inside the containers (Paulheim and Erdogan, 2010, p. 304).

9.2.2 *Implementing the Flex Container*

As discussed in section 9.1.1, adding a new technological platform to the framework requires adding a new container implementation. Therefore, we have added a Flex container in SoKNOS.

9.2.2.1 Selection of an Appropriate Library

For implementing the flex container, we have taken five libraries into consideration: *JFlash* (java net, 2006), *JFlashPlayer* (VersaEdge Software, 2011), *ComfyJ* (TeamDev Ltd., 2011), *DJ Project Native Swing* (Deckers, 2011), and *JDIC* (java net, 2008). While JFlash is a native Java implementation, JFlashPlayer and ComfyJ use ActiveX, and DJProject and JDIC embed a web browser displaying the Flex application via the respective browser plugin. As the popular *BlazeDS* is a library for facilitating communication between Flex front-ends and remote Java back-ends rather than components running on one machine (Coenraets, 2008), we have not taken BlazeDS into consideration.

To provide the necessary integration, those libraries should, at least, allow the display of a Flex component inside the Java container, and provide means to exchange messages, i.e. call Flex methods from Java and vice versa.

As JFlash is currently an alpha version which is probably discontinued (the last update dates back to 2006), it has been discarded in a preliminary evaluation. We have analyzed the remaining four more carefully with respect to stability, flexibility in message exchange between Java and Flex, and API simplicity, as well as availability of documentation. Table 9.2 sums up the results of this analysis.

All the four libraries proved reasonably stable in our analysis. JDIC is rather limited regarding message exchange, since the directed call of a specific Java method from Flex is only possible using some hand-crafted workarounds. Furthermore, the message exchange has to be manually coded using intermediate JavaScript, as shown in figure 9.3(b). ComfyJ also bears a massive coding overhead, since the callbacks from Flex are not encapsulated, but have to be manually coded, as shown in figure 9.3(c). Thus, only JFlashPlayer and DJ Project Native Swing provide a reasonably simple API.

Based on these findings, we have shortlisted only JFlashPlayer and DJ Project Native Swing for the implementation of our prototype. In more detailed tests, it turned out that drop events from Java to Flex cannot be captured precisely with DJ Project Native Swing (it can be detected that a drop event has occured *somewhere* within the Flex component, but not *where* exactly), thus not providing enough capabilities for implementing cross-technology drag and drop when different drop targets are involved within the same Flex component. The Flex container is therefore implemented with JFlashPlayer.

Library	License	Stability	Flexibility in Message Exchange	API Simplicity	Documentation
JFlashPlayer	Commercial	+	+	+	+
ComfyJ	Commercial	+	+	-	+
DJ Project	Open Source	+	-	+	+
JDIC	Open Source	+	-	-	+

Table 9.2: A comparison of four APIs for linking Flex and Java (Paulheim and Erdogan, 2010, p. 304)

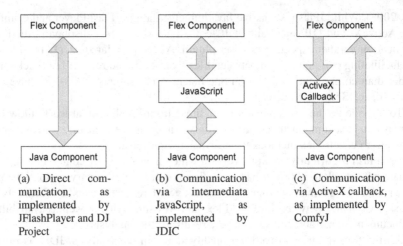

Fig. 9.3: Communication between Java and Flex components

9.2.2.2 Component Registration

As discussed in section 5.4.2, each container has to provide information about its components and their state.

As a prerequisite, the Flex application has to augment each component to be published with a unique identifier, e.g. a string or a number. This identifier is used to register and unregister the component at the container. The container maps that ID to a URI, so that it can provide the necessary information to the reasoner upon request.

To implement the component and state manager, two variants are possible: providing the necessary information redundantly in the Java implementation of the service, or passing the requests through to the underlying Flex application. In SoKNOS, we have chosen the first variant.

9.2.2.3 Object Exchange

Like components, information objects also get unique identifiers. Since Flex objects cannot be used in the Java-based framework and none of the libraries supports a direct object exchange between Java and Flex, an intermediate representation is needed. Thus, we use the JSON (JavaScript Object Notation) format, for which implementations both for Java and for Flex exist (as well as for numerous other platforms) (json org, 2011). To this end, we have introduced a new type of information object, the FlexInformationObject class.

Figure 9.4 demonstrates the object exchange between the Java container and the Flex application, using JSON as an intermediate format. The object converter also

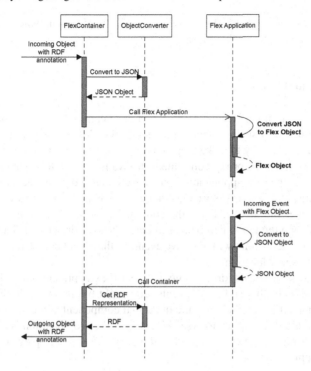

Fig. 9.4: Exchanging objects between the Java container and the Flex application using JSON as an intermediate format.

performs the mediation between the RDF, which follows the common ontology, and the Flex application's class model, as discussed in Chap. 7.

As for components and their states, the container has to provide the information objects to the reasoner. Since that data can be much more versatile than the component data, which has always a fixed structure, we have opted for only registering and unregistering the object IDs at the container, and dynamically pulling the data objects from the Flex application upon request.

9.2.2.4 Event Exchange

When an event is fired in Flex, a corresponding method on the container is called, which has the following parameters: type of event, the component's ID, and the objects that the event was performed with. The objects are transferred serialized as JSON strings (see above). These information are used to produce the required annotation of the event, using the object translation service to extract the necessary RDF from the objects.

For events sent to the Flex container by the reasoner, the contained objects are first transformed to JSON, which already conforms to the Flex application's class model.

Then, the corresponding method is called on the Flex application, which creates Flex objects from the JSON serializations.

9.2.2.5 Drag and Drop

Flex's own programming means for drag and drop cannot be used if the dropped object has not been dragged from the same Flex application, or vice versa. Therefore, a workaround is necessary to make drag and drop work in the Java-based framework.

As discussed above, a proxy component in Java is created for each drag source and drop target in the Flex application. Since Flex's drag and drop mechanism cannot be used, the drag start event is sensed manually, i.e., when the user presses the mouse button and moves the mouse. Then, the container is notified about the drag event having started, and the proxy component initiates the Java drag event. The ID of the dragged object is sent along with the Java event, so the object can be retrieved when it is dropped to some location.

Similarly to drag events, drop events inside a Flex application also have to be sensed manually. To this end, drop events are caught by the invisible proxy lying over the complete Flex application, and the actual component at the drop position is retrieved from the Flex application (see Fig. 9.5). If the drop position is a registered drop target, the respective event is produced in order have the drop event processed by the Flex application.

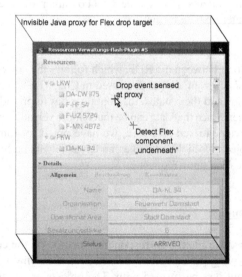

Fig. 9.5: Schematic view of a UI component and its proxy: If a drop is registered on the Java proxy, the corresponding Flex component "underneath" is detected.

9.2.3 Putting the Pieces Together

As discussed above, the use case from SoKNOS requires two sorts of cross-application interaction: brushing and linking, i.e. highlighting related information, and linking resources to measures via drag and drop.

For implementing those interactions, some adaptations had to be made to the underlying Flex application:

- The selection events of the underlying applications have to be forwarded to the respective containers. On the Flex container side, this is done by calling a Java method from the Flex application.
- The same holds for drag events.
- Drop events have to be recognized in the application. On the Flex side, this requires a method for finding a component at a given position when detecting a drop event on the proxy, so that the actual component can be determined.
- The Flex application has to register its components and information objects at the container by calling respective Java methods.
- The Flex application has to convert JSON objects to Flex objects. The conversion itself is done automatically by Flex, however, it has to be triggered when an object is to be transferred.
- To allow for drag and drop with user support, as discussed in section 5.4.2, the Flex application has to provide a method for highlighting a component, which is a potential drop location, and display a tool tip. The necessary event and the tool tip are provided by the reasoner.

With those adaptations, the desired actions could be implemented in SoKNOS.

9.3 Summary

This chapter has discussed the extension of the framework introduced in this book to support heterogeneous technologies. Using RDF and ontologies as an interlingua has been proven as an adequate means to bridge different technological platforms.

The SoKNOS case study has shown the details of cross-technology integration using the example of a Java and a Flex application. The observation is that with only a few adaptations, a Flex application could be hooked into the Java-based integration framework. This observation can be transferred to other technologies, given that there are libraries which serve as a technological bridge between Java and the target technology, like the JFlashPlayer library used to implement the prototype.

There are different other libraries which could be used to extend the framework in order to support more heterogeneous technologies. Examples are web-based applications that could be integrated via browser libraries (Deckers, 2011; The Lobo Project, 2009), or COM-based applications, such as Microsoft Office (TeamDev Ltd., 2011; Adler, 2004).

The current implementation of the Flex container uses JSON as an intermediate format. While there are comfortable libraries for converting Java and Flex objects from and to JSON, this format has some drawbacks as no references are allowed, thus making it impossible to encode larger object structures containing multiple references or cycles. However, this problem can be solved by using another intermediate format, such as JSON extended by references (Zyk, 2008), JRON (Hawke, 2010), YAML (Ben-Kiki et al, 2009), or XML.

Part III
The Future of Ontology-based UI Integration

Chapter 10
Improving Information Exploration

Abstract Integrated systems can consist of numerous applications containing massive amounts of data. Although integration is a useful step towards a better usability for the end user, it is possible to improve an integrated system's usability further. In this chapter, we discuss how the existing framework can be extended by the *Semantic Data Explorer*, which helps the user navigating the information contained in the different applications. This chapter is structured as follows: Sect. 10.1 introduces the Semantic Data Explorer and explains how the user can interact with it. Section 10.2 explains the implementation of the Semantic Data Explorer, and Sect. 10.3 presents a user study indicating the benefits of the Semantic Data Explorer for end users.

10.1 Interaction with the Semantic Data Explorer

Applications integrated on the user interface level can assist the user in exploring information contained in those applications. One possibility is the support of linking different views (Eick and Wills, 1995, pp. 445), as discussed in Sect. 6.3.1. Linking views, i.e., highlighting related information in other applications when selecting an object, can support the user in exploring information.

Despite the support provided to end users, the linking approach has its limits. When highlighting related information, the type of relation cannot be seen. Adding information about that relation, on the other hand, e.g. as a tool tip on the highlighted objects, can quickly lead to overloaded user interfaces and distract the user. When a large number of related objects is highlighted in parallel, the effect is also more distracting than helpful. Furthermore, linking only works for information objects that are currently visible on the screen. Information objects contained in hidden objects, such as inactive tabs, are not highlighted. Thus, the view gathered from linking may, on the one hand, be distracting, on the other hand be incomplete.

To overcome those limitations and improve usability for the end users of integrated systems, we have added an additional tool to the integration framework, i.e., the Semantic Data Explorer. It can provide a conceptual view on objects from the

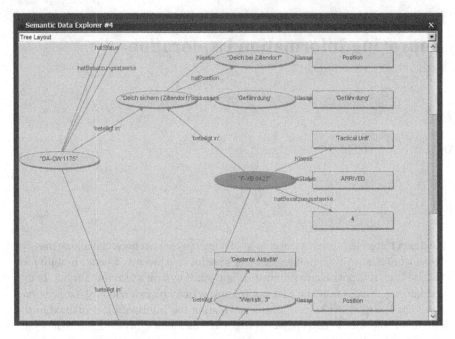

Fig. 10.1: Screen shot of the Semantic Data Explorer (Paulheim, 2011, p. 10)

application as a navigable semantic network, using the RDF standard visualization, i.e., ellipses for resources, boxes for data values (W3C, 2004c). Fig. 10.1 shows a screen shot of the Semantic Data Explorer.

Interaction-wise, the Semantic Data Explorer is integrated with the other applications in framework as follows:

- When the user drags and drops an object from an application onto the SDE, a graph view of that object is shown by the Semantic Data Explorer, containing the object itself and its directly connected neighbors. The graph shown by the Semantic Data Explorer is replaced when dropping a new object.
- Linked views also include the Semantic Data Explorer. In particular, when the user selects an object in an application, and that object is contained in the graph currently shown by the Semantic Data Explorer, the corresponding node in the graph is highlighted. Likewise, if the user selects a node in the graph, the corresponding objects in other applications are highlighted. This allows the user to keep track of information objects in the conceptual view provided by the Semantic Data Explorer, as well as in the original applications' user interfaces.
- Nodes in the graph view can be expanded and collapsed via double click. This allows the user to explore the information in an incremental way: Initially, the graph only shows the dropped object's direct neighbors. The user can then navigate to the information he is interested in.

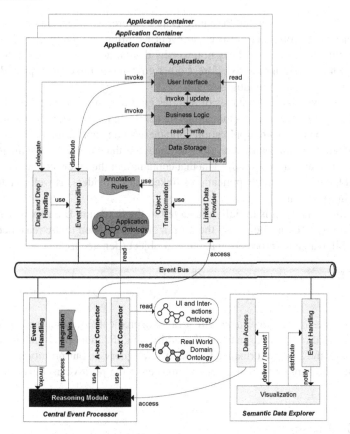

Fig. 10.2: Integration of the Semantic Data Explorer in the Framework (Paulheim, 2011, p. 7)

Since the Semantic Data Explorer is included in the linked views paradigm, using it in parallel with other integrated applications facilitates a *hybrid view* where the user can seamlessly switch between interacting with the Semantic Data Explorer and the integrated applications.

10.2 Architecture

The Semantic Data Explorer is integrated into the framework as a specialized container holding the visualization. The visualization itself was implemented using JGraph (JGraph, 2011). To support the interactions sketched above, the visualization component accepts supports dropping arbitrary objects, and it raises selection events each time a user selects a node in the graph.

Figure 10.2 shows how the Semantic Data Explorer is integrated into the framework. Like other containers, it uses an event handling service to coordinate with other applications. A particularly noteworthy design decision is that the Semantic Data Explorer does not directly address other containers' linked data providers, but interfaces the reasoning module instead.

There are two main advantages of that design. First, the Semantic Data Explorer does not need to know about applications that exist. In particular, it does not need to maintain an updated list of application containers when applications are instantiated by the integration framework. The other advantage is that upon querying the reasoner, the reasoner returns a view on the data that contains a unified view on the information extracted from the different application's linked data providers, as well as additional inferred information.

Each time an object is initially displayed in the Semantic Data Explorer, or the corresponding node is opened by the user, a query is passed to the reasoner which retrieves all available information about that object (denoted as :o):

$$
\text{SELECT ?r ?x1 ?x2 WHERE } \{ \ \{ \ :o \ ?r \ ?x1 \ \} \\
\text{UNION } \{ \ ?x2 \ ?r \ :o\} \ \} \qquad (10.1)
$$

That query is an *explorative query* with a variable predicate. As discussed in Sect. 8.4, using extended rules in the reasoner for addressing the individual linked data endpoints yields the best performance for that type of query. In our prototype, the query times could be kept lower than a second, thus enabling positive user experience.

10.3 Evaluation

To show that the Semantic Data Explorer provides a valuable extension to integrated information systems, we have conducted a user study for which we added the Semantic Data Explorer to SoKNOS and let a group of test persons solve different exercises with that group of tools, half of the exercises with the help of the Semantic Data Explorer, the other half without.

10.3.1 Scenario

For our evaluation, we used the set of applications described in Sect. 9.2: the *mission account* application which is used for viewing problems and measures, as well as assigned tactical units (such as fire brigade cars), and a resource management application used for browsing available tactical units, both from the operator's own organization as well as from other supporting organizations. Fig. 10.3 shows the two applications. Assignments of units and measures can be made by dragging and dropping a unit from the resource management application and dropping it onto a

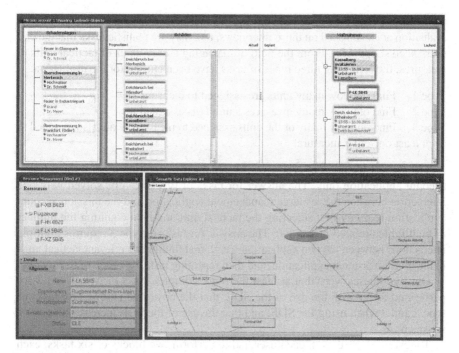

Fig. 10.3: Screenshot of the evaluation setup (Paulheim, 2011, p. 8). The setup consists of two applications – a mission account application (top) and a ressource application (bottom left) as well as the Semantic Data Explorer (bottom right). Items are parallely highlighted in different applications. The Semantic Data Explorer has been presented to the users for only half of the tasks.

measure in the mission account application. Technically, this creates a link between the data managed by the two applications. The link can be removed by dragging and dropping an assigned unit back to the resource management application.

The scenario of the evaluation deals with the assignment of operational resources to measures, e.g. sending helicopters to evacuate people from a roof top, or assigning fire brigade cars to individual areas of fire. Planning such an assignment is an important task in emergency management – an optimal assignment is needed for avoiding overload of units as well unnecessary idle times. To this end, the person doing the planning needs a good overview on the current assignments.

10.3.2 Evaluation Setup

In the course of the SoKNOS project, we conducted interviews with domain experts who deal with emergency management systems. From those interviews, the requirements for the prototype have been derived. The tasks the users had to perform in our evaluation are also based on those interviews, i.e., they are realistic tasks that the end users need support for. From the field of managing assignments of tactical units to measures, the following three types of tasks have been chosen for the evaluation:

Type 1   Find out how many units are assigned to measure M.
Type 2   Find out how many measures a unit U is assigned to.
Type 3   Find out how many of the units assigned to measure M are also assigned to at least one other measure.

The answer for tasks of type 1 can be obtained by looking it up in the mission account application only. The answer for tasks of type 2 can be solved with one interaction between the resource management application and the mission account application (e.g., by first selecting the tactical unit and then counting the number of highlighted related measures). The answer for tasks of type 3 requires multiple interactions between the two applications (e.g., first finding the relevant tactical units in the mission account application, and then repeating task 2 for each of those units).

Our hypotheses were that at least the more complex tasks of type 2 and 3 are performed faster with the use of the SDE, that the error rate is lower for tasks of type 2 and 3 when using the SDE, and that the use of the SDE increases the users' satisfaction.

To test our hypotheses, each user had to perform two blocks of six tasks, each block consisting of two tasks of each type. One block had to be performed using the SDE, the other without using the SDE. The test persons were split into two groups: One group started with the block of tasks using the SDE, the other with the block of tasks without using the SDE. The assignment of the individual tasks to the blocks was varied as well. When using the SDE, the users were advised to use it for all tasks, even if they felt they could perform those tasks without the SDE as well (and maybe even better). Furthermore, users were offered to use pen and paper if needed.

At the beginning of the evaluation, users were shown how to operate the system, in a way that an instructor showed them how to find the kind of information that was asked for later on the tasks. The group that started with the SDE was presented the whole system including the SDE at once, while the other group was presented the system without the SDE first, and got the introduction to the SDE at the beginning of the second block of tasks.

After each block of six tasks, the users were handed out a questionnaire for evaluating their user experience, using the questionnaire described by Laugwitz et al (2008, pp. 63). It consists of 20 questions which are used to quantify user experience according to five factors: attractiveness, perspicuity, efficiency, stimulation, and novelty.

The evaluation was performed with 22 participants between 22 and 52 years, 3 of which were female and 19 of which were male. The participants were researchers and students working in the SAP research lab who had significant experience with IT systems in general, and had only little knowledge of the SoKNOS scenario. When asked to self-assess their experience with ontologies and semantic networks, the

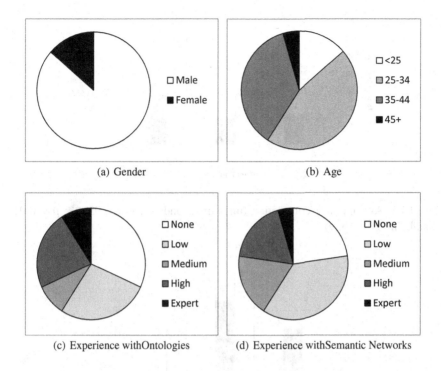

(a) Gender   (b) Age

(c) Experience withOntologies   (d) Experience withSemantic Networks

Fig. 10.4: Participants of the user study by age, gender, and self-assessment of prior knowledge about ontologies and semantic networks (Paulheim, 2011, p. 7)

majority ranked their experience below average (see figure 10.4). For each user, the evaluation, including filling out the questionnaires, took between 20 and 30 minutes.

When the users performed the tasks, the system recorded the times needed to perform the task and the number of errors. The instructor additionally recorded for which tasks the users made use of the offered pen and paper to take notes.

10.3.3 Evaluation Results

Figure 10.5 shows the average task completion times for the different types of tasks, each with and without SDE. It can be observed that the task completion time for tasks of type 2 and 3 are highly significantly reduced ($p < 0.01$ using a two-tailed t-test). Especially for the type 3 tasks, the task completion $p < 0.05$).

For solving the tasks of type 3 without the SDE, 17 out of 22 participants made use of pen and paper for taking down intermediate results, as opposed to none of the participants using the SDE. This shows that those tasks are particular difficult to

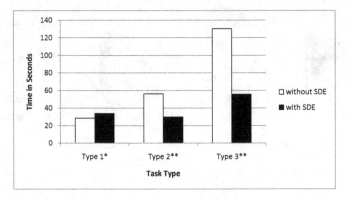

Fig. 10.5: Average task completion times in seconds (*: $p < 0.05$, **: $p < 0.01$) (Paulheim, 2011, p. 9)

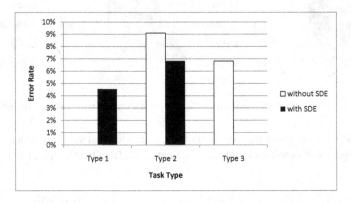

Fig. 10.6: Average error rates (Paulheim, 2011, p. 9). None of the results are statistically significant.

solve, and that there is a need for additional support which is provided by the SDE. For the other tasks, pen and paper was used by almost none of the participants.

Figure 10.6 shows the error rates (i.e. percentage of tasks of each type that have been solved incorrectly). For type 1 tasks, there are more errors with the SDE, while the error rate is lower for type 2 and 3 tasks. However, none of those results are statistically significant using a χ^2 test.

Figure 10.7 shows the results from the user experience questionnaires. We have compared the results of both times the users filled the questionnaire, once with and once without the SDE. It can be observed that the users rated the application with the SDE significantly more attractive, perspicuous, efficient, stimulating, and novel (all $p < 0.01$ using a two-tailed t-test).

To examine how much the Semantic Data Explorer helps users that are not familiar with ontologies and semantic web, we created a subset of our evaluation results containing only those 11 users that assessed their knowledge on ontologies *and* semantic

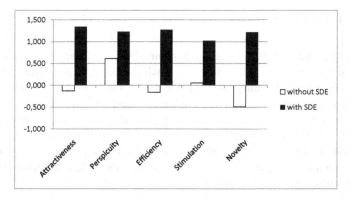

Fig. 10.7: Results of the questionnaires on user experience (Paulheim, 2011, p. 10). All differences are statistically significant with $p < 0.01$. The value space for each criterion ranges from -3 to $+3$.

networks less than medium. For that group of users, the reduction of task completion time for type 2 and type 3 tasks was still significant ($p < 0.01$). The evaluation of the user experience questionnaires proved improvements in attractiveness, efficiency, and novelty (all $p < 0.01$), while the improvements in perspicuity and stimulation could still be observed, but only on a non-statistically significant level. Neither the task completion times nor the questionnaire results of experts and non-experts differed significantly.

In summary, our original hypotheses on task completion times and on user satisfaction were supported by the evaluation. Our hypotheses on task error rates was not supported. A possible explanation is that the overall number of errors is very low, both with and without the SDE – less than 10% of all tasks were solved incorrectly in total. The participants were neither asked to perform the tasks as quickly nor as correct as possible, and most of them implicitly favored correct answers to quick task completion and took their time to answer the questions very thoroughly, which leads to a significant difference in task completion time, as discussed above, at a constant error rate.

The participants were asked for additional comments on possible improvements of the Semantic Data Explorer. One of the most often mentioned criteria was to use meaningful colors and symbols in the SDE – in the prototype, only the currently active node is highlighted in color, and all nodes, regardless of the type of object they represent, are drawn as ellipses, and data values are shown as rectangles. Other users opted for better labels to edges (which at the moment are marked with the rdfs:label of the corresponding relation), and a better arrangement of objects when the graph grows larger.

10.4 Summary

In this chapter, we have introduced the Semantic Data Explorer, an extension to the integration framework discussed in this book which allows for graphically exploring information contained in integrated applications in a *hybrid view*, i.e., using both a navigable graph view as well as the original applications. A user study has shown that the addition of such a graphical view significantly reduces the completion time of complex information gathering tasks, while, at the same time, increasing the users' satisfaction. Those results also hold when only considering users with no or little experience with ontologies and semantic networks, thus, they are suitable for end users without any particular training.

Chapter 11
Towards End-user User Interface Integration

Abstract The approach discussed in this book proposes the cooperation of different experts – domain experts, software engineers, ontology engineers – for developing an integrated system. The typical user of such an integrated system may be a domain expert, but neither a software engineer nor an ontology engineer in most cases. In the future, domain experts may want to create their own integrated applications. This chapter reviews the state of the art from an end user's perspective in Sect. 11.1 and discusses the necessary steps for enabling end users to do build their own ad hoc integrated systems in Sect. 11.2. In Sect. 11.3, we introduce a prototype tool which eases the creation of integrated systems based on the framework discussed in this book.

11.1 Current Approaches to UI Integration Revisited

In Chap. 2, we have discussed current approaches to application integration on the user interface level. Those encompass *portals*, *mashups*, a number of other *programming frameworks*, and a handful of academic prototypes.

While portals or programming frameworks such as Eclipse RCP or Microsoft CAB are targeted at professional software developers, the original aim of mashups is to enable end users to create ad hoc compositions of existing web applications (Yu et al, 2008, pp. 44). The vision foresees enabling end users to select web pages and design a mashup suitable to their current information needs with an easy to understand user interface.

Allowing end users to develop their own mashups requires a certain level of abstraction from the mashup's actual implementation, since understanding that implementation requires technical skills that the end user typically does not have. Grammel and Storey (2010, pp. 4) point out that there is a trade-off between the level of abstraction and the size of the solution space spanned by a tool. In other words: the higher a tool's level of abstraction, the lower the number of possible solutions that can developed with that tool.

Fig. 11.1: Screenshot of a dialog in Intel MashMaker (Intel Corporation, 2007)

A typical example for that trade-off between the level of abstraction and the size of the solution space is the layout of the resulting mashup. At a high level of abstraction, the user may select between a number of fixed layout templates, which allows for a very simple user interface, but limits the solution space exactly to the number of available templates. On the other hand of the scale, users may develop their own HTML and CSS templates – which provides them with a maximal degree of freedom, but at the price of no abstraction from the actual implementation.

While most approaches for mashups discussed in Sect. 2.3 provide a graphical user interface which hides the complexity of mashup development to a certain degree, end users have to perform tasks beyond their expertise in order to achieve more sophisticated mashups, such as creating XPath and regular expressions for extracting specific data values from applications, as shown in Fig. 11.1, or entering code in JavaScript.

The approach discussed in this book has introduced ontologies as an indirection and abstraction layer above the integrated applications. However, the use of ontologies is by no means a guarantee for a good user interface, despite the large body of work involving ontologies in user interface development, as discussed in Chap. 4. On the contrary, using ontologies as an intermediate layer only replaces the need to learn one sort of formalism (such as object-oriented programming) by another (such as description logics).

Implementing ontologies and ontology-based rules is a central activity which is necessary to perform application integration based on the approach introduced in this book. García-Barriocanal et al (2005) have shown that current ontology editing tools do not provide suitable user interfaces for end users. Thus, an additional level of abstraction is required for enabling end users to create their own integrated user interfaces, as shown in Fig. 11.2.

As an example, Fig. 11.3 depicts a screen shot of *SWRLTab*, a common editor for SWRL rules in Protégé (see Sect. 3.3.1). As can be seen, the user has to know the basic constructs of logic and rules in order to understand and work with the tool. In

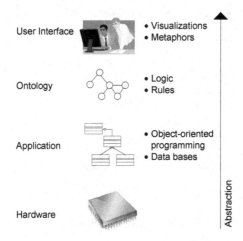

Fig. 11.2: Different levels of abstraction

contrast, *OntoStudio* (ontoprise GmbH, 2011b) uses a graphical editor for visualizing and editing rules, as shown in Fig. 11.4. Although it frees the user from learning the F-Logic rule syntax, it bears some difficulties as well, since it uses its own syntax of symbols and color codings, which the user has to learn.

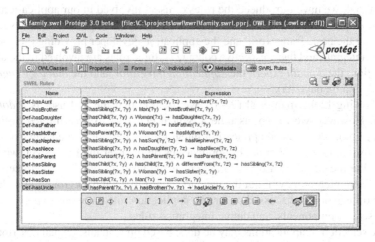

Fig. 11.3: Rule editing in Protégé with SWRLTab (Protégé Community of Practice, 2010)

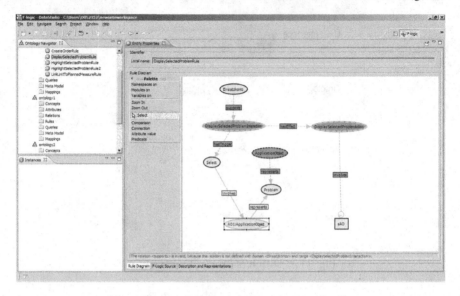

Fig. 11.4: Graphical rule editing in OntoStudio

11.2 Enabling End Users for Ad Hoc Integration

In Sect. 5.4, we have introduced the roles of users involved in our application integration framework, and the tasks they perform. Besides the framework developer providing the basic framework, and the application developer providing the applications to integrate and their respective containers, three roles are involved in the actual integration: the *domain expert*, the *application integrator*, and the *ontology engineer* (see Fig. 5.5 on page 95).

Following Lieberman et al (2006), we assume that the end user is a *domain expert*. However, we cannot assume a typical end user to be a trained *ontology engineer*, nor an expert in application integration. Therefore, to enable end users to perform tailored integration of applications on the user interface level, we have to provide means for end users to take over the tasks of ontology engineers and application integrators without the need to acquire special background knowledge. In our framework as discussed so far, the application integrator has to perform two tasks: select components, and define integration rules.

The selection of applications may be done based on manuals, textual descriptions, which may also include screens hots. The integrator may also try out the applications beforehand. However, to facilitate integration, it is not only necessary to know what an application is capable of, but also which possibilities it provides for facilitating integration. The main information is the provision about information on the *events* an application is capable of producing, and the *operations* it is capable of performing. As discussed in Sect. 5.3, both are described in our approach using ontologies.

The application developer defines a wiring from events and operations in the application's API to concepts defined in the respective ontologies. In our first prototype implementation, this is done in a hard wired fashion, but it is equally possible to define the wiring in an external file, e.g., in XML, and interpret it at run-time, or to use that file for generating the respective glue code.

Given that the wiring is defined in a structured way, it can be displayed to the end user to let her know which events and operations the application is capable of providing and consuming, as depicted in Fig. 11.5. This allows for selecting a subset of applications that allow for the definition of meaningful interactions. Information from the ontologies may be used for providing explaining tool tips, as shown in the figure, or to allow the user to switch into an ontology browsing mode for further exploring the semantics of an event or an operation.

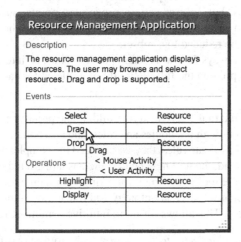

Fig. 11.5: Displaying the events and operations of an application to the integrator

When the user has selected a set of applications to integrate, the next step is to define a set of integration rules. From the SoKNOS project, our experience was that even software developers have difficulties to write the corresponding logic rules without additional instructions or training, so it is completely unlikely that this task can be done by an end user. Furthermore, as shown in the previous section, existing rule editing tools often only provide complicated user interface which require at least a partial understanding of the underlying logic formalisms.

In addition to application integrators, software developers may also not be experts in ontology engineering, as discussed in Babitski et al (2011, pp. 192). Thus, there is not only a need for tools supporting the end user performing the integration, but also for supporting developers in tasks involving ontologies, i.e., providing application ontologies for their software components, and wiring ontologies to those application's APIs and data models.

11.3 Towards a Visual, Ontology-based Tool for User Interface Integration

With these considerations in mind, we have developed a prototype tool for enabling skilled developers (and, in the future, also end users) to create their own integrated applications. The following insights were the essential guidelines for the development:

- The ontologies used are grounded in top level ontologies, which provide ontological modeling guidance and ensure formal correctness. However, the top level is not useful for the end user. Therefore, any displaying of ontology concepts may omit the top level.
- Likewise, end users and developers will typically not make arbitrary extensions to the ontologies, but only at certain predefined points, such as adding new sub categories to a well-defined set of categories. Thus, the ontology editing capabilities may be reduced to a subset.
- Interaction rules always follow a certain pattern. Thus, an interface for end users does not need to provide the full flexibility of a rule editor capable of producing *any* kind of rule.

Those insights point to the core idea for building the prototype tool: although end users may have to work with ontologies and rules, and also build their own extensions to ontologies as well as create rules, they do not need the complexity of a full-fledged ontology editor. Instead, the tool may be designed as a restricted ontology editor.

Furthermore, as the tool is designed for a single domain, i.e., the integration of applications, and not as a universal ontology and rule editor, it may be developed as a *domain specific* tool. This allows for more intuitive naming of functionalities:

- Instead of *adding categories to the ontology*, the tool may offer functionalities such as *add new user interface component* or *add new domain object*.
- Instead of *adding conditions to rules*, the tool may offer functionalities such as *add trigger to interaction* or *restrict domain object types with which the interaction may be performed*.

Furthermore, some logic constructs are only needed in order to support correct reasoning, such as the introduction of skolem functions (see Sect. 5.2.5). Other concepts have been introduced for the sake of ontological correctness. For instance, a condition may be "a select action is performed with an information object representing a customer". While this is correct and in accordance with the top level ontology, most users will colloquially say that "the action is performed with a customer [object]". Thus, the indirection of information objects may also be omitted in the user interface.

These considerations lead to a simplified user interface for creating interaction rules, as shown in Fig. 11.6, which depicts a prototype of a graphical user interface. A rule is divided into two main parts – a *cause* and an *effect* (rather than using the logic programming terms *head* and *body*). The user may create rules by dragging

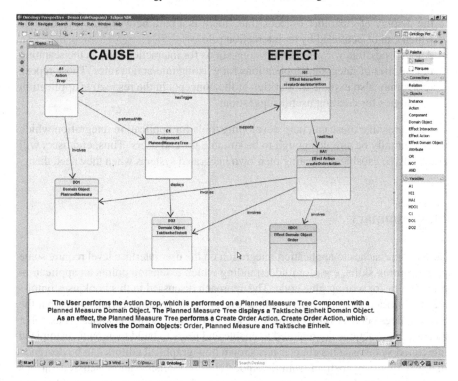

Fig. 11.6: A simplified editor interface for interaction rules

and dropping objects, such as components or business objects used in conditions, from a palette into the rule and connect them to other parts of the rule.

In order to improve the learning and understanding of the graphical editor, each rule can be output in text form, as shown at the bottom of Fig. 11.6. That text output provides a more natural way of displaying an interaction rule to the end user, as it does not require any understanding of the graphical formalisms of an editor.

First tests with end users who had moderate programming skills, but no knowledge about ontologies, logic programming, and rule languages, have delivered promising results. Anyway, to provide end users with means to create their own integrated systems and interaction rules, there is still some way to go. Some future steps to push the limits of user interface integration towards the end user will comprise:

- Adding wizards that guide the end user to creating their interaction rules, which may at least partially replace the visual editor. Wizards may be used to generate initial interaction rules, which may refined in a graphical editor, thus addressing the problem that a wizard may be less powerful than a full editor.
- An intelligent assistant may suggest interactions to the end user. Those suggestions may be generated from computing paths between two application ontologies: e.g., one application supports the selection of customer objects, the other one supports

the display of customer objects, thus, there is a path between the two actions which can be activated by an interaction rule.

- Another possible way of creating suggestions for interaction rules is the scanning repositories of integrated applications for existing interaction rules. Those repositories may also exploit similarities of the concepts in the respective application ontologies for creating useful suggestions.

Measures like these can help developing tools for application integration which will eventually be simple enough to be suitable for end users. Thus, end users will ultimately be capable of creating their own integrated systems when they need them.

11.4 Summary

Current approaches to application integration on the user interface level require some programming skills, e.g., for understanding which extension points an application provides, or for writing glue code. The approach discussed in this book uses ontologies to abstract from the programming level, but still requires certain skills that the end user does not necessarily bring, e.g., knowledge of description logics. Thus, other means of abstractions are required to enable end users to build their own customized integrated systems. This chapter has shown how graphical editors can be designed in a way that they abstract from the underlying formalisms, and discussed various means for lifting the level of abstraction to the end user, while trying to avoid to give up too much of the expressive power of the underlying mechanisms.

Chapter 12
Conclusion and Outlook

Abstract In this book, we have introduced an approach for integrating applications on the user interface layer. Current state of the art approaches to UI integration, such as portals and mashups, have some shortcomings, as missing formal models of the integrated components make the integration a tedious manual task and lead to integrated systems which are hard to maintain. The approach discussed in this book aims at remedying those shortcomings by employing formal ontologies and rules.

12.1 Achievements

Software is typically built in three layers: the data source layer, the business logic layer, and the user interface layer. While ontologies have been widely and successfully used for integration of software applications on the data source and the business logic layer, the employment of ontologies for integration on the user interface layer is a novel approach. In this book, we have presented an in-depth study on how ontologies may be employed for integration on the user interface layer.

With a prototype implementation, we have shown that ontology-based integration on the user interface level is feasible. As this prototype has been used in a large-scale research project for building an industrial strength demonstrator for an emergency management application, the approach does not only work in theory, but that it is also feasible to build functional applications with the framework.

One central result is the development of a concise formal ontology of the domain of user interfaces and interactions. This ontology is aligned to the widely accepted top level ontology DOLCE and contains a fine-grained formal characterization of user interface components and interactions. Several user interface description languages have been taken into account for building the ontology. As we have sketched a number of use cases where such an ontology can be employed for improving user interfaces and/or their development, we are confident that this ontology is a valuable contribution to the community of researchers and practitioners in the field.

An aspect that is particularly important when using ontologies and reasoning at run-time is to ensure that low performance does not decrease the overall usability of the system. In Chap. 8, we have shown various implementation variants for using reasoning at run-time while still ensuring adequate overall performance, and presented a generalized architecture for reasoning on data acquired from running software systems. As bad performance is often a show stopper for ontology-based applications in general, the results achieved in this section provide helpful guidelines when designing and implementing such applications.

Data exchange between applications is an essential requirement for application integration. Although ontologies have been recognized to be a suitable means for implementing such an exchange, state of the art approaches for implementing such an exchange based on ontologies are limited, as they assume and require a certain similarity between the class model and the ontology used for exchange. In this book, we have introduced a novel approach which does not rely on such similarities, but allows for arbitrary mappings between class models and ontologies.

A common shortcoming of state of the art UI integration approaches is the lack of support for integrating technologically heterogeneous components. In this book, we have shown that the framework developed is capable of overcoming this limitation, and presented a case study including components developed with Flex and Java.

To demonstrate how the usability of integrated applications can be further improved, we have introduced the Semantic Data Explorer which has been developed on top of the framework discussed in this book. It provides a light-weight visualization of the data contained in the integrated applications. With a user study, we have demonstrated how the Semantic Data Explorer supports users in conducting complex knowledge acquisition tasks.

A long-term vision is the enabling of end users to create their own customized, tailored integrated systems in an ad hoc fashion. As current tools for mashup development as well as tools for editing ontologies demand too much technical knowledge and are thus not suitable for end users, a new type of tools is required. In this book, we have sketched a number of ideas of what such a tool could like.

12.2 Summary of Evaluations

There have been different evaluations discussed in this book to show that the approach introduced can be used in practice for application integration on the user interface layer. As the performance of the integrated application is a paramount usability criterion, performance has been a widely tested characteristic of the approach. Reasoning and semantic event processing form the central, and at the same time, the most complex step in the approach. Therefore, the run-time performance of this step has been evaluated with particular care.

In the performance evaluation, we have shown that only an approach that pulls A-Box instance data dynamically from the application scales up to a larger number of highly dynamic integrated applications, while pushing that data into a separately maintained A-Box does not. Furthermore, the performance could be improved by introducing local caches for instance data. Depending on the nature of the queries that are to be answered, different strategies of connecting the A-Box wrappers to the reasoner are adequate. Overall, the event processing times could be kept below one second even for a larger set of integrated applications, thus, reasonable performance is ensured.

The suitability of the approach for exchanging data objects based on ontologies and rules has been shown both qualitatively and quantitatively. The class model and the domain ontology used in the SoKNOS project deviated in many ways, and, unlike most state of the art approaches, the rule-based annotation mechanism introduced in this book was capable of dealing with all of those deviations. Furthermore, a quantitative evaluation has shown that the performance overhead generated by processing the mapping rules is negligible.

In Chap. 10, we have introduced the Semantic Data Explorer, which was developed to improve the usability of integrated systems and leverage the semantic annotation of data contained in the integrated applications. With a user study, we have shown that the completion time of complex knowledge acquisition tasks as well as the user's satisfaction with the system could be significantly improved. These results also hold for users that are not particularly trained with ontologies and semantic networks. The user study thus shows that ontologies and semantic technologies can also generate benefits for non-expert end users.

With the emergency management system SoKNOS, a running case study was pursued throughout the book. This system was built using the framework introduced in this book and used for various demonstrations and evaluations with users from the emergency management domain. This case study demonstrates the applicability of the approach to a real world use case.

The SoKNOS prototype itself has undergone various evaluations with end users from the application domain, i.e., the police, fire brigades, and the German Federal Agency for Technical Relief (Technisches Hilfswerk, THW). Those domain experts were presented the prototypes at different stages of the project, asked to fulfill some typical tasks, and questioned for their experiences. Using the AMUSE method (Doerr et al, 2007, pp. 101), the key findings were (Probst and Ziegert, 2010, pp. 489):

- Throughout all the institutions, the reception of the SoKNOS prototype was very positive (between 0.5 and 1.5 on a scale from -2 to +2).
- The final prototype was evaluated significantly better than the first prototype, the main reasons being the increased amount of functionality, and improvements with respect to performance.
- Looking into detailed dimensions of usability, the evaluations of *utility* and *voluntary use* were particularly well. *Ease of use*, *effectiveness*, *productivity*, and *joy of use* were also rated positively, while the ratings with respect to *trust* were rather mixed, mainly since the prototype was presented to the end users as a result of ongoing research rather than a market-ready product.

Although none of the tasks and questions were directly concerned with the underlying integration framework, the positive reception of the SoKNOS prototype is at least partly influenced by a sound integration of the different applications. In fact, many features used in the evaluation were only possible with an integrated system, as they spanned different applications and therefore relied on the integration. Furthermore, a careful implementation of the integration framework, e.g., with respect to performance, was paramount for positive reception of usability. Thus, these evaluations show that the integration framework discussed in this book does not only follow a sound approach and validates according to academic measures, but is also feasible for building real-world applications.

12.3 Open Research Issues

With this book, we have laid out an approach for using ontologies for integrating applications on the user interface level. While this approach has proven to be practical, it opens up a variety of questions and future directions, both in improving the development process of integrated user interfaces, as well as enhancing the capabilities of such integrated user interfaces themselves.

12.3.1 Improving the Development Process of User Interface Integration

Creating an integrated system from different applications requires the software engineer to perform a couple of steps, such as the creation of an application ontology, the definition of integration rules, the wiring of event types to method calls, and the definition of rules for mapping the application's data model to a real world domain ontology. As discussed in Sect. 5.4, some of those tasks require very special knowledge, e.g., of ontologies and F-Logic. To ease these tasks, a visual developer's tool is currently designed which will help the software developers concerned with the integration perform the integration without the need for a deep understanding of ontologies and F-Logic. A first sketch of that tool has been presented in Chap. 11.

Given that such a tool is intuitive enough to understand and use, the vision of end users creating their own customized integrated systems and mashups becomes more concrete. While current mashup tools require a fair amount of programming skills and are therefore hardly suitable for end users, a tool built upon formal models and hiding the implementation in favor of a consumable representation could help in achieving the vision of enabling end users to dynamically combine the applications they need for their tasks at hand.

One assumption that we have made in this book is that the applications to integrated have been pre-selected and prepared by an engineer responsible for the integration. A next step would be the use of repositories such as *KOntoR* (Happel et al, 2006, pp. 349, see Sect. 4.4.3), which allow for dynamically searching for and integrating applications at run-time. With such a combination, users might formulate queries when searching for applications for certain tasks, and applications might be dynamically added that are considered useful in the user's current context.

An approach using repositories and dynamic registration would be especially appealing when transferring the framework discussed in this book to the web. Although some major technical obstacles have to be addressed for that step, such as the implementation of high-performance reasoning in a browser without server round trips and the provision of suitable web-based wrappers for non web-based legacy systems, such a web-based integration tool would allow for more flexible integration of applications, assembled by using constantly updated repositories and application stores on the web.

Technically, the demand for more dynamic application integration raises some further interesting challenges. With the current version of our reference implementation, it is not possible to add new applications at run-time without restarting the integrated system. While solutions using application containers that are generated on demand can be thought of, issues that have to be taken care are, e.g., dynamic loading and unloading of application ontologies (which also covers T-Box concepts, not only A-Box axioms, as discussed in Chap. 8).

12.3.2 Enhancing the Capabilities of Integrated User Interfaces

The approach discussed in book has used ontologies and rules for formally describing the interaction capabilities of the integrated applications. In Sect. 4.3.3, we have laid out that ontologies may be used for providing user assistance and form a self-explaining application. To this end, using the information encoded in the different ontologies and rules for rendering graphical and/or textual hints for users could provide the user with assistance in learning to work with an integrated system. Highlighting and augmenting drop targets upon a drag action, as discussed in Sect. 6.3.2 is a first step in this direction, which, however, is only the tip of the iceberg of what is possible. Prototypes and user studies in this field are likely to reveal extensive possibilities of employing ontologies for improving the usability and learnability of user interfaces.

The approach discussed in this book has mainly looked at user interfaces from a software engineering perspective, which is reflected in the ontology developed. With the advent of ubiquitous computing and multi modal user interfaces that go beyond the classic WIMP (window, icon, menu, pointing device) paradigms (van Dam, 1997, pp. 63), a consistent next step would be the extension of the approach to integrating not only software user interfaces, but user interfaces consisting of and running on different devices. The techniques of using ontologies and rules for describing user interfaces and controlling interactions between components are a good candidate for supporting such an integration (see, e.g., Foundation for Intelligent Phyiscal Agents, 2002), and we have already foreseen the extensibility of our ontology with respect to different modalities. However, various challenges will have to be addressed, e.g., the distribution of the reasoning process across devices with limited processing capability.

New interaction paradigms may also bring new challenges. Event-based mechanisms, such as the one pursued in this book, are well suited for certain types of user interfaces. In WIMP user interfaces, a limited set of discrete events (such as a mouse click) are usually sufficient to formally describe what the user does and how the system is supposed to react. Other interaction paradigms may be different by nature, such as using gestures with mobile devices, which evoke a continuous interaction with a system. Although it is possible in general to use ontologies and rules for describing such forms interactions, the required means for processing may be different from the event-driven architecture developed in this book, as pointed out, e.g., by Shaer and Jacob (2009, p. 5).

Besides the evolution from classic WIMP to post-WIMP user interfaces, another major upcoming trend is the development of multi-user systems, using, e.g., multi touch tables or walls, which can be used in a collaborative fashion (Hawkey et al, 2005, pp. 31). While the approach discussed in this book is targeted at single-user interaction, formalizing and efficiently supporting multi-user interaction with integrated user interfaces will open up new challenges.

So far, we have assumed that an integrated user interface will look the same and provide the same interaction capabilities for each user. Providing custom-tailored integrated user interfaces would be one further step towards better usability and acceptance of integrated systems. As integration rules may contain arbitrary conditions, it is possible to formulate integration rules stating that an interaction is possible, e.g., only if the user has some specific rights (e.g., by employing an additional ontology of users and users' rights, such as the one introduced by Kagal et al, 2003). Another possibility would be to take into account the user context by detecting the user's current task (Schmidt et al, 2010, pp. 251) and offering specific interactions only in a given context.

12.3.3 Possible Influence on Related Fields

The results discussed in this book have been motivated by the topic of application integration on the user interface level, and they have been implemented in a prototype addressing that problem. However, many of the results may be useful in other fields of research as well.

Chapter 6 has introduced a formal ontology of the domain of user interfaces and interactions. Many applications of such an ontology outside of the field of UI integration can be thought of, such as annotated repositories of UI components, automated translation between UI modeling languages, and self-explaining UIs, as well as supporting adaptivity of user interface by formal models.

Chapter 7 has discussed a flexible, non-intrusive approach for exchanging objects between applications. Such an approach is useful not only for integration on the user interface level, but also for integration on the business-logic level, where business objects have to be exchanged between applications, rather than simply mutually granting access rights to the applications' data sources. Semantic-web enabled service buses in service oriented architectures may be one future application of such an approach. Furthermore, the approach allows for homogeneous views on heterogeneous IT systems, using a tool like the semantic data explorer introduced in Chap. 10.

Chapter 8 has taken a deeper look at different architectures for making data from running applications accessible to a reasoner for semantic event processing. Such event processing is not only relevant in integrated UIs, but also in other fields, such as business process orchestration or complex event detection. Furthermore, reasoning on data in applications can also be used for various other purposes, such as ontology-based consistency checking, or assisted navigation in integrated applications.

Chapter 9 has shown how ontologies and annotated events can help crossing technological barriers between UI components. Being targeted mainly at software components, such an exchange format may be useful in also crossing hardware heterogeneities, as discussed above. The findings from this chapter may serve as a useful basis for designing the next generation of ubiquitous computing devices which may dynamically coordinate for facilitating emergent interaction (Andersson et al, 2002).

12.4 Concluding Remarks

With this book, we have discussed an approach of using ontologies and formal rules for improving the process of user interface integration and the quality of the resulting integrated systems, both in terms of maintainability for the developer and in terms of usability for the end users. We have laid out the theoretical foundations, as well as presented various in-depth considerations of detail aspects. The list of open research issues shows that there is a potential for widely adopting that approach, both by a wider audience and on a larger variety of platforms, and for improving the development process of integrated user interfaces as well as enhancing their interaction capabilities.

When discussing the topic of this book, and the employment of ontologies in software in general, with colleagues who do not have an ontology background, their most frequent comments were: too academic, too impractical, too poor performance, too bad usability. While working on this book, only the first comment has been proven correct: ontologies are indeed a topic of academia, and they are a subject of ongoing research. As far as the other three comments are concerned, the results discussed in this book proves them wrong. Ontologies can be employed for efficiently solving practical problems. Ontology-based software may have bad performance when designed badly – which holds true for any kind of software, ontology-based or not – but carefully designing the software architecture can lead to significant performance gains and remedy those problems. Finally, usability can even be improved by using ontologies, e.g., by allowing for new forms of integrated user interfaces, and by supporting information exploration in heterogeneous systems.

So, in summary, this book has shown how ontologies and formal rules can be used to address a practical software engineering problem, and, by pursuing the approach down to an implemented prototype used for a real-world case study, shown that the approach is practically feasible and useful. On a wider scale, it can serve as an example that, despite a large number of objections that one may face, ontologies are mature enough to be employed in real-world settings outside of researchers' sandboxes.

List of Abbreviations

AI   Artificial Intelligence
AJAX   Asynchronous JavaScript And XML
API   Application Programming Interface
AUI   Abstract User Interface]
BFO   Basic Formal Ontology
BMBF   Bundesministerium für Bildung und Forschung (German Federal Ministry of Education and Research)
BPEL   Business Process Execution Language
CAB   Composite UI Application Block
CCT   Concur[rent] Task Trees
CIDL   Component Interface Description Language
COM   Component Object Model
CSS   Cascading Style Sheet
CUI   Concrete User Interface
DIG   DL Implementation Group
DAML   DARPA Markup Language
DARPA   Defense Advanced Research Projects Agency
DHTML   Dynamic HTML
DOLCE   Descriptive Ontology for Linguistic and Cognitive Engineering
DL   Description Logics
DnS   Descriptions and Situations
DTD   Document Type Definition
EBNF   Extended Backus Naur Form
ECA   Event Condition Action
EMF   Eclipse Modeling Framework
EMML   Enterprise Mashup Markup Language
ER   Entity Relationship
F-Logic   Frame Logic
FOAF   Friend of a Friend
GFO   General Formal Ontology
HCI   Human Computer Interaction

HTML   HyperText Markup Language
HTTP   HyperText Transport Protocol
ISO   International Organization for Standardization
JavaCC   Java Compiler Compiler
JDIC   Java Desktop Integration Components
JSF   Java Server Faces
JNI   Java Native Interface
JRON   JavaScript RDF Object Notation
JSON   JavaScript Object Notation
JSP   Java Server Pages
JSR   Java Specification Request
JQL   Java Query Language
KIF   Knowledge Interchange Format
LINQ   Language Integrated Query
LISP   List Processing
LZX   The XML based language used in OpenLaszlo; a resolution of the abbreviation is not given.
MARIA   Model-based lAnguage foR Interactive Applications
MDA   Model Driven Architecture
MDL   MashArt Description Language
MXML   The XML based language used in Adobe Flex; it is likely that it originally stands for Macromedia XML.
N3   Notation 3
OASIS   Organization for the Advancement of Structured Information Standards
OIL   Ontology Inference Layer
OMA   Open Mashup Alliance
OMG   Object Management Group
OWL   Web Ontology Language
OWL DL   OWL Description Logics
OWL-S   Semantic Markup for Web Services (not really an abbreviation)
PROTON   PROTo ONtology
RCP   Rich Client Platform
RIF   Rule Interchange Format
RDF   Resource Description Framework
RDF-S   Resource Description Framework Schema
RMI   Remote Method Invocation
RSS   Really Simple Syndication
RuleML   Rule Markup Language
SAWSDL   Semantic Annotations for WSDL
SCA   Service Component Architecture
SOA   Service Oriented Architecture
SOAP   Simple Object Access Protocol
SoKNOS   Service-orientierte Architekturen für Netzwerke im Bereich Öffentlicher Sicherheit (Service oriented architectures for networks in the public security area)
SOS   Sensor Observation Service
SQL   Structured Query Language

SPARQL   SPARQL Protocol And RDF Query Language (a recursive acronym)
SUMO   Suggested Upper Merged Ontology
SWRL   Semantic Web Rule Language
THW   Technisches Hilfswerk (Federal Agency for Technical Relief)
UCL   Universal Composition Language
UI   User Interface
UIDL   User Interface Description Language
UIML   User Interface Markup Language
UISDL   User Interface Service Description Language
UML   Universal Modeling Language
URI   Uniform Resource Identifier
UsiXML   USer Interface eXtensible Markup Language
W3C   World Wide Web Consortium
WAI ARIA   Web Accessibility Initiative – Accessible Rich Internet Applications
WIMP   Window, Icon, Menu, Pointing Device
WML   Wireless Markup Language
WSDL   Web Service Description Language
WSDL-S   Web Services Semantics (not really an abbreviation)
WSML   Web Service Modeling Language
WSMO   Web Service Modeling Ontology
WSMX   Web Service Execution Environment
XAML   eXtensible Application Markup Language
XBL   XML Binding Language, also eXtensible Bindings Language
XIML   eXtensible Interface Markup Language
XML   eXtensible Markup Language
XPIL   eXtensible Presentation Integration Language
XSLT   eXtensible Stylesheet Language Transformation
XUL   XML User Interface Language
YAML   YAML Ain't Markup Language (a recursive acronym)

List of Figures

2.1   Different levels of integration 10
2.2   The design space of UI integration 15

3.1   The semantic web stack 29
3.2   Different syntaxes for RDF 30
3.3   Example OWL ontology....................................... 31
3.4   The linked open data cloud 32
3.5   Example F-Logic ontology................................... 34
3.6   Ontology types based on the degree of formality 35
3.7   Classification of ontologies based on their level of abstraction 38
3.8   Classification of ontologies in software engineering 39
3.9   Comparison of different ontology engineering methodologies 42
3.10 The top level categories of DOLCE 44
3.11 The top level categories of SUMO 46
3.12 The taxonomy of Cyc's upper level ontology................... 47
3.13 The system and top level categories of PROTON 48
3.14 Screenshot of the ontology editor Protégé 50
3.15 Screenshot of the Linked Data explorer Tabulator............... 51
3.16 Examples for integration on the different layers 56
3.17 Ontology-based database integration 57

4.1   Characterization schema for ontology-enhanced user interfaces 63

5.1   Characterization of the approach............................. 84
5.2   Ontologies used in the integration framework 86
5.3   Improving modularity with event annotations 91
5.4   Schematic view of an application and the logical representation of
      its state 93
5.5   Roles in and tasks in UI integration 95
5.6   High level view on the implementation of the integration framework. 97

5.7   Screenshot of the event inspector, showing the annotation of an
      event in RDF 98
5.8   Object exchange between applications 100
5.9   Overview of the SoKNOS prototype. 102
5.10 Screenshot of the SoKNOS prototype with a set of UI modules and
      possible interactions 104
5.11 Coordinating interaction in the integration framework 106
5.12 The SoKNOS toolbox 108
5.13 The link storage extension in the integration framework 110
5.14 The update service extension in the integration framework 111
5.15 Ontologies used in the SoKNOS project. 112
5.16 Six use cases for semantic technologies covered in the SoKNOS
      project. 115

6.1   Overview of examined UI description languages 120
6.2   A screenshot of the Teresa toolkit 124
6.3   Distribution of UI component definitions across different UI
      description languages 127
6.4   Ontologies reused for building the ontology of user interfaces and
      interactions 129
6.5   Core concepts of the Core Ontology of Software 130
6.6   Different realizations of a slider user interface component. 133
6.7   The top level of the ontology of the user interfaces and interactions
      domain 139
6.8   Excerpt from the detail level ontology, showing the top categories of
      UI components 140
6.9   Example for user activities and their mapping to hardware devices . . 143
6.10 A-Box statements processed by the reasoner 146

7.1   Example for mapping a Java class to an ontology 152
7.2   Multi-purpose class 153
7.3   Artificial class 154
7.4   Class for relation 154
7.5   Multi-purpose relation with a flag 155
7.6   Multi-purpose relation with background knowledge 155
7.7   Skipping categories in chains of relations 156
7.8   Shortcut including a subclass relation 156
7.9   Non-atomic data types 157
7.10 Counting attributes 157
7.11 Example class model that can lead to very large annotations 165
7.12 Example for a template for restricting an object's annotation 166
7.13 Architecture diagram of object exchange between applications via
      dynamic annotation 167
7.14 Excerpt from the common SoKNOS class model and the SoKNOS
      domain ontology 170

7.15 Excerpts from two class models and the corresponding part in the
      SoKNOS domain ontology.................................... 171
7.16 Runtime behavior of creating annotations for Java objects.......... 174
7.17 Runtime behavior of creating Java objects from annotations 174

8.1   Performance of a naive implementation of semantic event processing 178
8.2   Framework architecture using global vs. local event processing 181
8.3   Event processing performance comparison between using global and
      local processing 182
8.4   Framework architecture using a push-based vs. a pull-based approach 183
8.5   Event processing performance comparison between pushing and
      pulling instance data 184
8.6   Different variants for using caches 185
8.7   Event processing times for different types of caches.............. 186
8.8   Performance evaluation of different designs of connector rules...... 187
8.9   Generalized architecture for reasoning about data from running
      applications 189
8.10 Query times for selected query types 191
8.11 Evaluation of robustness of different caching approaches regarding
      A-Box dynamics 192

9.1   Drag and drop across heterogeneous components using Java proxies . 197
9.2   Two heterogeneous, integrated UIs 200
9.3   Communication between Java and Flex components 202
9.4   Exchanging objects between the Java container 203
9.5   Schematic view of a UI component and its proxy 204

10.1 Screen shot of the Semantic Data Explorer 210
10.2 Integration of the Semantic Data Explorer in the Framework 211
10.3 Screenshot of the evaluation setup............................. 213
10.4 Participants of the user study 215
10.5 Average task completion times in seconds 216
10.6 Average error rates 216
10.7 Results of the questionnaires on user experience................. 217

11.1 Screenshot of a dialog in Intel MashMaker 220
11.2 Different levels of abstraction 221
11.3 Rule editing in Protégé with SWRLTab 221
11.4 Graphical rule editing in OntoStudio 222
11.5 Displaying the events and operations of an application to the integrator 223
11.6 A simplified editor interface for interaction rules 225

List of Tables

2.1 Comparison of popular portal frameworks 17
2.2 Comparison of popular mashup platforms 19
2.3 Comparison of other commercial and established UI integration
     approaches 20
2.4 Comparison of research prototypes for UI integration 24

3.1 Size of the DOLCE ontologies and extensions 45

4.2 Summary of approaches for ontology-enhanced UIs 75

6.1 Concepts from user interface standards and their alignment to the
     reused ontologies 131
6.2 Relations of the top level ontology already covered by the reused
     ontologies 135
6.3 Relations of the top level ontology that have been added 137

7.1 Mismatches observed between the common SoKNOS class model
     and the SoKNOS domain ontology. 169

8.1 Queries used for performance evaluation 190

9.1 Issues to address when stepping from Java-only to multi-technology
     integration. 196
9.2 A comparison of four APIs for linking Flex and Java. 201

References

Aasman J (2008) Unification of Geospatial Reasoning, Temporal Logic, & Social Network Analysis in Event-Based Systems. In: DEBS '08: Proceedings of the Second International Conference on Distributed Event-Based Systems, ACM, pp 139–145

Abdelnur A, Heppner S (2003) JSR 168: Portlet Specification. http://www.jcp.org/en/jsr/detail?id=168, accessed April 12th, 2011.

Abrams M, Phanouriou C, Batongbacal AL, Williams SM, Shuster JE (1999) UIML: an appliance-independent XML user interface language. Computer Networks 31(11-16):1695 – 1708

Adler D (2004) The JACOB Project: A JAva-COM Bridge. http://danadler.com/jacob/, accessed April 12th, 2011.

Adobe Systems Inc (2011) Adobe Flex. http://www.adobe.com/products/flex/, accessed April 12th, 2011.

Agnew B (2006) Java Object Querying Using JXPath. http://today.java.net/pub/a/today/2006/08/03/java-object-querying-using-jxpath.html, accessed April 12th, 2011.

Alasoud A, Haarslev V, Shiri N (2009) An Empirical Comparison of Ontology Matching Techniques. Journal of Information Science 35(4):379–397

Alferes JJ, Eckert M, May W (2009) Evolution and Reactivity in the Semantic Web. In: Bry F, Maluszynski J (eds) Semantic Techniques for the Web, LNCS, vol 5500, pp 161–200

Alishevskikh A (2011) RDFBeans. http://rdfbeans.sourceforge.net/, accessed April 12th, 2011.

Altova (2011) SemanticWorks Semantic Web tool - Visual RDF and OWL editor. http://www.altova.com/semanticworks.html, accessed April 12th, 2011.

Aßmann U, Zschaler S, Wagner G (2006) Ontologies, Meta-models, and the Model-Driven Paradigm. In: (Calero et al, 2006), chap 9, pp 249–273

Aßmann U, Bartho A, Wende C (eds) (2010) Reasoning Web - Semantic Technologies for Software Engineering, LNCS, vol 6325, Springer

Amsden J (2001) Levels Of Integration - Five ways you can integrate with the Eclipse Platform. http://www.eclipse.org/articles/Article-Levels-Of-Integration/levels-of-integration.html, accessed April 12th, 2011.

Andersson N, Broberg A, Bränberg A, Janlert LE, Jonsson E, Holmlund K, Pettersson J (2002) Emegent Interaction - A Pre-study. Tech. rep., Department of Computing Science, Umeå University, Sweden

Angele J, Lausen G (2009) Ontologies in F-Logic. In: (Staab and Studer, 2009), chap 3, pp 45–70

Angele J, Erdmann M, Wenke D (2008) Ontology-Based Knowledge Management in Automotive Engineering Scenarios. In: (Hepp et al, 2008), pp 245–264

Anicic D, Stojanovic N (2008) Towards Creation of Logical Framework for Event-Driven Information Systems. In: Cordeiro J, Filipe J (eds) ICEIS 2008 - Proceedings of the Tenth International

Conference on Enterprise Information Systems, Volume ISAS-2, Barcelona, Spain, June 12-16, 2008, pp 394–401

Ankolekar A, Krötzsch M, Tran T, Vrandecic D (2007a) The Two Cultures: Mashing Up Web 2.0 and the Semantic Web. In: (Williamson et al, 2007), pp 825–834

Ankolekar A, Paolucci M, Srinivasan N, Sycara K (2007b) Tools for Semantic Web Services. In: Studer R, Grimm S, Abecker A (eds) Semantic Web Services - Concepts, Technologies and Applications, Springer, chap 11, pp 311–337

Antoniou G, Bikakis A (2007) DR-Prolog: A System for Defeasible Reasoning with Rules and Ontologies on the Semantic Web. IEEE Transactions on Knowledge and Data Engineering 19:233–245

Antoniou G, Damásio CV, Grosof B, Horrocks I, Kifer M, Maluszynski J, Patel-Schneider PF (2005a) Combining Rules and Ontologies. A survey. Deliverable I3-D3, REWERSE

Antoniou G, Franconia E, van Harmelen F (2005b) Introduction to Semantic Web Ontology Languages. In: (Eisinger and Maluszynski, 2005), pp 1–21

Apache Software Foundation (2010) Welcome to Pluto. http://portals.apache.org/pluto/, accessed April 12th, 2011.

de Araújo SFC, Schwabe D (2009) Explorator: a tool for exploring RDF data through direct manipulation. In: Bizer C, Heath T, Berners-Lee T, Idehen K (eds) Proceedings of the WWW2009 Workshop on Linked Data on the Web, CEUR-WS, vol 538

Ardissono L, Felfernig A, Friedrich G, Jannach D, Zanker M, Schäfer R (2002) A Framework for Rapid Development of Advanced Web-based Configurator Applications. In: van Harmelen F (ed) Proceedings of the 15th Eureopean Conference on Artificial Intelligence, ECAI'2002, Lyon, France, July 2002, IOS Press, pp 618–622

Aroyo L, Traverso P, Ciravegna F, Cimiano P, Heath T, Hyvönen E, Mizoguchi R, Oren E, Sabou M, Simperl EPB (eds) (2009) The Semantic Web: Research and Applications (ESWC 2009), LNCS, vol 5554, Springer

Aroyo L, Antoniou G, Hyvönen E, ten Teije A, Stuckenschmidt H, Cabral L, Tudorache T (eds) (2010) The Semantic Web: Research and Applications (ESWC 2010), Part II, LNCS, vol 6089, Springer

Arpírez JC, Corcho O, Fernández-López M, Gómez-Pérez A (2001) WebODE: a scalable workbench for ontological engineering. In: K-CAP '01: Proceedings of the 1st international conference on Knowledge capture, ACM, pp 6–13

Artz D, Gil Y (2007) A Survey of Trust in Computer Science and the Semantic Web. Journal of Web Semantics 5(2):58–71

Atkinson C, Gutheil M, Kiko K (2006) On the Relationship of Ontologies and Models. In: Brockmans S, Jung J, Sure Y (eds) Workshop on Meta-Modelling (WoMM), GI, LNI, vol 96, pp 47–60

Auer S, Dietzold S, Lehmann J, Hellmann S, Aumueller D (2009) Triplify: Light-Weight Linked Data Publication from Relational Databases. In: WWW '09: Proceedings of the 18th international conference on World wide web, ACM, pp 621–630

Babitski G, Bergweiler S, Hoffmann J, Schön D, Stasch C, Walkowski AC (2009a) Ontology-Based Integration of Sensor Web Services in Disaster Management. In: Proceedings of the 3rd International Conference on GeoSpatial Semantics, Springer, GeoS '09, pp 103–121

Babitski G, Probst F, Hoffmann J, Oberle D (2009b) Ontology Design for Information Integration in Catastrophy Management. In: Proceedings of the 4th International Workshop on Applications of Semantic Technologies (AST'09)

Babitski G, Probst F, Walkowski A, Bergweiler S, Schön D, Oberle D, Hutter D, Kleser G, Hoffmann J, Paulheim H (2009c) SoKNOS Deliverable D10.7: Finaler Demonstrator

Babitski G, Bergweiler S, Grebner O, Paulheim DOH, Probst F (2011) SoKNOS - Using Semantic Technologies in Disaster Management Software. In: The Semantic Web: Research and Applications (ESWC 2011), Part II, pp 183–197

Bailey J, Bry F, Furche T, Schaffert S (2005) Web and Semantic Web Query Languages: A Survey. In: (Eisinger and Maluszynski, 2005), pp 35–133

Bandelloni R, Paternò F, Santoro C (2008) Reverse Engineering Cross-Modal User Interfaces for Ubiquitous Environments. In: Gulliksen J, Harning MB, Palanque P, Veer GC, Wesson J (eds) Engineering Interactive Systems, Springer, pp 285–302

Barrasa J, Óscar Corcho, Gómez-Pérez A (2004) R2O, an Extensible and Semantically Based Database-to-ontology Mapping Language. http://www.cs.man.ac.uk/~ocorcho/documents/SWDB2004_BarrasaEtAl.pdf, accessed April 12th, 2011.

Batini C, Lenzerini M, Navathe SB (1986) A Comparative Analysis of Methodologies for Database Schema Integration. ACM Computing Surveys 18(4):323–364

Bechhofer S, Carroll JJ (2004) Parsing OWL DL: Trees or Triples? In: Proceedings of the 13th international conference on World Wide Web, ACM Press, pp 266–275

Bechhofer S, Möller R, Crowther P (2003a) The DIG Description Logic Interface. In: Proceedings of the International Workshop on Description Logics (DL-2003)

Bechhofer S, Volz R, Lord PW (2003b) Cooking the Semantic Web with the OWL API. In: Fensel D, Sycara KP, Mylopoulos J (eds) The Semantic Web - ISWC 2003, Second International Semantic Web Conference, Springer, LNCS, vol 2870, pp 659–675

Bechhofer S, Hauswirth M, Hoffmann J, Koubarakis M (eds) (2008) The Semantic Web: Research and Applications (ESWC 2008), LNCS, vol 5021, Springer

Behrends E, Fritzen O, May W, Schenk F (2006) Combining ECA Rules with Process Algebras for the Semantic Web. In: RULEML '06: Proceedings of the Second International Conference on Rules and Rule Markup Languages for the Semantic Web, IEEE Computer Society, pp 29–38

Ben-Kiki O, Evans C, döt Net I (2009) YAML Ain't Markup Language Version 1.2. http://yaml.org/spec/1.2/spec.html, accessed April 12th, 2011.

Benatallah B, Nezhad HRM (2007) Service Oriented Architecture: Overview and Directions. In: Börger E, Cisternino A (eds) Advances in Software Engineering, Springer, LNCS, vol 5316, pp 116–130

Bénel A, Zhou C, Cahier JP (2010) Beyond Web 2.0 ... and Beyond the Semantic Web. In: Randall D, Salembier P (eds) From CSCW to Web 2.0: European Developments in Collaborative Design, Computer Supported Cooperative Work, Springer London, pp 155–171

Berners-Lee T (1998) Relational Databases on the Semantic Web. http://www.w3.org/DesignIssues/RDB-RDF.html, accessed April 12th, 2011.

Berners-Lee T (2009) Semantic Web and Linked Data. http://www.w3.org/2009/Talks/0120-campus-party-tbl/, accessed April 12th, 2011.

Berners-Lee T, Connolly D (1993) Hypertext Markup Language (HTML). http://www.w3.org/MarkUp/draft-ietf-iiir-html-01.txt, accessed April 12th, 2011.

Berners-Lee T, Connolly D (2011) Notation3 (N3): A readable RDF syntax. http://www.w3.org/TeamSubmission/n3/, accessed April 12th, 2011.

Berners-Lee T, Hendler J, Lassila O (2001) The Semantic Web. Scientific American 284(5):34–43

Berners-Lee T, Fielding RT, Masinter L (2005) RFC 3986 - Uniform Resource Identifier (URI): Generic Syntax. http://tools.ietf.org/html/rfc3986, accessed April 12th, 2011.

Berners-Lee T, Chen Y, Chilton L, Connolly D, Dhanaraj R, Hollenbach J, Lerer A, Sheets D (2006) Tabulator: Exploring and Analyzing linked data on the Semantic Web. In: (Rutledge et al, 2006)

Birsan D (2005) On plug-ins and extensible architectures. ACM Queue 3(2):40–46

Bizer C, Schultz A (2009) The Berlin SPARQL Benchmark. International Journal on Semantic Web and Information Systems 5(2):1–24

Bizer C, Seaborne A (2004) D2RQ - Treating Non-RDF Databases as Virtual RDF Graphs. In: International Semantic Web Conference 2004 - Posters

Bizer C, Westphal D (2007) Developers Guide to Semantic Web Toolkits for different Programming Languages. http://www4.wiwiss.fu-berlin.de/bizer/toolkits/, accessed April 12th, 2011.

Bizer C, Heath T, Idehen K, Berners-Lee T (eds) (2008) Proceedings of the WWW2008 Workshop on Linked Data on the Web, CEUR-WS, vol 369

Bizer C, Heath T, Berners-Lee T (2009) Linked Data - The Story So Far. International Journal on Semantic Web and Information Systems 5(3):1–22

Blechar M (2010) Hype Cycle for Application Development. http://www.gartner.com/
    DisplayDocument?id=1412014, accessed April 12th, 2011.

Blechar M, Norton D, Natis YV, Knipp E, Murphy TE, Malinverno P, Duggan J, Sholler D,
    Murphy J, Altman R, Driver M (2010) IT Market Clock for Application Development, 2010.
    http://www.gartner.com/DisplayDocument?doc_cd=206032, accessed April
    12th, 2011.

Boley H, Kifer M, Pătrânjan PL, Polleres A (2007) Rule Interchange on the Web. In: Antoniou G,
    Aßmann U, Baroglio C, Decker S, Henze N, Pătrânjan PL, Tolksdorf R (eds) Reasoning Web,
    LNCS, vol 4636, Springer Berlin / Heidelberg, pp 269–309

Boley H, Paschke A, Tabet S, Grosof B, Bassiliades N, Governatori G, Hirtle D, Shafiq O (2010)
    Schema Specification of RuleML 1.0. http://ruleml.org/1.0/, accessed April 12th,
    2011.

Bontcheva K, Wilks Y (2004) Automatic Report Generation from Ontologies: The MIAKT Ap-
    proach. In: 9th International Conference on Applications of Natural Language to Information
    Systems, pp 324–335

Bottazzi E, Catenacci C, Gangemi A, Lehmann J (2006) From Collective Intentionality to Intentional
    Collectives: an Ontological Perspective. Cognitive Systems Research 7(2-3):192–208

Bowley D (2009) Rapid Portlet Development with WebSphere Portlet Factory: Step-by-Step Guide
    for Building Your Own Portlets. IBM Press

Brickley D, Miller L (2010) FOAF Vocabulary Specification 0.98. http://xmlns.com/foaf/
    spec/, accessed April 12th, 2011.

Broekstra J, Kampman A, van Harmelen F (2002) Sesame: A Generic Architecture for Storing and
    Querying RDF and RDF Schema. In: (Horrocks and Hendler, 2002), pp 54–68

de Bruijn J, Kerrigan M, Zaremba M, Fensel D (2009) Semantic Web Services. In: (Staab and
    Studer, 2009), chap 29, pp 617–636

Burel G, Cano AE, Lanfranchi V (2009) Ozone Browser: Augmenting the Web with Semantic
    Overlays. In: Bizer C, Auer S, Grimnes GA (eds) 5th Workshop on Scripting and Development
    for the Semantic Web

Calì A, Calvanese D, Grau BC, Giacomo GD, Lembo D, Lenzerini M, Lutz C, Milano D,
    Möller R, Poggi A, Sattler U (2005) State of the Art Survey - Deliverable D01 of the
    TONES project. http://www.inf.unibz.it/tones/index.php?option=com_
    docman&task=docclick&Itemid=45&bid=11&limitstart=0&limit=20,
    accessed April 12th, 2011.

Calero C, Ruiz F, Piattini M (eds) (2006) Ontologies for Software Engineering and Software
    Technology. Springer

Calvary G, Coutaz J, Thevenin D, Bouillon L, Florins M, Limbourg Q, Souchon N, Vanderdonckt J,
    Marucci L, Paternò F, Santoro C (2002) The CAMELEON Reference Framework. Deliverable 1.1
    of the CAMELEON Project. http://giove.isti.cnr.it/projects/cameleon/
    pdf/CAMELEON%20D1.1RefFramework.pdf, accessed April 12th, 2011.

Calvary G, Coutaz J, Thevenin D, Limbourg Q, Bouillon L, Vanderdonckt J (2003) A Unifying
    Reference Framework for multi-target user interfaces. Interacting with Computers 15(3):289–308

Calvary G, Graham TCN, Gray P (eds) (2009) Proceedings of the 1st ACM SIGCHI Symposium on
    Engineering Interactive Computing Systems (EICS 2010), ACM

Cardoso J (2007) The Semantic Web Vision: Where Are We? IEEE Intelligent Systems 22(5):84–88

Carr L, Hall W, Bechhofer S, Goble C (2001) Conceptual linking: ontology-based open hypermedia.
    In: WWW '01: Proceedings of the 10th international conference on World Wide Web, ACM, pp
    334–342

Carroll JJ, Dickinson I, Dollin C, Reynolds D, Seaborne A, Wilkinson K (2004) Jena: Implementing
    the Semantic Web Recommendations. In: Feldman SI, Uretsky M, Najork M, Wills CE (eds)
    Proceedings of the 13th international conference on World Wide Web - Alternate Track Papers
    & Posters, ACM, pp 74–83

Catarci T, Dongilli P, Mascio TD, Franconi E, Santucci G, Tessaris S (2004) An Ontology Based
    Visual Tool for Query Formulation Support. In: de Mántaras RL, Saitta L (eds) 16th European
    Conference on Artificial Intelligence ECAI, IOS Press, pp 308–312

Chappell D (2007) Introducing SCA. http://www.davidchappell.com/articles/Introducing_SCA.pdf, accessed April 12th, 2011.

Cheyer A, Park J, Giuli R (2005) IRIS: Integrate. Relate. Infer. Share. In: (Decker et al, 2005)

Cimiano P, Mädche A, Staab S, Völker J (2010) Ontology Learning. In: (Staab and Studer, 2009), pp 245–267

Codd EF (1985a) Does Your DBMS Run By the Rules? ComputerWorld October 21st

Codd EF (1985b) Is Your DBMS Really Relational? ComputerWorld October 14th

CodeWeavers Inc (2011) WineHQ - Run Windows applications on Linux, BSD, Solaris and Mac OS X. http://www.winehq.org/, accessed April 12th, 2011.

Coenraets C (2008) Getting Started with BlazeDS. http://www.adobe.com/devnet/livecycle/articles/blazeds_gettingstarted.html, accessed April 12th, 2011.

Cohen M, Schwabe D (2010) RExplorator - supporting reusable explorations of Semantic Web Linked Data. In: (Polleres and Chen, 2010)

Collberg C, Thomborson C, Low D (1997) A Taxonomy of Obfuscating Transformations. Tech. Rep. 148, University of Auckland, Department of Computer Science

Coskun G, Heese R, Luczak-Rösch M, Oldakowski R, Paschke A, Schäfermeier R, Streibel O (2009) Towards a Corporate Semantic Web. In: Proceedings of I-KNOW '09 and I-SEMANTICS '09, pp 602–610

Coutaz J, Lachenal C, Dupuy-Chessa S (2003) Ontology for Multi-surface Interaction. In: Proceedings of IFIP INTERACT03: Human-Computer Interaction, IFIP Technical Committee No 13 on Human-Computer Interaction, pp 447–454

Cowan T (2008) Jenabean: Easily bind JavaBeans to RDF. http://www.ibm.com/developerworks/java/library/j-jenabean.html, accessed April 12th, 2011.

Cruz IF, Antonelli FP, Stroe C (2009) AgreementMaker: efficient matching for large real-world schemas and ontologies. In: Proceedings of the VLDB Endowment, vol 2, pp 1586–1589

Cycorp, Inc (2002) OpenCyc Selected Vocabulary and Upper Ontology. http://www.cyc.com/cycdoc/vocab/upperont-diagram.html, accessed April 12th, 2011.

Cycorp Inc (2011) OpenCyc.org. http://www.opencyc.org/, accessed April 12th, 2011.

Cyganiak R, Jentzsch A (2010) Linking Open Data cloud diagram. http://lod-cloud.net/, accessed April 12th, 2011.

van Dam A (1997) Post-WIMP user interfaces. Commun ACM 40(2):63–67

Daniel F, Matera M (2008) Mashing Up Context-Aware Web Applications: A Component-Based Development Approach. In: WISE '08: Proceedings of the 9th international conference on Web Information Systems Engineering, Springer, LNCS, vol 5175, pp 250–263

Daniel F, Yu J, Benatallah B, Casati F, Matera M, Saint-Paul R (2007) Understanding UI Integration: A Survey of Problems, Technologies, and Opportunities. IEEE Internet Computing 11(3):59–66

Daniel F, Casati F, Benatallah B, Shan MC (2009) Hosted Universal Composition: Models, Languages and Infrastructure in mashArt. In: ER '09: Proceedings of the 28th International Conference on Conceptual Modeling, Springer, pp 428–443

Davies J, Weeks R, Krohn U (2004) QuizRDF: Search Technology for the Semantic Web. Hawaii International Conference on System Sciences 4:40,112

Decker S, Erdmann M, Fensel D, Studer R (1999) Ontobroker: Ontology Based Access to Distributed and Semi-Structured Information. In: Meersman R, Tari Z, Stevens SM (eds) Database Semantics - Semantic Issues in Multimedia Systems, IFIP TC2/WG2.6 Eighth Working Conference on Database Semantics (DS-8), Rotorua, New Zealand, January 4-8, 1999, Kluwer, IFIP Conference Proceedings, vol 138, pp 351–369

Decker S, Park J, Quan D, Sauermann L (eds) (2005) Proceedings of the ISWC 2005 Workshop on The Semantic Desktop - Next Generation Information Management & Collaboration Infrastructure, CEUR-WS, vol 175

Deckers C (2011) The DJ Project Native Swing Website. http://djproject.sourceforge.net/ns/index.html, accessed April 12th, 2011.

Dentler K, Cornet R, ten Teije A, de Keizer N (2011) Comparison of Reasoners for large Ontologies in the OWL 2 EL Profile. Semantic Web - Interoperability, Usability, Applicability 1(1-5)

Desbiens F, Moskovits P, Weckerle P (2010) Oracle WebCenter 11g Handbook: Build Rich, Customizable Enterprise 2.0 Applications. McGraw-Hill Osborne Media

Desiderata Software (2008) EZ JCom. http://www.ezjcom.com/, accessed April 12th, 2011.

Dettborn T, König-Ries B, Welsch M (2008) Using Semantics in Portal Development. In: Proceedings of the 4th International Workshop on Semantic Web Enabled Software Engineering, pp 109–110

Díaz O, Iturrioz J, Irastorza A (2005) Improving portlet interoperability through deep annotation. In: WWW '05: Proceedings of the 14th international conference on World Wide Web, ACM, pp 372–381

Dix A, Hussein T, Lukosch S, Ziegler J (eds) (2010) Proceedings of the First Workshop on Semantic Models for Adaptive Interactive Systems (SEMAIS)

Doan A, Halevy AY (2005) Semantic Integration Research in the Database Community: A Brief Survey. AI Magazine 26(1):83–94

Doerr J, Hartkopf S, Kerkow D, Landmann D, Amthor P (2007) Built-in User Satisfaction - Feature Appraisal and Prioritization with AMUSE. In: 15th IEEE International Requirements Engineering Conference, pp 101 –110

Domingue J, Motta E (1999) A Knowledge-Based News Server Supporting Ontology-Driven Story Enrichment and Knowledge Retrieval. In: EKAW '99: Proceedings of the 11th European Workshop on Knowledge Acquisition, Modeling and Management, Springer, pp 103–120

Dou D, LePendu P (2006) Ontology-based integration for relational databases. In: SAC '06: Proceedings of the 2006 ACM symposium on Applied computing, ACM, pp 461–466

Drabent W (2010) Hybrid Reasoning with Non-monotonic Rules. In: (Aßmann et al, 2010), pp 28–61

Döweling S, Probst F, Ziegert T, Manske K (2009) SoKNOS - An Interactive Visual Emergency Management Framework. In: Amicis RD, Stojanovic R, Conti G (eds) GeoSpatial Visual Analytics, Springer, NATO Science for Peace and Security Series C: Environmental Security, pp 251–262

Dzbor M (2008) Best of Both: Using Semantic Web Technologies to Enrich User Interaction with the Web and Vice Versa. In: Geffert V, Karhumäki J, Bertoni A, Preneel B, Návrat P, Bieliková M (eds) SOFSEM 2008: Theory and Practice of Computer Science, 34th Conference on Current Trends in Theory and Practice of Computer Science, Springer, LNCS, vol 4910, pp 34–49

Eberhart A (2002) Automatic Generation of Java/SQL Based Inference Engines from RDF Schema and RuleML. In: (Horrocks and Hendler, 2002), pp 102–116

Eick SG, Wills GJ (1995) High Interaction Graphics. European Journal of Operational Research 84:445–459

Eisinger N, Maluszynski J (eds) (2005) Reasoning Web, First International Summer School 2005, Msida, Malta, July 25-29, 2005, Tutorial Lectures, LNCS, vol 3564, Springer

Ennals R (2010) Intel Mash Maker: Mashups for the Masses. http://software.intel.com/en-us/articles/intel-mash-maker-mashups-for-the-masses/, accessed April 12th, 2011.

Ennals R, Brewer E, Garofalakis M, Shadle M, Gandhi P (2007) Intel Mash Maker: Join the Web. SIGMOD Record 36:27–33

Ennals RJ, Garofalakis MN (2007) MashMaker: mashups for the masses. In: Proceedings of the 2007 ACM SIGMOD international conference on Management of data, ACM, SIGMOD '07, pp 1116–1118

Erling O, Mikhailov I (2009) RDF Support in the Virtuoso DBMS. In: Pellegrini T, Auer S, Tochtermann K, Schaffert S (eds) Networked Knowledge - Networked Media, Studies in Computational Intelligence, vol 221, Springer, pp 7–24

ESRI Inc (2010) ArcGIS: A Complete Integrated System. http://www.esri.com/software/arcgis/index.html, accessed April 12th, 2011.

ESRI Inc (2011) ArcObjects Java API. http://edndoc.esri.com/arcobjects/9.2/Java/api/arcobjects/, accessed April 12th, 2011.

Euzenat J, Shvaiko P (2007) Ontology Matching. Springer

Euzenat J, Ferrara A, Hollink L, Isaac A, Joslyn C, Malaisé V, Meilicke C, Nikolov A, Pane J, Sabou M, Scharffe F, Shvaiko P, Spiliopoulos V, Stuckenschmidt H, Sváb-Zamazal O, Svátek V, dos Santos CT, Vouros GA, Wang S (2009) Results of the Ontology Alignment Evaluation Initiative 2009. In: Shvaiko P, Euzenat J, Giunchiglia F, Stuckenschmidt H, Noy NF, Rosenthal A (eds) Proceedings of the 4th International Workshop on Ontology Matching (OM-2009), CEUR Workshop Proceedings, vol 551

Euzenat J, Ferrara A, Meilicke C, Pane J, Scharffe F, Shvaiko P, Stuckenschmidt H, Sváb-Zamazal O, Svátek V, Trojahn C (2010) Results of the Ontology Alignment Evaluation Initiative 2010. In: (Shvaiko et al, 2010)

Evans AS (1998) Reasoning with UML class diagrams. In: 2nd IEEE Workshop on Industrial Strength Formal Specification Techniques, pp 102 –113

Feldt KC (2007) Programming Firefox. O'Reilly

Fensel D, Lausen H, Polleres A, de Bruijn J, Stollberg M, Roman D, Domingue J (2007a) Enabling Semantic Web Services. Springer

Fensel D, Lausen H, Polleres A, de Bruijn J, Stollberg M, Roman D, Domingue J (2007b) Introduction to WSMO. In: (Fensel et al, 2007a), chap 5, pp 57–81

Fensel D, Lausen H, Polleres A, de Bruijn J, Stollberg M, Roman D, Domingue J (2007c) WSML - a Language for WSMO. In: (Fensel et al, 2007a), chap 7, pp 83–110

Fernández M, Gómez-Pérez A, Juristo N (1997) METHONTOLOGY: From Ontological Art Towards Ontological Engineering. In: Proceedings of the AAAI97 Spring Symposium, pp 33–40

Finin T (2001) Re: NAME: SWOL versus WOL. http://lists.w3.org/Archives/Public/www-webont-wg/2001Dec/0169.html, accessed April 12th, 2011.

Fischer P, Haddorp H, Stober T (2006) Building Composite Applications and Templates in Web-Sphere Portal V6. http://download.boulder.ibm.com/ibmdl/pub/software/dw/wes/pdf/0608_stober-CompositeApps.pdf, accessed April 12th, 2011.

Fluit C, Sabou M, Harmelen FV (2003) Supporting User Tasks through Visualisation of Light-weight Ontologies. In: Handbook on Ontologies in Information Systems, Springer, pp 415–434

Foundation for Intelligent Phyiscal Agents (2002) FIPA Device Ontology Specification. http://www.fipa.org/specs/fipa00091/index.html, accessed April 12th, 2011.

Fowler M (2003) Patterns of Enterprise Application Architecture. Addison Wesley

Franz Inc (2010) AllegroGraph RDFStore Web 3.0's Database. http://www.franz.com/agraph/allegrograph/, accessed April 12th, 2011.

Friedl J (2006) Mastering Regular Expressions. O'Reilly

Fritz C, Kirschner C, Reker D, Wisplinghoff A, Paulheim H, Probst F (2010) Geospatial Web Mining for Emergency Management. In: GIScience 2010 - Extended Abstracts

Furtado E, Furtado JJV, Silva WB, Rodrigues DWT, da Silva Taddeo L, Limbourg Q, Vanderdonckt J (2002) An Ontology-Based Method for Universal Design of User Interfaces. In: Task Models and Diagrams For User Interface Design (TAMODIA 2002), pp 25–31

Gabrilovich E, Finkelstein L (2001) JNI-C++ Integration Made Easy. C/C++ Users Journal 19:10–21

Gaffar A, Javahery H, Seffah A, Sinnig D (2003) A Pattern Framework for Eliciting and Delivering UCD Knowledge and Practices. In: Proceedings of the Tenth International Conference on Human-Computer Interaction, Lawrence Erlbaum Associates, pp 108–112

Gangemi A, Mika P (2003) Understanding the Semantic Web through Descriptions and Situations. In: On The Move to Meaningful Internet Systems 2003: CoopIS, DOA, and ODBASE, LNCS, vol 2888, Springer, pp 689–706

Gangemi A, Presutti V (2009) Ontology Design Patterns. In: (Staab and Studer, 2009), pp 221–243

Gangemi A, Guarino N, Masolo C, Oltramari A, Schneider L (2002) Sweetening Ontologies with DOLCE. In: Proceedings of the 13th International Conference on Knowledge Engineering and Knowledge Management. Ontologies and the Semantic Web, Springer, pp 166–181

Gangemi A, Borgo S, Catenacci C, Lehmann J (2005) Task Taxonomies for Knowledge Content. http://www.loa-cnr.it/Papers/D07_v21a.pdf, accessed April 12th, 2011.

García-Barriocanal E, Sicilia MA, Sánchez-Alonso S (2005) Usability evaluation of ontology editors. Knowledge Organization 32(1):1–9

Gartner (2007) Gartner Identifies the Top 10 Strategic Technologies for 2008. http://www.gartner.com/it/page.jsp?id=530109, accessed April 12th, 2011.

Gartner (2008) Gartner Identifies the Top 10 Strategic Technologies for 2009. http://www.gartner.com/it/page.jsp?id=777212, accessed April 12th, 2011.

Gašević D, Djurić D, Devedžić V (2006) Model Driven Architecture and Ontolology Development. Springer

Genesereth MR, Fikes RE (1992) Knowledge Interchange Format Version 3.0 Reference Manual. Tech. Rep. Logic-92-1, Stanford University, Computer Science Department, Logic Group

Gennari JH, Musen M, Fergerson RW, Grosso WE, Crubézy M, Eriksson H, Noy NF, Tu SW (2003) The Evolution of Protégé: An Environment for Knowledge-Based System Development. International Journal of Human-Computer Studies 58(1):89–123

Gerber A, van der Merwe A, Barnard A (2008) A Functional Semantic Web Architecture. In: (Bechhofer et al, 2008), pp 273–287

Gómez-Pérez A, Fernández-López M, Corcho O (2004) Ontological Engineering. Advanced Information and Knowledge Processing, Springer

Goessner S (2007) JSONPath - XPath for JSON. http://goessner.net/articles/JsonPath/, accessed April 12th, 2011.

Google Inc (2010) Google Mashup Editor. http://code.google.com/gme/, accessed April 12th, 2011.

Gootzit D, Phifer G, Valdes R, Knipp E (2009) Magic Quadrant for Horizontal Portals. http://www.gartner.com/technology/media-products/reprints/oracle/article95/article95.html, accessed April 12th, 2011.

Goyal S, Westenthaler R (2004) RDF Gravity (RDF Graph Visualization Tool). http://semweb.salzburgresearch.at/apps/rdf-gravity/, accessed April 12th, 2011.

Grammel L, Storey MA (2010) A Survey of Mashup Development Environments. In: Chignell M, Cordy J, Ng J, Yesha Y (eds) The Smart Internet, LNCS, vol 6400, Springer Berlin / Heidelberg, pp 137–151

Grenon P, Smith B, Goldberg L (2004) Biodynamic Ontology: Applying BFO in the Biomedical Domain. In: Pisanelli DM (ed) Ontologies in Medicine, IOS Press, pp 20–38

Gribova V (2007) Automatic Generation of Context-Sensitive Help Using a User Interface Project. In: Gladun VP, Markov KK, Voloshin AF, Ivanova KM (eds) Proceedings of the 8th International Conference "Knowledge-Dialogue-Solution", vol 2, pp 417–422

Griffin E (2008) Foundations of Popfly: Rapid Mashup Development. Apress

Gruber TR (1995) Toward Principles for the Design of Ontologies Used for Knowledge Sharing. International Journal Human-Computer Studies 43(5-6):907–928

Grüninger M, Fox MS (1995) Methodology for the Design and Evaluation of Ontologies. In: IJCAI'95, Workshop on Basic Ontological Issues in Knowledge Sharing, April 13, 1995

Guarino N (ed) (1998) Formal Ontology and Information Systems, IOS Press

Guarino N, Giaretta P (1995) Ontologies and Knowledge Bases: Towards a Terminological Clarification. In: Mars NJI (ed) Towards Very Large Knowledge Bases: Knowledge Building and Knowledge Sharing, IOS Press, Amsterdam, pp 25–32

Guarino N, Welty CA (2009) An Overview of OntoClean. In: (Staab and Studer, 2009), chap 10, pp 201–220

Guarino N, Masolo C, Vetere G (1999) OntoSeek: Content-Based Access to the Web. IEEE Intelligent Systems 14(3):70–80

Guarino N, Smith B, Welty C (eds) (2001) FOIS '01: Proceedings of the international conference on Formal Ontology in Information Systems, ACM

Guerrero-Garcia J, Gonzalez-Calleros JM, Vanderdonckt J, Munoz-Arteaga J (2009) A Theoretical Survey of User Interface Description Languages: Preliminary Results. In: LA-WEB '09: Proceedings of the 2009 Latin American Web Congress (la-web 2009), IEEE Computer Society, pp 36–43

Guruge A (2002) Corporate Portals Empowered with XML and Web Services. Digital Press

Gutierrez-Pulido JR, Garcia-Ruiz MA, Herrera R, Cabello E, Legrand S, Elliman D (2006) Ontology languages for the semantic web: A never completely updated review. Knowledge Based Systems 19(7):489–497

Haarslev V, Möller R (2003) Racer: A Core Inference Engine for the Semantic Web. In: Proceedings of the 2nd International Workshop on Evaluation of Ontology-based Tools (EON2003), pp 27–36

Haase P, Broekstra J, Eberhart A, Volz R (2004) A Comparison of RDF Query Languages. In: McIlraith SA, Plexousakis D, van Harmelen F (eds) The Semantic Web – ISWC 2004, Springer Berlin / Heidelberg, LNCS, vol 3298, pp 502–517

Haase P, Lewen H, Studer R, Tran DT, Erdmann M, d'Aquin M, Motta E (2008) The NeOn Ontology Engineering Toolkit. In: WWW 2008 Developers Track

Handschuh S, Heath T, Thai V (eds) (2009) Workshop on Visual Interfaces to the Social and the Semantic Web (VISSW2009), CEUR-WS, vol 443

Happel HJ, Seedorf S (2006) Applications of Ontologies in Software Engineering. In: Workshop on Semantic Web Enabled Software Engineering (SWESE)

Happel HJ, Korthaus A, Seedorf S, Tomczyk P (2006) KOntoR: An Ontology-enabled Approach to Software Reuse. In: Zhang K, Spanoudakis G, Visaggio G (eds) Proceedings of the Eighteenth International Conference on Software Engineering & Knowledge Engineering (SEKE), pp 349–354

Harris S, Gibbins N (2003) 3Store: Efficient Bulk RDF Storage. In: Volz R, Decker S, Cruz IF (eds) First International Workshop on Pracitical and Scalable Semantic Systems, CEUR Workshop Proceedings, vol 89

Harris S, Shadbolt N (2005) SPARQL Query Processing with Conventional Relational Database Systems. In: Dean M, Guo Y, Jun W, Kaschek R, Krishnaswamy S, Pan Z, Sheng QZ (eds) Web Information Systems Engineering - WISE 2005 Workshops, Springer, LNCS, vol 3807, pp 235–244

Harth A (2010) VisiNav: A system for visual search and navigation on web data. Web Semantics: Science, Services and Agents on the World Wide Web 8(4):348 – 354

Hasselbring W (2000) Information System Integration. Communications of the ACM 43(6):32–38

Hastrup T, Cyganiak R, Bojars U (2008) Browsing Linked Data with Fenfire. In: (Bizer et al, 2008)

Hawke S (2010) From JSON to RDF in Six Easy Steps with JRON. http://decentralyze.com/2010/06/04/from-json-to-rdf-in-six-easy-steps-with-jron/, accessed April 12th, 2011.

Hawkey K, Kellar M, Reilly D, Whalen T, Inkpen KM (2005) The Proximity Factor: Impact of Distance on Co-located Collaboration. In: Proceedings of the 2005 international ACM SIGGROUP conference on Supporting group work, ACM, GROUP '05, pp 31–40

van Heijst G, Schreiber ATG, Wielinga BJ (1997) Using Explicit Ontologies in KBS Development. International Journal of Human-Computer Studies 46(2-3):183–292

Heim P, Ziegler J, Lohmann S (2008) gFacet: A Browser for the Web of Data. In: Auer S, Dietzold S, Lohmann S, Ziegler J (eds) Proceedings of the International Workshop on Interacting with Multimedia Content in the Social Semantic Web (IMC-SSW'08), CEUR WS, vol 417, pp 49–58

Henninger S, Keshk M, Kinworthy R (2003) Capturing and Disseminating Usability Patterns with Semantic Web Technology. In: CHI 2003 Workshop: Concepts and Perspectives on HCI Patterns

Hepp M (2007) Ontologies: State of the Art, Business Potential, and Grand Challenges. In: Hepp M, Leenheer PD, de Moorand York Sure A (eds) Ontology Management: Semantic Web, Semantic Web Services, and Business Applications, Springer, chap 1, pp 3–22

Hepp M, Leenheer PD, Moor AD, Sure Y (eds) (2008) Ontology Management, Semantic Web and Beyond, vol 7. Springer

Heppner S (2008) JSR 286: Portlet Specification 2.0. http://www.jcp.org/en/jsr/detail?id=286, accessed April 12th, 2011.

Herman I, Melançon G, Marshall MS (2000) Graph Visualization and Navigation in Information Visualization: A Survey. IEEE Transactions on Visualization and Computer Graphics 6(1):24–43

Herre H (2009) General Formal Ontology (GFO) : A Foundational Ontology for Conceptual Modelling. In: Poli R, Obrst L (eds) Theory and Applications of Ontology, vol 2, Springer

Hesse W (2005) Ontologies in the Software Engineering Process. In: Lenz R, Hasenkamp U, Hasselbring W, Reichert M (eds) Proceedings of the 2nd GI-Workshop on Enterprise Application Integration (EAI), CEUR-WS.org, CEUR Workshop Proceedings, vol 141

Heymans S, Ma L, Anicic D, Zhilei M, Steinmetz N, Pan Y, Mei J, Fokoue A, Kalyanpur A, Kershenbaum A, Schonberg E, Srinivas K, Feier C, Hench G, Wetzstein B, Keller U (2008) Ontology Reasoning with Large Data Repositories. In: (Hepp et al, 2008), chap 4, pp 89–128

Hildebrand M, van Ossenbruggen J (2009) Configuring Semantic Web Interfaces by Data Mapping. In: (Handschuh et al, 2009)

Hillairet G, Bertrand F, Lafaye JY (2008) Bridging EMF applications and RDF data sources. In: Kendall EF, Pan JZ, Sabbouh M, Stojanovic L, Bontcheva K (eds) Proceedings of the 4th International Workshop on Semantic Web Enabled Software Engineering (SWESE)

Hirsch C, Hosking J, Grundy J (2009) Interactive Visualization Tools for Exploring the Semantic Graph of Large Knowledge Spaces. In: (Handschuh et al, 2009)

Horrocks I, Hendler JA (eds) (2002) The Semantic Web - ISWC 2002, LNCS, vol 2342, Springer

Hoyer V, Fischer M (2008) Market Overview of Enterprise Mashup Tools. In: ICSOC '08: Proceedings of the 6th International Conference on Service-Oriented Computing, Springer, pp 708–721

Hussein T, Münter D (2010) Automated Generation of Faceted Navigation Interfaces Using Semantic Models. In: (Dix et al, 2010)

Huynh D, Mazzocchi S, Karger DR (2005) Piggy Bank: Experience the Semantic Web Inside Your Web Browser. In: Gil Y, Motta E, Benjamins VR, Musen MA (eds) International Semantic Web Conference, Springer, LNCS, vol 3729, pp 413–430

Hyvönen E, Styrman A, Saarela S (2002) Ontology-Based Image Retrieval. In: Hyvönen E, Klemettinen M (eds) Towards the semantic Web and Web services. Proceedings of the XML Finland 2002 Conference, HIIT Publications, pp 15–27

IBM Corporation (2008) IBM Web Portal software from WebSphere. http://www.ibm.com/websphere/portal, accessed April 12th, 2011.

IBM Corporation (2010) IBM Enterprise Mashups - IBM Mashup Center. http://www.ibm.com/software/info/mashup-center/, accessed April 12th, 2011.

Igarashi T, Zeleznik B (2007) Sketch-Based Interaction. IEEE Computer Graphics and Applications 27(1):26–27

Intel Corporation (2007) Extractors in Intel Mash Maker. http://software.intel.com/en-us/articles/extractors-in-intel-mash-maker/, accessed May 3rd, 2011.

International Organization for Standardization (ISO) (1996) ISO/IEC 14977: Information technology – Syntactic metalanguage – Extended BNF. http://www.iso.org/iso/iso_catalogue/catalogue_tc/catalogue_detail.htm?csnumber=26153, accessed April 12th, 2011.

JackBe Corporation (2011) Presto: The Real-Time Intelligence Solution. http://www.jackbe.com/products/, accessed April 12th, 2011.

Jay R (2008) SAP NetWeaver Portal Technology: The Complete Reference. McGraw-Hill Osborne Media

JBoss Community (2011) GateIn Portal. http://www.jboss.org/gatein/, accessed April 12th, 2011.

Jean-Mary YR, Shironoshita EP, Kabuka MR (2009) Ontology Matching with Semantic Verification. Web Semantics: Science, Services and Agents on the World Wide Web 7(3):235–251

JGraph (2011) JavaScript and Java Diagram Library Components. http://www.jgraph.com/, accessed April 12th, 2011.

Jin Z, Hongqiao Z, Zhuoning C, Xiaoguang Y (2009) A Framework for Supporting Business, Data and User Interface Integration between Multiple CAD and PDM Systems. In: International Conference on Measuring Technology and Mechatronics Automation, IEEE, vol 2, pp 3 –7

Junghans M, Agarwal S, Studer R (2010) Towards Practical Semantic Web Service Discovery. In: (Aroyo et al, 2010), pp 15–29

Kagal L, Finin T, Joshi A (2003) A policy language for a pervasive computing environment. In: Proceedings of the IEEE 4th International Workshop on Policies for Distributed Systems and Networks.

Kalfoglou Y, Schorlemmer M (2005) Ontology Mapping: The State of the Art. In: Kalfoglou Y, Schorlemmer M, Sheth A, Staab S, Uschold M (eds) Semantic Interoperability and Integration, Internationales Begegnungs- und Forschungszentrum für Informatik (IBFI), Schloss Dagstuhl, Germany, no. 04391 in Dagstuhl Seminar Proceedings

Kaljurand K, Fuchs NE (2007) Verbalizing OWL in Attempto Controlled English. In: Golbreich C, Kalyanpur A, Parsia B (eds) Proceedings of the OWLED 2007 Workshop on OWL: Experiences and Directions, Innsbruck, Austria, June 6-7, 2007, CEUR WS, vol 258

Kalyanpur A, Pastor DJ, Battle S, Padget JA (2004) Automatic Mapping of OWL Ontologies into Java. In: Maurer F, Ruhe G (eds) Proceedings of the Sixteenth International Conference on Software Engineering & Knowledge Engineering (SEKE'2004), Banff, Alberta, Canada, June 20-24, 2004, pp 98–103

Kalyanpur A, Parsia B, Sirin E, Grau BC, Hendler J (2006) Swoop: A Web Ontology Editing Browser. Journal of Web Semantics 4(2):144–153

Karim S, Tjoa AM (2006) Towards the Use of Ontologies for Improving User Interaction for People with Special Needs. In: Miesenberger K, Klaus J, Zagler WL, Karshmer AI (eds) 10th International Conference on Computers Helping People with Special Needs (ICCHP), Springer, LNCS, vol 4061, pp 77–84

Katifori A, Halatsis C, Lepouras G, Vassilakis C, Giannopoulou EG (2007) Ontology Visualization Methods - A Survey. ACM Comput Surv 39(4)

Kiryakov A, Simov KI, Dimitrov M (2001) OntoMap: Portal for Upper-Level-Ontologies. In: (Guarino et al, 2001), pp 47–58

Kiryakov A, Ognyanov D, Manov D (2005) OWLIM - a Pragmatic Semantic Repository for OWL. In: Proceedings of the International Workshop on Scalable Semantic Web Knowledge Base Systems (SSWS 2005), LNCS, vol 3807, pp 182–192

Knight A, Dai N (2002) Objects and the Web. IEEE Software 19(2):51–59

Knipp E, Valdes R, Bradley A (2009) Open Mashup Alliance Needs More Support to Create Standardization. http://www.gartner.com/DisplayDocument?doc_cd=171619, accessed April 12th, 2011.

Kobilarov G, Dickinson I (2008) Humboldt: Exploring Linked Data. In: (Bizer et al, 2008)

Kodaganallur V (2004) Incorporating Language Processing into Java Applications: A JavaCC Tutorial. IEEE Software 21:70–77

Kohlhase A, Kohlhase M (2009) Semantic Transparency in User Assistance Systems. In: Proceedings of the 27th annual ACM international conference on Design of Communication. Special Interest Group on Design of Communication (SIGDOC-09), Bloomingtion,, IN, United States, ACM Special Interest Group for Design of Communication, ACM Press, pp 89–96

Korpipää P, Häkkilä J, Kela J, Ronkainen S, Känsälä I (2004) Utilising context ontology in mobile device application personalisation. In: MUM '04: Proceedings of the 3rd international conference on Mobile and ubiquitous multimedia, ACM, pp 133–140

Kotsalis D (2009) Managing Non-Native Widgets in Model-Based UI Engineering. In: (Calvary et al, 2009), pp 313–316

Laahs K, McKenna E, Vickers D (2001) Microsoft SharePoint Portal Server: Building Knowledge Sharing Applications. Digital Press

Lanzenberger M, Sampson J, Rester M (2009) Visualization in Ontology Tools. In: Complex, Intelligent and Software Intensive Systems, International Conference, IEEE Computer Society, pp 705–711

Larsson A, Ingmarsson M, Sun B (2007) A Development Platform for Distributed User Interfaces. In: Proceedings of the Nineteenth International Conference on Software Engineering & Knowledge Engineering (SEKE'2007), Boston, Massachusetts, USA, July 9-11, 2007, Knowledge Systems Institute Graduate School, pp 704–709

Lassila O, McGuinness D (2001) The Role of Frame-Based Representation on the Semantic Web. Linköping Electronic Articles in Computer and Information Science 6(5)

Laszlo Systems (2006) OpenLaszlo - An Open Architecture Framework for Advanced Ajax Applications. http://www.openlaszlo.org/whitepaper/LaszloWhitePaper.pdf, accessed April 12th, 2011.

Laugwitz B, Held T, Schrepp M (2008) Construction and Evaluation of a User Experience Questionnaire. In: Holzinger A (ed) HCI and Usability for Education and Work, 4th Symposium of the Workgroup Human-Computer Interaction and Usability Engineering of the Austrian Computer Society (USAB 2008), Springer, LNCS, vol 5298, pp 63–76

Lawson JY (2008) OpenInterface Platform - Description Languages Specification. https://forge.openinterface.org/frs/download.php/75/DL_spec.pdf, accessed April 12th, 2011.

Lawson JYL, Al-Akkad AA, Vanderdonckt J, Macq B (2009) An Open Source Workbench for Prototyping Multimodal Interactions Based on Off-The-Shelf Heterogeneous Components. In: (Calvary et al, 2009), pp 245–254

Lee A (2010) Exploiting Context for Mobile User Experience. In: (Dix et al, 2010)

Lee C, Park S, Lee D, won Lee J, Jeong OR, goo Lee S (2008) A Comparison of Ontology Reasoning Systems Using Query Sequences. In: ICUIMC '08: Proceedings of the 2nd international conference on Ubiquitous information management and communication, ACM, pp 543–546

Lee R (2004) Scalability Report on Triple Store Applications. http://simile.mit.edu/reports/stores/stores.pdf, accessed April 12th, 2011.

Lei Y, Motta E, Domingue J (2003) Design of customized web applications with OntoWeaver. In: K-CAP '03: Proceedings of the 2nd international conference on Knowledge capture, ACM, pp 54–61

Lenat DB (1995) CYC: a Large-Scale Investment in Knowledge Infrastructure. Communications of the ACM 38(11):33–38

Ley M (2009) DBLP - Some Lessons Learned. In: Proceedings of the Very Large Data Bases (VLDB) Endowment, vol 2, pp 1493–1500

Li J, Tang J, Li Y, Luo Q (2009) RiMOM: A Dynamic Multistrategy Ontology Alignment Framework. IEEE Transactions on Knowledge and Data Engineering 21(8):1218–1232

Lieberman H, Paternò F, Klann M, Wulf V (2006) End-User Development: An Emerging Paradigm. In: Lieberman H, Paternò F, Wulf V (eds) End User Development, Human-Computer Interaction Series, vol 9, Springer, pp 1–8

Limbourg Q, Vanderdonckt J, Michotte B, Bouillon L, Florins M, Trevisan D (2004) USIXML: A User Interface Description Language for Context-Sensitive User Interfaces. In: Developing User Interfaces with XML: Advances on User Interface Description Languages, pp 55–62

Linthicum DS (1999) Enterprise Application Integration. Addison Wesley

Liu B, Hu B (2005) An Evaluation of RDF Storage Systems for Large Data Applications. In: International Conference on Semantics, Knowledge and Grid, IEEE Computer Society, pp 59–61

Liu B, Chen H, He W (2005) Deriving User Interface from Ontologies: A Model-Based Approach. In: ICTAI '05: Proceedings of the 17th IEEE International Conference on Tools with Artificial Intelligence, IEEE Computer Society, pp 254–259

Liu X, Hui Y, Sun W, Liang H (2007) Towards Service Composition based on Mashups. In: IEEE Congress on Services, pp 332–339

Lohmann S, Heim P, Stegemann T, Ziegler J (2010) The RelFinder User Interface: Interactive Exploration of Relationships between Objects of Interest. In: IUI '10: Proceeding of the 14th international conference on Intelligent user interfaces, ACM, pp 421–422

Luo S, Wang Y, Guo J (2009) Research on Ontology-Based Usable User Interface Layout Approach. In: IEEE International Conference on Intelligent Computing and Intelligent Systems, 2009. ICIS 2009., vol 1, pp 234–238

Luther M, Liebig T, Böhm S, Noppens O (2009) Who the Heck is the Father of Bob? In: (Aroyo et al, 2009), pp 66–80

Lutz C (2002) Reasoning about Entity Relationship Diagrams with Complex Attribute Dependencies. In: Proceedings of the International Workshop in Description Logics 2002 (DL2002), no. 53 in CEUR WS, pp 185–194

Mascardi V, Cordì V, Rosso P (2007) A Comparison of Upper Ontologies. In: Baldoni M, Boccalatte A, Paoli FD, Martelli M, Mascardi V (eds) 8th AI*IA/TABOO Joint Workshop "From Objects to Agents" (WOA), Seneca Edizioni Torino, pp 55–64

Masolo C, Borgo S, Gangemi A, Guarino N, Oltramari A (2003) WonderWeb Deliverable D18 – Ontology Library (final). http://wonderweb.semanticweb.org/deliverables/documents/D18.pdf, accessed April 12th, 2011.

Matuszek C, Cabral J, Witbrock M, Deoliveira J (2006) An introduction to the syntax and content of Cyc. In: Proceedings of the 2006 AAAI Spring Symposium on Formalizing and Compiling Background Knowledge and Its Applications to Knowledge Representation and Question Answering, pp 44–49

Maximilien EM, Singh MP (2004) A Framework and Ontology for Dynamic Web Services Selection. IEEE Internet Computing 8(5):84–93

Meijer E, Beckman B, Bierman G (2006) LINQ: Reconciling Objects, Relations and XML in the .NET Framework. In: Proceedings of the 2006 ACM SIGMOD International Conference on Management of Data, p 706

Mendes PN, McKnight B, Sheth AP, Kissinger JC (2008) TcruziKB: Enabling Complex Queries for Genomic Data Exploration. In: ICSC '08: Proceedings of the 2008 IEEE International Conference on Semantic Computing, IEEE Computer Society, pp 432–439

Microsoft Corporation (2005) Smart Client - Composite UI Application Block. http://msdn.microsoft.com/en-us/library/ff648747.aspx, accessed April 12th, 2011.

Microsoft Corporation (2010a) Prism (Composite Client Application Guidance). http://msdn.microsoft.com/en-us/library/ff648465.aspx, accessed April 12th, 2011.

Microsoft Corporation (2010b) SharePoint 2010 - the Business Collaboration Platform for the Enterprise and the Internet. http://sharepoint.microsoft.com/, accessed April 12th, 2011.

Microsoft Corporation (2011a) COM: Component Object Model Technologies. http://www.microsoft.com/com/default.mspx, accessed April 12th, 2011.

Microsoft Corporation (2011b) The Official Microsoft Silverlight Site. http://www.silverlight.net/, accessed April 12th, 2011..

Microsoft Corporation (2011c) XAML Overview (WPF). http://msdn.microsoft.com/en-us/library/ms752059.aspx, accessed April 12th, 2011.

Miller GA (1995) WordNet: a lexical database for English. Commununications of the ACM 38(11):39–41

Miller RB (1968) Response time in man-computer conversational transactions. In: AFIPS '68: Proceedings of the Fall Joint Computer Conference, Part I, ACM, pp 267–277

Mirizzi R, Ragone A, Noia TD, Sciascio ED (2010) Semantic Wonder Cloud: Exploratory Search in DBpedia. In: Daniel F, Facca FM (eds) Current Trends in Web Engineering - 10th International Conference on Web Engineering ICWE 2010 Workshops, Springer, LNCS, vol 6385, pp 138–149

Mizoguchi R, Kozaki K (2009) Ontology Engineering Environments. In: (Staab and Studer, 2009), pp 315–336

Möller K, Heath T, Handschuh S, Domingue J (2007) Recipes for Semantic Web Dog Food - The ESWC and ISWC Metadata Projects. In: Aberer K, Choi KS, Noy N, Allemang D, Lee KI, Nixon L, Golbeck J, Mika P, Maynard D, Mizoguchi R, Schreiber G, Cudré-Mauroux P (eds) The Semantic Web, Springer Berlin / Heidelberg, LNCS, vol 4825, pp 802–815

Möller R, Haarslev V (2009) Tableau-based Reasoning. In: (Staab and Studer, 2009), pp 509–528

Moore MM, Rugaber S, Seaver P (1994) Knowledge-Based User Interface Migration. In: ICSM '94: Proceedings of the International Conference on Software Maintenance, IEEE Computer Society, pp 72–79

Motik B (2009) Resolution-Based Reasoning for Ontologies. In: (Staab and Studer, 2009), pp 529–550

Motik B, Sattler U (2006) A Comparison of Reasoning Techniques for Querying Large Description Logic ABoxes. In: Hermann M, Voronkov A (eds) Logic for Programming, Artificial Intelligence, and Reasoning, LNCS, vol 4246, Springer Berlin / Heidelberg, pp 227–241

Motik B, Horrocks I, Rosati R, Sattler U (2006) Can OWL and Logic Programming Live Together Happily Ever After? In: Cruz IF, Decker S, Allemang D, Preist C, Schwabe D, Mika P, Uschold M, Aroyo L (eds) The Semantic Web - ISWC 2006, Springer, LNCS, vol 4273, pp 501–514

Motik B, Shearer R, Horrocks I (2009) Hypertableau Reasoning for Description Logics. Journal of Artificial Intelligence Research 36:165–228

Mozilla (2011a) Gecko. https://developer.mozilla.org/en/Gecko, accessed April 12th, 2011.

Mozilla (2011b) XUL. https://developer.mozilla.org/en/XUL, accessed April 12th, 2011.

Murth M, Kühn E (2009) Knowledge-based coordination with a reliable semantic subscription mechanism. In: SAC '09: Proceedings of the 2009 ACM symposium on Applied Computing, ACM, pp 1374–1380

Murugesan S (2007) Understanding Web 2.0. IT Professional 9:34–41

Myers BA, Rosson MB (1992) Survey on user interface programming. In: CHI '92: Proceedings of the SIGCHI conference on Human factors in computing systems, ACM, pp 195–202

Naur P, Randell B (1968) Software Engineering: Report of a conference sponsored by the NATO Science Committee, Garmisch, Germany, 7-11 Oct. 1968, Brussels, Scientific Affairs Division, NATO

Nazarian R (2009) Von Türstehern und Torwächtern - Marktübersicht Portlet-Technologien. JavaSpektrum 1:26–29

java net (2006) JFlash Website. https://jflash.dev.java.net/, accessed April 12th, 2011.

java net (2008) JDIC - JDesktop Integration Components Website. https://jdic.dev.java.net/, accessed April 12th, 2011.

Niles I, Pease A (2001) Towards a Standard Upper Ontology. In: (Guarino et al, 2001), pp 2–9

Niles I, Terry A (2004) The MILO: A general-purpose, mid-level ontology. In: International conference on information and knowledge engineering (IKE'04), pp 15–19

Nilsson EG, Nordhagen EK, Oftedal G (1990) Aspects of systems integration. In: ISCI '90: Proceedings of the first international conference on systems integration on Systems integration '90, IEEE Press, pp 434–443

North C, Shneiderman B (2000) Snap-together visualization: a user interface for coordinating visualizations via relational schemata. In: AVI '00: Proceedings of the working conference on Advanced visual interfaces, ACM, pp 128–135

Nottingham M, Sayre R (2005) RFC 4287 - The Atom Syndication Format. http://tools.ietf.org/html/rfc4287, accessed April 12th, 2011.

Noy NF (2004) Semantic Integration: A Survey Of Ontology-Based Approaches. SIGMOD Rec 33(4):65–70

OASIS (2007) Web Services Business Process Execution Language Version 2.0. http://docs.oasis-open.org/wsbpel/2.0/OS/wsbpel-v2.0-OS.html, accessed April 12th, 2011.

OASIS (2009) User Interface Markup Language (UIML) Version 4.0. http://docs.oasis-open.org/uiml/v4.0/uiml-4.0.html, accessed April 12th, 2011. Page numbers follow the PDF version: http://docs.oasis-open.org/uiml/v4.0/cs01/uiml-4.0-cs01.pdf

Oberle D, Lamparter S, Grimm S, Vrandečić D, Staab S, Gangemi A (2006) Towards Ontologies for Formalizing Modularization and Communication in Large Software Systems. Applied Ontology 1(2):163–202

Oberle D, Grimm S, Staab S (2009) An Ontology for Software. In: (Staab and Studer, 2009), chap 18, pp 383–402

Ogrinz M (2009) Mashup Patterns - Designs and Examples for the Modern Enterprise. Addison-Wesley

OMG (2003) MDA Guide Version 1.0.1. http://www.omg.org/cgi-bin/doc?omg/03-06-01.pdf, accessed April 12th, 2011.

ontoprise GmbH (2011a) OntoBroker Website. http://www.ontoprise.de/en/products/ontobroker/, accessed April 12th, 2011.

ontoprise GmbH (2011b) ontoprise:OntoStudio. http://www.ontoprise.de/en/products/ontostudio/, accessed April 12th, 2011.

Open Mashup Alliance (2009) EMML Changes Everything: Profitability, Predictability & Performance through Enterprise Mashups. http://openmashup.org/whitepaper/docs/oma_whitepaper_120309.pdf, accessed April 12th, 2011.

openRDF (2009) ELMO. http://www.openrdf.org/doc/elmo/1.5/, accessed April 12th, 2011.

Oracle Corporation (2010) Drag and Drop Subsystem for the Java 2 Platform Standard Edition 5.0. http://java.sun.com/javase/6/docs/technotes/guides/dragndrop/spec/dnd1.html, accessed April 12th, 2011.

Oracle Corporation (2011) Oracle WebLogic Portal. http://www.oracle.com/us/products/middleware/user-interaction/059320.html, accessed April 12th, 2011.

Oren E, Delbru R, Gerke S, Haller A, Decker S (2007) ActiveRDF: object-oriented semantic web programming. In: (Williamson et al, 2007), pp 817–824

json org (2011) Introducing JSON. http://www.json.org/, accessed April 12th, 2011.

Pajntar B, Grobelnik M (2008) SearchPoint - a New Paradigm of Web Search. In: WWW 2008 Developers Track

Parallels Holdings Ltd (2011) Parallels Desktop 6 for Mac. http://www.parallels.com/products/desktop/, accessed April 12th, 2011.

Parnas DL (1972) On the criteria to be used in decomposing systems into modules. Commun ACM 15(12):1053–1058

Parreiras FS, Saathoff C, Walter T, Franz T, Staab S (2009) APIs à gogo: Automatic Generation of Ontology APIs. In: Proceedings of the International Conference on Semantic Computing, IEEE Computer Society, pp 342–348

Paschke A, Kozlenkov A, Boley H (2007) A Homogenous Reaction Rules Language for Complex Event Processing. In: 2nd International Workshop on Event Driven Architecture and Event Processing Systems (EDA-PS 2007)

Paternò F, Santoro C, Mäntyjärvi J, Mori G, Sansone S (2008a) Authoring Pervasive Multimodal User Interfaces. International Journal on Web Engineering and Technology 4(2):235–261

Paternò F, Santoro C, Spano LD (2008b) XML Languages for User Interface Models - Deliverable D2.1 of the ServFace Project. http://www.servface.org/index.php?option=com_docman&task=doc_download&gid=5&Itemid=61, accessed April 12th, 2011.

Paternò F, Santoro C, Spano LD (2009) MARIA: A Universal, Declarative, Multiple Abstraction-Level Language for Service-Oriented Applications in Ubiquitous Environments. ACM Transactions on Computer-Human Interaction 16(4):1–30

Paternò F, Mancini C, Meniconi S (1997) ConcurTaskTrees: A Diagrammatic Notation for Specifying Task Models. In: INTERACT '97: Proceedings of the IFIP TC13 Interantional Conference on Human-Computer Interaction, Chapman & Hall, Ltd., pp 362–369

Paton NW, Stevens R, Baker P, Goble CA, Bechhofer S, Brass A (1999) Query processing in the TAMBIS bioinformatics source integration system. In: Eleventh International Conference on Scientific and Statistical Database Management, pp 138–147

Paulheim H (2010a) Efficient Semantic Event Processing: Lessons Learned in User Interface Integration. In: (Aroyo et al, 2010), pp 60–74

Paulheim H (2010b) Seamlessly Integrated, but Loosely Coupled - Building UIs from Heterogeneous Components. In: ASE '10: Proceedings of the IEEE/ACM International Conference on Automated Software Engineering, ACM, pp 123–126

Paulheim H (2011) Improving the Usability of Integrated Applications by Using Visualizations of Linked Data. In: Proceedings of the International Conference on Web Intelligence, Mining and Semantics (WIMS'11), ACM

Paulheim H, Erdogan A (2010) Seamless Integration of Heterogeneous UI Components. In: (Sukaviriya et al, 2010), pp 303–308

Paulheim H, Probst F (2010a) Application Integration on the User Interface Level: an Ontology-Based Approach. Data & Knowledge Engineering Journal 69(11):1103–1116

Paulheim H, Probst F (2010b) Improving UI Integration with Formal Semantics. In: (Dix et al, 2010)

Paulheim H, Probst F (2010c) Ontology-Enhanced User Interfaces: A Survey. International Journal on Semantic Web and Information Systems 6(2):36–59

Paulheim H, Probst F (2011) A Formal Ontology on User Interfaces – Yet Another User Interface Description Language? In: Hussein T, Lukosch S, Paulheim H, Ziegler J, Calvary G (eds) Proceedings of the Second Workshop on Semantic Models for Adaptive Interactive Systems (SEMAIS), to appear

Paulheim H, Döweling S, Tso-Sutter K, Probst F, Ziegert T (2009) Improving Usability of Integrated Emergency Response Systems: The SoKNOS Approach. In: Proceedings "39. Jahrestagung der Gesellschaft für Informatik e.V. (GI) - Informatik 2009", LNI, vol 154, pp 1435–1449

Paulheim H, Fengel J, Rebstock M (2011a) Context-Sensitive Semantic Synchronization Enablement in Electronic Negotiations. Group Decision and Negotiation To appear.

Paulheim H, Plendl R, Probst F, Oberle D (2011b) Mapping Pragmatic Class Models to Reference Ontologies. In: The 2011 IEEE 27th International Conference on Data Engineering Workshops - 2nd International Workshop on Data Engineering meets the Semantic Web (DESWeb), pp 200–205

Pease A (2011) Suggested Upper Merged Ontology (SUMO). http://www.ontologyportal.org/, accessed April 12th, 2011.

Peng Z, Chen H, Rao J, Liu Y, Wang L, Chen J (2010) Semantic-based Mobile Mashup Platform. In: (Polleres and Chen, 2010)

Pietschmann S (2009) A Model-Driven Development Process and Runtime Platform for Adaptive Composite Web Applications. International Journal On Advances in Internet Technology 2(4):277–288

Pietschmann S, Voigt M, Meißner K (2009a) Dynamic Composition of Service-Oriented Web User Interfaces. In: Proceedings of the 4th International Conference on Internet and Web Applications and Services (ICIW 2009), IEEE, pp 217–222

Pietschmann S, Voigt M, Rümpel A, Meißner K (2009b) CRUISe: Composition of Rich User Interface Services. In: Gaedke M, Grossniklaus M, Díaz O (eds) Proceedings of the 9th International Conference on Web Engineering (ICWE 2009), Springer, LNCS, vol 5648, pp 473–476

Platt DS (2008) Programming Microsoft Composite Application Block and Smart Client Software. Microsoft Press

Polleres A, Chen H (eds) (2010) Proceedings of the ISWC 2010 Posters & Demonstrations Track: Collected Abstracts, CEUR-WS, vol 658

Potter R, Wright H (2006) An Ontological Approach to Visualization Resource Management. In: Doherty GJ, Blandford A (eds) Interactive Systems. Design, Specification, and Verification, 13th International Workshop, DSVIS 2006, Dublin, Ireland, July 26-28, 2006. Revised Papers, Springer, LNCS, vol 4323, pp 151–156

Probst F, Ziegert T (2010) SoKNOS Deliverable D1.10 - Ausführliche SoKNOS Dokumentation

Protégé Community of Practice (2010) SWRLEditor FAQ. http://protege.cim3.net/cgi-bin/wiki.pl?SWRLEditorFAQ, accessed May 4th, 2011.

Puerta A, Eisenstein J (2001) XIML: A Universal Language for User Interfaces. http://www.ximl.org/documents/XimlWhitePaper.pdf, accessed April 12th, 2011.

Puerta A, Eisenstein J (2002) XIML: a common representation for interaction data. In: IUI '02: Proceedings of the 7th international conference on Intelligent user interfaces, ACM, pp 214–215

Puleston C, Parsia B, Cunningham J, Rector A (2008) Integrating Object-Oriented and Ontological Representations: A Case Study in Java and OWL. In: (Sheth et al, 2008), pp 130–145

Quasthoff M, Meinel C (2009) Design Pattern for Object Triple Mapping. In: 2009 IEEE International Conference on Services Computing (SCC 2009), 21-25 September 2009, Bangalore, India, IEEE Computer Society, pp 443–450

Rafatirad S, Gupta A, Jain R (2009) Event composition operators: ECO. In: EiMM '09: Proceedings of the 1st ACM international workshop on Events in multimedia, ACM, pp 65–72

Rao R (2009) JBoss Portal Server Development. Packt Publishing

Rauschmayer A (2005) Semantic-Web-Backed GUI Applications. In: Proceedings of the ISWC 2005 Workshop on End User Semantic Web Interaction

Rebstock M, Fengel J, Paulheim H (2008) Ontologies-based Business Integration. Springer

Red Hat, Inc (2011) Cygwin Information and Installation. http://www.cygwin.com/, accessed April 12th, 2011.

RedWhale Software (2000) The XIML Specification. Available as part of the XIML Starter Kit version 1, available at http://www.ximl.org/download/step1.asp, accessed April 12th, 2011.

Reed S (2007) Semantic Annotation for Persistence. In: Proceedings of AAAI2007's Workshop on Semantic e-Science

Ross PE (2005) 5 Commandments. IEEE Spectrum 40(12):30–35

RSS Advisory Board (2009) RSS 2.0 Specification (version 2.0.11). http://www.rssboard.org/rss-specification, accessed April 12th, 2011.

Rubel D (2006) The Heart of Eclipse. ACM Queue 4(8):36–44

Ruiz F, Hilera JR (2006) Using Ontologies in Software Engineering and Technology. In: (Calero et al, 2006), chap 2, pp 49–102

Russell S, Norvig P (2010) Artificial Intelligence: A Modern Approach, 3rd edn. Pearson Education

Rutledge L, mc schraefel, Bernstein A, Degler D (eds) (2006) Procedings of the The 3rd International Semantic Web User Interaction Workshop (SWUI06) Workshop

Sahoo SS, Halb W, Hellmann S, Idehen K, Jr TT, Auer S, Sequeda J, Ezzat A (2009) A Survey of Current Approaches for Mapping of Relational Databases to RDF. http://www.w3.org/2005/Incubator/rdb2rdf/RDB2RDF_SurveyReport.pdf, accessed April 12th, 2011.

SAP AG (2011) SAP - Components & Tools of SAP Netweaver: SAP Netweaver Portal. http://www.sap.com/platform/netweaver/components/portal/index.epx, accessed April 12th, 2011.

Sauermann L, Bernardi A, Dengel A (2005) Overview and Outlook on the Semantic Desktop. In: (Decker et al, 2005)

Saxon S (2003) XPath Querying Over Objects with ObjectXPathNavigator. http://msdn.microsoft.com/en-us/library/ms950764.aspx, accessed April 12th, 2011.

Scerri S, Davis B, Handschuh S, Hauswirth M (2009) Semanta - Semantic Email Made Easy. In: (Aroyo et al, 2009), pp 36–50

Schefström D (1999) System Development Environments: Contemporary Concepts. In: Schefström D, van den Broek G (eds) Tool Integration - Environments and Frameworks, John Wiley & Sons Ltd.

Scheifler RW, Gettys J (1986) The X Window System. ACM Transactions on Graphics 5(2):79–109

Schmidt B, Stoitsev T, Mühlhäuser M (2010) Activity-centric Support for Weakly-structured Business Processes. In: (Sukaviriya et al, 2010), pp 251–260

Schmidt KU, Anicic D, Stühmer R (2008a) Event-driven Reactivity: A Survey and Requirements Analysis. In: Proceedings of the 3rd International Workshop on Semantic Business Process Management

Schmidt KU, Dörflinger J, Rahmani T, Sahbi M, Stojanovicand L, Thomas SM (2008b) An User Interface Adaptation Architecture for Rich Internet Applications. In: (Bechhofer et al, 2008), pp 736–750

Schmitt N, Niepert M, Stuckenschmidt H (2010) BRAMBLE: A Web-based Framework for Interactive RDF-Graph Visualisation. In: (Polleres and Chen, 2010)

mc schraefel, Karger D (2006) The Pathetic Fallacy of RDF. In: (Rutledge et al, 2006)

Seaborne A, Steer D, Williams S (2007) SQL-RDF. http://www.w3.org/2007/03/RdfRDB/papers/seaborne.html, accessed April 12th, 2011.

Seeling C, Becks A (2003) Exploiting metadata for ontology-based visual exploration of weakly structured text documents. In: Seventh International Conference on Information Visualization (IV 2003), pp 652–657

Sergevich KA, Viktorovna GV (2003) From an Ontology-Oriented Approach Conception to User Interface Development. International Journal "Information Theories and Applications" 10(1):89–98

Shadbolt N, Berners-Lee T, Hall W (2006) The Semantic Web Revisited. IEEE Intelligent Systems 21(3):96–101

Shaer O, Jacob RJ (2009) A Specification Paradigm for the Design and Implementation of Tangible User Interfaces. ACM Transactions on Computer-Human Interaction 16:1–39

Shahzad SK, Granitzer M (2010) Ontological Framework Driven GUI Development. In: Proceedings of I-KNOW, pp 198–206

Sheth AP, Staab S, Dean M, Paolucci M, Maynard D, Finin TW, Thirunarayan K (eds) (2008) The Semantic Web - ISWC 2008, LNCS, vol 5318, Springer

Shneiderman B (1984) Response Time and Display Rate in Human Performance with Computers. ACM Computing Surveys 16(3):265–285

Shvaiko P, Euzenat J (2008) Ten Challenges for Ontology Matching. In: On the Move to Meaningful Internet Systems: OTM 2008, Springer, LNCS, vol 5332, pp 1164–182

Shvaiko P, Euzénat J, Giunchiglia F, Stuckenschmidt H, Mao M, Cruz IF (eds) (2010) Proceedings of the The Fifth International Workshop on Ontology Matching (OM-2010), CEUR-WS, vol 689

Pinheiro da Silva P, McGuinness D, Del Rio N, Ding L (2008) Inference Web in Action: Lightweight Use of the Proof Markup Language. In: (Sheth et al, 2008), pp 847–860

Silva V (2009) Practical Eclipse Rich Client Platform Projects. Apress

Simon R, Kapsch MJ, Wegscheider F (2004) A Generic UIML Vocabulary for Device- and Modality Independent User Interfaces. In: WWW Alt. '04: Proceedings of the 13th international World Wide Web conference on Alternate track papers & posters, ACM, pp 434–435

Sirin E, Parsia B, Grau BC, Kalyanpur A, Katz Y (2007) Pellet: A practical OWL-DL reasoner. Journal of Web Semantics: Science, Services and Agents on the World Wide Web 5(2):51–53

Skovronski J, Chiu K (2006) An Ontology-Based Publish Subscribe Framework. In: Proceedings of the 8th International Conference on Information Integration and Web-based Applications & Services (iiWAS2006)

Software AG (2011) ARIS MashZone - Cool Business Mashups. http://www.mashzone.com/, accessed April 12th, 2011.

SoKNOS Consortium (2009) SoKNOS – Service-orientierte ArchiteKturen zur Unterstützung von Netzwerken im Rahmen Oeffentlicher Sicherheit. http://www.soknos.de/, accessed April 12th, 2011.

Sonntag D, Deru M, Bergweiler S (2009) Design and Implementation of Combined Mobile and Touchscreen-based Multimodal Web 3.0 Interfaces. In: Arabnia HR, de la Fuente D, Olivas JA (eds) Proceedings of the 2009 International Conference on Artificial Intelligence (ICAI 2009), CSREA Press, pp 974–979

Souchon N, Vanderdonckt J (2003) A Review of XML-compliant User Interface Description Languages. In: Interactive Systems. Design, Specification, and Verification, Springer, LNCS, vol 2844, pp 377–391

Sousa K (2009) Model-Driven Approach for User Interface - Business Alignment. In: (Calvary et al, 2009), pp 325–328

Sowa JF (2000) Knowledge Representation: Logical, Philosophical, and Computational Foundations. Brooks Cole Publishing Co.

Spahn M, Kleb J, Grimm S, Scheidl S (2008) Supporting business intelligence by providing ontology-based end-user information self-service. In: OBI '08: Proceedings of the first international workshop on Ontology-supported business intelligence, ACM, pp 1–12

Spyns P, Meersmanand R, Jarrar M (2002) Data modelling versus ontology engineering. SIGMOD Rec 31(4):12–17

Staab S, Studer R (eds) (2009) Handbook on Ontologies, 2nd edn. International Handbooks on Information Systems, Springer

Stachowiak H (1973) Allgemeine Modelltheorie. Springer

Stadlhofer B, Salhofer P (2008) SeGoF: semantic e-government forms. In: Proceedings of the 2008 international conference on Digital government research, Digital Government Society of North America, pp 427–428

Steinberg D, Budinsky F, Paternostro M, Merks E (2008) EMF: Eclipse Modeling Framework, 2nd edn. Addison Wesley

Story H (2009) Sommer - Semantic Object (Medata) Mapper. https://sommer.dev.java.net/, accessed April 12th, 2011.

Stuckenschmidt H, Klein M (2003) Integrity and Change in Modular Ontologies. In: Proceedings of the 18th International Joint Conference on Artificial intelligence, pp 900–905

Stühmer R, Anicic D, Sen S, Ma J, Schmidt KU, Stojanovic N (2009) Lifting Events in RDF from Interactions with Annotated Web Pages. In: Bernstein A, Karger DR, Heath T, Feigenbaum L, Maynard D, Motta E, Thirunarayan K (eds) The Semantic Web - ISWC 2009, Springer, LNCS, vol 5823, pp 893–908

Su X, Ilebrekke L (2006) A Comparative Study of Ontology Languages and Tools. In: Pidduck A, Ozsu M, Mylopoulos J, Woo C (eds) Advanced Information Systems Engineering, LNCS, vol 2348, Springer Berlin / Heidelberg, pp 761–765

Sukaviriya N, Vanderdonckt J, Harrison M (eds) (2010) Proceedings of the 2nd ACM SIGCHI Symposium on Engineering Interactive Computing Systems (EICS 2010), ACM

Sun Microsystems (2010) Annotations. http://java.sun.com/j2se/1.5.0/docs/guide/language/annotations.html, accessed April 12th, 2011.

Sure Y, Erdmann M, Angele J, Staab S, Studer R, Wenke D (2002) OntoEdit: Collaborative Ontology Development for the Semantic Web. In: Horrocks I, Hendler J (eds) The Semantic Web - ISWC 2002, Springer Berlin / Heidelberg, LNCS, vol 2342, pp 221–235

Swartz A (2002) TRAMP: Makes RDF look like Python data structures. http://www.aaronsw.com/2002/tramp/, accessed April 12th, 2011.

Szyperski C (2002) Component Software - Beyond Object-Oriented Programming, 2nd edn. ACM Press

Tane J, Schmitz C, Stumme G (2004) Semantic resource management for the web: an e-learning application. In: WWW Alt. '04: Proceedings of the 13th international World Wide Web conference on Alternate track papers & posters, ACM, pp 1–10

TeamDev Ltd (2011) ComfyJ Website. http://www.teamdev.com/comfyj/, accessed April 12th, 2011.

Terenziani P, Anselma L (2003) Towards a Temporal Reasoning Approach Dealing with Instance-of, Part-of, and Periodicity. In: Proceedings of the 10th International Symposium on Temporal Representation and Reasoning, and Fourth International Conference on Temporal Logic, pp 37–46

Terziev I, Kiryakov A, Manov D (2005) Base upper-level ontology (BULO) Guidance. http://proton.semanticweb.org/D1_8_1.pdf, deliverable D1.8.1 of the SEKT project. Accessed April 12th, 2011.

Teymourian K, Paschke A (2009) Towards semantic event processing. In: DEBS '09: Proceedings of the Third ACM International Conference on Distributed Event-Based Systems, ACM, pp 1–2

The Dojo Foundation (2011) The Dojo Toolkit - Unbeatable JavaScript Tools. http://dojotoolkit.org/, accessed April 12th, 2011.

The Lobo Project (2009) The Lobo Project: Home of Lobo (Java Web Browser) and Cobra (HTML Rendering Engine). http://lobobrowser.org/, accessed April 12th, 2011.

Tsarkov D, Horrocks I (2006) FaCT++ Description Logic Reasoner: System Description. In: Furbach U, Shankar N (eds) Automated Reasoning, LNCS, vol 4130, Springer Berlin / Heidelberg, pp 292–297

Turhan AY (2010) Reasoning and Explanation in EL and in Expressive Description Logics. In: (Aßmann et al, 2010), pp 1–27

UIMLorg (2000) Formal Vocabulary Definitions of UIML Vocabularies. http://uiml.org/toolkits/, accessed April 12th, 2011.

Unicode Inc (2011) Unicode 6.0.0. http://www.unicode.org/versions/Unicode6.0.0/, accessed April 12th, 2011.

Uschold M, Grüninger M (1996) Ontologies: Principles, Methods and Applications. Knowledge Engineering Review 11:93–136

Uschold M, Grüninger M (2004) Ontologies and Semantics for Seamless Connectivity. SIGMOD Record 33(4):58–64

Uschold M, Jasper R (1999) A framework for understanding and classifying ontology applications. In: Proceedings of the IJCAI99 Workshop on Ontologies, pp 16–21

Uschold M, King M (1995) Towards a Methodology for Building Ontologies. In: Workshop on Basic Ontological Issues in Knowledge Sharing

UsiXML Consortium (2007) USer Interface eXtensible Markup Language V1.8 Reference Manual. http://www.usixml.org/index.php?mod=download&file=usixml-doc/UsiXML_v1.8.0-Documentation.pdf, accessed April 12th, 2011.

Vanderdonckt J (2000) XIML Specification of a simple dictionary. Available as part of the XIML Starter Kit version 1, available at http://www.ximl.org/download/step1.asp, accessed April 12th, 2011.

Vanderdonckt J (2005) A MDA-Compliant Environment for Developing User Interfaces of Information Systems. In: Proceedings of the 17th Conference on Advanced Information Systems Engineering (CAiSE'05), Springer, pp 13–17

VersaEdge Software (2011) JFlashPlayer Web Page. http://www.jpackages.com/jflashplayer, accessed April 12th, 2011.

Voigt K, Ivanov P, Rummler A (2010) MatchBox: Combined Meta-model Matching for Semi-automatic Mapping Generation. In: Proceedings of the 2010 ACM Symposium on Applied Computing, ACM, pp 2281–2288

Völkel M, Sure Y (2005) RDFReactor - From Ontologies to Programmatic Data Access. In: Posters and Demos at International Semantic Web Conference (ISWC) 2005, Galway, Ireland

Völkel M, Krötzsch M, Vrandecic D, Haller H, Studer R (2006) Semantic Wikipedia. In: WWW '06: Proceedings of the 15th international conference on World Wide Web, ACM, pp 585–594

W3C (2001) DAML+OIL Web Ontology Language. http://www.w3.org/Submission/2001/12/, accessed April 12th, 2011.

W3C (2004a) OWL-S: Semantic Markup for Web Services. http://www.w3.org/Submission/OWL-S/, accessed April 12th, 2011.

W3C (2004b) OWL Web Ontology Language Overview. http://www.w3.org/TR/owl-features/, accessed April 12th, 2011.

W3C (2004c) RDF Primer. http://www.w3.org/TR/rdf-primer/, accessed April 12th, 2011.

W3C (2004d) RDF Vocabulary Description Language 1.0: RDF Schema. http://www.w3.org/TR/rdf-schema/, accessed April 12th, 2011.

W3C (2004e) Resource Description Framework (RDF): Concepts and Abstract Syntax. http://www.w3.org/TR/rdf-concepts/, accessed April 12th, 2011.

W3C (2004f) SWRL: A Semantic Web Rule Language Combining OWL and RuleML. http://www.w3.org/Submission/SWRL/, accessed April 12th, 2011.

W3C (2005a) Web Service Execution Environment (WSMX). http://www.w3.org/Submission/WSMX/, accessed April 12th, 2011.

W3C (2005b) Web Service Modeling Language (WSML). http://www.w3.org/Submission/WSML/, accessed April 12th, 2011.

W3C (2005c) Web Service Modeling Ontology (WSMO). http://www.w3.org/Submission/WSMO/, accessed April 12th, 2011.

W3C (2005d) Web Service Semantics - WSDL-S. http://www.w3.org/Submission/WSDL-S/, accessed April 12th, 2011.

W3C (2007a) RDF Validation Service. http://www.w3.org/RDF/Validator/, accessed April 12th, 2011.

W3C (2007b) Semantic Annotations for WSDL and XML Schema. http://www.w3.org/TR/sawsdl/, accessed April 12th, 2011.

W3C (2007c) SOAP Specifications. http://www.w3.org/TR/soap/, accessed April 12th, 2011.

W3C (2007d) Web Services Description Language (WSDL) Version 2.0. `http://www.w3.`
`org/TR/wsdl20/`, accessed April 12th, 2011.

W3C (2008a) Best Practice Recipes for Publishing RDF Vocabularies. `http://www.w3.org/`
`TR/swbp-vocab-pub/`, accessed April 12th, 2011.

W3C (2008b) Extensible Markup Language (XML) 1.0 (Fifth Edition). `http://www.w3.org/`
`TR/xml/`, accessed April 12th, 2011.

W3C (2008c) RDFa in XHTML: Syntax and Processing. `http://www.w3.org/TR/`
`rdfa-syntax/`, accessed April 12th, 2011.

W3C (2008d) SPARQL Query Language for RDF. `http://www.w3.org/TR/`
`rdf-sparql-query/`, accessed April 12th, 2011.

W3C (2009a) OWL 2 Web Ontology Language – New Features and Rationale. `http://www.w3.`
`org/TR/2009/REC-owl2-new-features-20091027/`, accessed April 12th, 2011.

W3C (2009b) OWL 2 Web Ontology Language - Manchester Syntax. `http://www.w3.org/`
`TR/owl2-manchester-syntax/`, accessed April 12th, 2011.

W3C (2009c) OWL 2 Web Ontology Language - Structural Specification and Functional-Style
Syntax. `http://www.w3.org/TR/owl2-syntax/`, accessed April 12th, 2011.

W3C (2009d) SPARQL New Features and Rationale. `http://www.w3.org/TR/`
`sparql-features/`, accessed April 12th, 2011.

W3C (2009e) XForms 1.1. `http://www.w3.org/TR/xforms/1`, accessed April 12th, 2011.

W3C (2010a) Cascading Style Sheets Level 2 Revision 1 (CSS 2.1) Specification. `http://www.`
`w3.org/TR/CSS2/`, accessed April 12th, 2011.

W3C (2010b) RIF Overview. `http://www.w3.org/TR/rif-overview/`, accessed April
12th, 2011.

W3C (2010c) Voice Extensible Markup Language (VoiceXML) 3.0. `http://www.w3.org/`
`TR/voicexml30/`, accessed April 12th, 2011.

W3C (2010d) XML Path Language (XPath) 2.0 (Second Edition). `http://www.w3.org/TR/`
`xpath20/`, accessed April 12th, 2011.

W3C (2011a) Accessible Rich Internet Applications (WAI-ARIA) 1.0. `http://www.w3.org/`
`TR/wai-aria/`, accessed April 12th, 2011.

W3C (2011b) HTML5 – A vocabulary and associated APIs for HTML and XHTML. `http:`
`//www.w3.org/TR/html5/`, accessed April 12th, 2011.

Wagner A, Curran P, O'Brien R (1995) Drag Me, Drop Me, Treat Me Like an Object. In: CHI
'95: Proceedings of the SIGCHI conference on Human factors in computing systems, ACM, pp
525–530

Wagner J, Babi F, Bednar P (2009) Java RDF framework for knowledge repository. In: 7th International Symposium on Applied Machine Intelligence and Informatics (SAMI 2009), pp 99
–102

Wang J, Jin B, Li J (2004) An ontology-based publish/subscribe system. In: Middleware '04:
Proceedings of the 5th ACM/IFIP/USENIX international conference on Middleware, Springer
New York, Inc., pp 232–253

Wang Y, Haase P, Bao J (2007) A Survey of Formalisms for Modular Ontologies. In: International
Joint Conference on Artificial Intelligence 2007 (IJCAI'07) Workshop SWeCKa

Wege C (2002) Portal Server Technology. IEEE Internet Computing 6(3):73–77

Weiss W, Hausenblas M, Sprung G (2008) Visual Exploration, Query, and Debugging of RDF
Graphs. In: Semantic Web User Interaction at CHI 2008

Weithöner T, Liebig T, Luther M, Böhn S, von Henke F, Noppens O (2007) Real-World Reasoning
with OWL. In: Franconi E, Kifer M, May W (eds) The Semantic Web: Research and Applications,
LNCS, vol 4519, Springer Berlin / Heidelberg, pp 296–310

Westermann U, Jain R (2007) Toward a Common Event Model for Multimedia Applications. IEEE
MultiMedia 14(1):19–29

Wiederhold G, Genesereth M (1997) The Conceptual Basis for Mediation Services. IEEE Expert
12(5):38 –47

Wilkinson K, Sayers C, Harumi K, Reynolds D (2003) Efficient RDF Storage and Retrieval in Jena2. In: Cruz IF, Kashyap V, Decker S (eds) Proceedings of the First International Workshop on Semantic Web and Databases, pp 131–150

Williamson CL, Zurko ME, Patel-Schneider PF, Shenoy PJ (eds) (2007) Proceedings of the 16th International Conference on World Wide Web, WWW 2007, Banff, Alberta, Canada, May 8-12, 2007, ACM

Willis D, Pearce D, Noble J (2006) Efficient Object Querying for Java. In: Thomas D (ed) ECOOP 2006 – Object-Oriented Programming, LNCS, vol 4067, Springer Berlin / Heidelberg, pp 28–49

Wireless Application Protocol Forum, Ltd (2001) Wireless Markup Language Version 2.0. http://www.openmobilealliance.org/tech/affiliates/wap/wap-238-wml-20010911-a.pdf, accessed April 12th, 2011.

Xu P, Wang Y, Cheng L, Zang T (2010) Alignment Results of SOBOM for OAEI 2010. In: (Shvaiko et al, 2010)

Yahoo! Inc (2011) Pipes: Rewire the web. http://pipes.yahoo.com/pipes/, accessed April 12th, 2011.

Yee R (2008) Pro Web 2.0 Mashups: Remixing Data and Web Services. Apress

Young GO, Daley E, Gualtieri M, Lo H, Ashour M (2008) The Mashup Opportunity – How To Make Money In The Evolving Mashup Ecosystem. http://www.forrester.com/rb/Research/mashup_opportunity/q/id/44213/t/2, accessed April 12th, 2011.

Yu J, Benatallah B, Saint-Paul R, Casati F, Daniel F, Matera M (2007) A framework for rapid integration of presentation components. In: (Williamson et al, 2007), pp 923–932

Yu J, Benatallah B, Casati F, Daniel F (2008) Understanding Mashup Development. IEEE Internet Computing 12(5):44–52

Zyk C (2008) JSON Referencing in Dojo. http://www.sitepen.com/blog/2008/06/17/json-referencing-in-dojo/, accessed April 12th, 2011.

Index

.NET, 17, 19, 20, 22, 157
3Store, 54

A-Box, 28, 88, 89, 182
  caching, 185
  connector, 100, 105, 107, 182, 188, 199
  Dynamic A-Box, 192
  pushing vs. pulling data, 100, 182
ABAP, 16
Abstract user interface, 120, 123, 126, 129
ActiveX, 201
agogo, 52
AJAX, 16
AllegroGraph, 55
Apache
  Pluto, 15
Application integration
  levels, 9
  on the business logic level, 10, 58
  on the data source level, 9, 56, 113
  on the user interface level, 9, 59
ArcGIS, 171
ARIS, 18
Atom, 18, 19
Autocomplete, 69

BlazeDS, 201
BPEL, 58
Brushing and linking, 21, 102, 200

C/C++, 22
Cache
  eager, 185, 192
  lazy, 185, 192
Cameleon reference framework, 14, 119
CIDL, 22
Class

artificial, 153, 159, 162
  for relation, 153, 160
  multi-purpose, 153, 159, 162
Clipping, 18
Closed world assumption, 33, 40, 87, 132
ComfyJ, 200
Composite application, 2
Concrete user interface, 120, 126
Container, 95, 96, 105
CRUISe, 22
CSS, 121, 220
Cyc, 46
  OpenCyc, 46

DAML+OIL, 30, 53
Datalog, 179
DJ Project Native Swing, 200
Dojo, 16
DOLCE, 43, 112, 128, 132, 133
  DDPO, 44, 128
  DnS, 44, 128, 136
  Functional participation, 128
  Information objects, 44, 128
  Spatial relation, 128
  Temporal relation, 128
Drag and drop, 96, 99, 103, 105, 148
  across different technologies, 197

Eclipse, 20
  Modeling Framework (EMF), 53
ELMO, 53
Emergency management, 4, 101
Enterprise application integration, 10
Enterprise Mashup Markup Language (EMML), 18
Entity Relationship (ER), 40
Event detection, 178

Event processing, 3, 4, 13, 16, 17, 19, 85, 96,
    98, 178
  across different technologies, 196
  centralized, 85
  local vs. global, 180
  logic-based, 178
  publish/subscribe, 20, 24, 179
  Semantic event processing, 90, 145, 177, 178,
    188
  with server round trip, 15, 84
Extensibility, 80

F-Logic, 33, 34, 54, 58, 59, 88, 93, 144, 179,
    188, 221
Faceted browsing, 50, 67
Fenfire, 50
Final user interface, 120
Flex, 3, 23, 96, 199
FOAF, 151
Front-end composition, 9

GateIn Portal, 15
Google Mashup Editor, 18

Heterogeneity
  of data models, 14, 25, 81
  technological, 13, 22, 25, 81, 99
HTML, 13, 18, 19, 23, 24, 29, 120, 220

IBM
  Mashup Center, 19
  WebSphere Portal, 16
Information Clustering, 64
Information hiding, 80
Integration
  on the glass, 9
  on the implementation level, 25
  on the presentation level, 9
Integration dilemma, 3
Intel MashMaker, 18
iView, 16

JackBe Presto, 18
Java, 3, 17, 20, 22, 94, 96
  annotations, 53, 151
  Applet, 23
  Swing, 197
JavaScript, 15, 16, 18, 23, 201, 220
JBoss Portal, 15
JDIC, 201
JENA, 168
Jena, 53, 54
JFlash, 200
JFlashPlayer, 200

JQL, 157
JSF, 17
JSON, 157, 196, 202
JSONPath, 198
JSP, 17, 19
JSR-286, 15
JXPath, 157, 167

KAON2, 54
KIF, 33

Linked data, 31, 96, 100, 151
  browser, 50
  Linked open data cloud, 32
  Storing links, 109
Linked views, 103, 147, 209
LINQ, 157
Look and feel, 12
Loose coupling, 3, 146
LZX, 123

Mapping
  class model to ontology, 151, 157
  ontology to class model, 161
MARIA XML, 123, 129, 136, 137
mashArt, 23
Mashup, 2, 3, 17, 71, 83, 219
  Enterprise mashup, 2
  of data, 18
  of user interfaces, 18
  Web mashup, 1
MashZone, 18
Matlab, 22
MDA, 23, 39, 52, 72
MDL, 23
Method integration, 10
Microsoft
  CAB, 19
  COM, 21, 24
  Popfly, 18
  Prism, 20
  SharePoint, 16
MILO, 45
Mixup, 23
Model, 39
Modularity, 80, 85, 91

Non-atomic data type, 156, 160, 163
Non-intrusiveness, 52, 166

Object exchange, 99, 107
OntoBroker, 88, 94, 113, 183
Ontobroker, 54
OntoClean, 42

OntoJava, 52
Ontological Engineering, 40
Ontology
  Application ontology, 37, 89, 94
  as inter-lingua, 27, 55
  Definitions, 28
  design pattern, 42, 130
  Domain ontology, 37, 85, 92, 94, 112
  editor, 49
  for describing events, 179
  for emergency management, 112
  formal, 36
  Generic ontology, 37
  in application integration, 55
  in philosophy, 27
  in software engineering, 38
  informal, 36
  interaction with, 62
  Languages, 28
  learning, 41
  matching, 55
  Methodology for developing, 40
  modular, 85, 91
  programming framework, 52, 151
  Representation ontology, 37
  Storage, 54
  Task ontology, 37
  top level, 42
  Top-level ontology, 37, 89
  types, 35
  verbalization, 64
  visualization, 49, 62, 117
  vs. model, 39
OntoStudio, 221
Open Mashup Alliance (OMA), 18
Open world assumption, 33, 40, 87
OpenInterface Workbench, 22
Oracle
  WebLogic Portal, 16
otm-j, 151
OWL, 30, 31, 49, 53–55, 138
  Lite, 174
  OWL 2, 32
  OWL DL, 30, 54, 58
  OWL Full, 30
  OWL Lite, 30
OWL API, 53
OWL-S, 58
OWL2Java, 52
OWLIM, 54

Performance, 4, 14, 81, 173, 177
Piping, 18
Plausibility checking, 68, 116

Portal, 15, 71, 83
Portlet, 15
Presentation integration, 9
Prolog, 33, 55
Protégé, 49
  SWRLTab, 220
PROTON, 46

Query
  explorative, 192
  target-oriented query, 192

RDF, 29, 31, 53, 54, 98, 99, 151, 157, 158, 161,
    162, 188, 198
  blank node, 29, 160, 163, 165
  Notation 3 (N3), 29
  RDF-XML, 29, 49
  Schema, 30, 52, 53
  template, 165, 167
  visualization, 210
RDFa, 29, 67, 179
RDFReactor, 52
Reactivity, 177
Reasoning, 33, 68
  DIG interface, 35, 54
  for validating ontologies, 34
  logic programming based, 34
  monotonic, 87
  non-monotonic, 87
  on events, 106, 145
  on running systems, 4
  tableau-based, 34
  with hypothesized instances, 88, 150
Regular expression, 158, 159, 220
Relation
  multi-purpose, 154, 159, 162
  shortcut, 154, 160, 162
RelFinder, 51
Reuse, 12
RSS, 18, 19
Rule, 32
  Connector rule, 114, 186
  Datalog, 93
  ECA, 92, 179
  F-Logic, 33, 114
  Integration rule, 92, 96, 105, 106, 143
  Mapping rule, 95, 114
  RIF, 32
  RuleML, 32, 52, 93
  SWRL, 32, 49, 54, 59
RuleML, 179

SAP NetWeaver Portal, 16
SAWSDL, 58

SCA, 58
Scalability, 173, 191
Screen scraping, 12, 67
Seamless integration, 3, 13, 17, 81, 102
Semantic annotation
    of events, 89
Semantic desktop, 57, 68, 188
Semantic Web, 28
Sensor data, 115
Sesame, 54
Silverlight, 3, 20
Skolem function, 88, 107, 144, 224
Snap-Together, 21
SOAP, 58
SPARQL, 32, 52, 54, 56, 69, 161, 168, 179, 188
Speech interaction, 114
SUMO, 45, 46
SWRL, 220

T-Box, 28, 96, 107, 182
    Connector, 189
Tabulator, 50
TeresaXML, 123
Tight coupling, 3
Triple store, 54

UCL, 23
UIML, 125, 129, 133
UISDL, 22, 23
UML, 37, 40, 133
Unicode, 29
URI, 20, 29, 31, 100, 105, 158
    generation, 167
Usability, 5, 12, 81, 102
User interface
    for multiple users, 232

Multi-modal, 231
User interface description language, 119
User interface integration, 9
    design space of, 14
UsiXML, 23, 126, 129, 136, 137

VB Script, 16
Virtuoso, 54
visR, 51

W3C, 28
WAI ARIA, 65, 125, 129, 136, 137
Web 2.0, 1
Web service, 13, 58
    Semantic web service, 58
WIMP, 231
WIMP interface, 126
Wiring, 18
Wirth's law, 177
Wrapper, 82
WSDL, 22, 58
WSDL-S, 58
WSMO, 58
WSMX, 58

X Window, 10
XForms, 120
XIML, 122, 129, 133
XML, 17–19, 24, 29, 36, 49, 196
    schema, 37, 133
XPath, 18, 19, 157, 158, 167, 198, 220
XPIL, 23
XSLT, 23, 24
XUL, 122

Yahoo! Pipes, 18